QUEEN OF THE PLAZA

Books by Paul Lewis

QUEEN OF THE PLAZA

LADY OF FRANCE

QUEEN OF CAPRICE

THE GENTLE FURY

QUEEN
OF THE PLAZA

A Biography of Adah Isaacs Menken

by

PAUL LEWIS

FUNK & WAGNALLS COMPANY, INC.

NEW YORK

For
Marion

"I see her yet, that dark-eyed one"
—"A Memory"
Adah Isaacs Menken

CONTENTS

CONTENTS

QUEEN OF THE PLAZA

CHAPTER I

OPENING NIGHT

The Queen of the World in her young strength and beauty*

—"Pro Patria"

NEW YORK CITY was in a ferment on June 13, 1861, as was all of the United States. Only three months earlier Abraham Lincoln had been inaugurated as President, and one week later, in Montgomery, Alabama, the Congress of the Confederate States of America had adopted a Constitution, by unanimous vote, proclaiming the sovereignty of the states that had formed that confederation. From that time, the outbreak of civil war had been inevitable, and the first shots had been fired at Fort Sumter, at Charleston, South Carolina, on April 12.

For two months, New York had been breathing fire. Recruiting sergeants, accompanied by drummers, had become a familiar sight in the streets, and men in blue uniforms were no longer a novelty. Every day brought its fresh sensations. The ports of the Confederacy were blockaded, and only five days earlier, on June 8, Tennessee had become the eleventh state to secede from the Union and

---

*The poetry quotations that precede each chapter are all taken from Adah Isaacs Menken's book of poetry, *Infelicia*.

[3]

join the Confederacy. There were rumors that Congress would soon pass a bill taxing incomes to support the war effort. No battles had yet been fought, but ladies were already forming societies to roll bandages.

People sometimes escaped from the pressures of the war. New Yorkers were critical of a new novel just published by Oliver Wendell Holmes, *Elsie Venner*. Boston retorted that New York neither understood nor appreciated Holmes. Philadelphia, sniffing at New York's cultural tastes, said that only a city that liked raw sensationalism would support Dion Boucicault's play *Colleen Bawn*, first produced the previous year and still playing to capacity audiences.

New York cheerfully and blandly admitted the charge. Her citizens willingly granted that they enjoyed the unusual, the bizarre and the quaint. The *Sun*, an aggressive newspaper that sold for a penny and mirrored the tastes of the masses who could read, had declared in a recent editorial: "Boston and Philadelphia are conscious of their cultural heritage. In those dusty cities people attend the theater, read books and listen to music out of a sense of duty. That duty impels these worthies to suffer through many a dull evening. We of New York are not fettered by such conventional restrictions. We seek pleasure in literature, the arts and drama for the sake of that pleasure itself, ever mindful, to be sure, that the bounds of propriety and good taste are observed."

Now the city was promised a new treat, rare and titillating. And no one was certain whether the "bounds of propriety and good taste" would burst at their well-worn seams.

At a little after 7:00 P.M. a crowd began to gather at Broadway and Broome Street to stare at bill-posters and other signs decorating the front of the city's largest theater, the Broadway, which had a seating capacity of almost fif-

teen hundred. A decorous announcement placed on a
stand was somewhat misleading:

First Performance This Evening
at 8:00 O'Clock
MAZEPPA
or
The Wild Horse of Tartary
One of the Most Popular Plays of the
Past One Hundred Years
featuring as its star
MISS ADAH ISAACS MENKEN
Revised and Rewritten from an Unknown Original
by the Distinguished Dramatist, H. M. Milner
Also Featuring in the Glittering Cast
ADRIAN MURPHY   T. P. BATES
ROBERT TELL ROBERTSON

Another placard announced the price scale for seats,
which was the maximum being charged for plays starring
such celebrated performers as Edwin Booth. Boxes, which
accommodated six to eight persons, were selling for ten
dollars, orchestra chairs for one dollar each. Reserved
seats in the family circle and parquette were seventy-five
cents. Unreserved seats in the family circle, so named because of a reluctance in the theatrical world to call a balcony by its right name, were fifty cents. These, the cheapest
seats, had been filled soon after the box office had opened
at 6:00 P.M.

A large, hand-lettered placard announced:

Positively No Free List During Miss Menken's Engage-
ment
                                George Wood, Manager

That placard, and an illustrated poster in the front of the lobby, were the clues that indicated the Broadway was about to have a new hit. The poster displayed a mammoth black stallion, teeth bared, rearing, with its front legs furiously pawing the air. Lashed to the animal's back was a cleverly concealed figure of a woman who appeared to be nude. All that could be seen of her on close examination, however—and the recruits in blue, teen-aged urchins and other youths studied the drawing with great care— were her bare arms, shoulders, and long legs. Black hair, waist length, streamed behind her, and on her pretty face was an expression of terror.

The hand of Boucicault was plainly evident. Any play that hoped to succeed in New York had to include two elements that had made Boucicault popular. Unabashed melodrama predominated, and somewhere during the performance a touch of realism on a grand scale was required. Audiences demanded a diet that would jolt the emotions and leave them round-eyed with wonder.

Mazeppa, a tired failure of a play that had first been tried by Clara Woodhull in 1833, was known to the critics as a limp melodrama, a pseudo-historical venture concerning heroic, wild Tartars and villainous Poles in eastern Europe. The plot was paper-thin, the characters transparent, the dialogue wooden. The story, which was too involved for any but the most meticulously alert theatergoer to follow closely, concerned the efforts of proud, freedomloving Tartars, a semicivilized mountain people, to escape from the bondage imposed on them by Polish armies who had invaded their homeland.

There were two principal roles. One was that of Mazeppa, a Tartar girl who hated her people's oppressors and was willing to take any risk for the cause of freedom. The other was that of Cassimir, the proud, patriotic Tartar leader. Cassimir is captured by the Poles, who tie him to a wild horse and send the beast thundering off into the mountains. There Cassimir meets his death, but the struggle of his followers continues, and Mazeppa vows to finish the work that he has begun.

Theatrical insiders, as wise in the 1860's as they are a century later, knew that the star, Adah Isaacs Menken, was playing both roles. Titters and raised eyebrows had greeted the revelation after the play had tried out in Albany, for Adah Isaacs Menken was no gifted, bright-eyed newcomer, but a woman of twenty-five or more, who had consistently demonstrated during the two years she had been working in New York that she was an actress of little talent.

The *Sun* summed up her career in brutal words: "We recall Miss Menken on our stages in one or another roles that were mercifully brief. She is a dreadful actress."

Some of the insiders concluded that George Wood, the owner-manager of the Broadway Theater, who, following the custom of the period, produced the plays that appeared at his edifice, had taken leave of his senses. Others were not so sure. It was reported that when the play had been presented at the Green Street Theater in Albany on June 3, Adah had actually been lashed to a horse that had thundered around a runway built in a semicircle out into the auditorium.

It was a fact that such a runway had been erected in the Broadway Theater. And it was known that a four-year-old mare, Black Bess, had been taken to the theater late in the afternoon. An actress who dared to attempt such a feat was sure to draw audiences.

But the excitement caused by Adah's opening in *Mazeppa* stemmed from even more sensational gossip, which no one could confirm or deny. According to persistent rumors, she was totally unclad when strapped to the horse.

Even Horace Greeley, the peripatetic editor-publisher

of the New York *Tribune,* had deigned to take notice of the whispers. A firm advocate of equal rights for women, he was nevertheless a stern moralist who thought the theater immoral, and only in recent years had he revoked his ban on theatrical advertising in the *Tribune.* Obsessed by the Civil War, he still had found time to state in an editorial: "We cannot believe that the actress scheduled to appear before our citizenry in *Mazeppa* would so shock and revolt decent people by exposing her body in the nude."

It was obvious, as the crowds in front of the theater grew larger, that few New Yorkers shared Greeley's conviction. At 7:15, the assistant manager of the Broadway, G. T. Collins, came out of the box office and tacked up a sign: "All seats for this performance have been sold. Tickets may be purchased for the next four weeks at the prevailing rates. Evening performances at 8.00 P.M., matinees at 1:30 P.M."

The doors leading into the auditorium were locked, and inside the theater the tension was even greater than that of an ordinary opening night. James Murdoch, the noted actor-director, watched critically as an assistant led the mare, Black Bess, up a sturdy, spiral runway that led from the stage to the rear of the theater before curving back again. George Gilbert, the stage manager, conferred frantically with stagehands and property men, with constant interruptions as members of the cast notified him they had arrived.

Murdoch, who had conceived the idea of a woman being carried by the horse, was justifiably nervous. There had been an accident during the pre-Albany rehearsal that had almost killed the star when a horse, locally hired, had tumbled from the runway. And during one performance of the week-long Albany engagement, Black Bess had lost her footing, recovering just in time to avoid plunging headlong into the audience. If the beast fell tonight, injuring one or more celebrated spectators, Murdoch knew he would be forced to leave New York and seek a new career elsewhere. He had eaten no food all day, and was pale, exhausted, and irritable.

A few minutes before 7:30, George Wood descended from a carriage at the front of the theater. A short, plump man with an ever-present smile and small, hard eyes, he surveyed the crowd. Following him from the carriage were two newspapermen. One, former editor of the Brooklyn *Daily Eagle* and, subsequently, of the Brooklyn *Daily Freeman*, was an untidy eccentric—Walt Whitman. He was known in literary circles for a remarkable volume of poetry published six years earlier, *Leaves of Grass*, which had created considerable controversy. No one in the crowd knew him.

Scores recognized his companion, however. Ed James, a man with a florid face, a shock of prematurely white hair, and the build of a professional athlete, was the editor of the New York *Clipper,* a nineteenth-century combination of *Variety, Sports Illustrated,* and the *Daily Racing Form.* Like Wood, he studied the crowd before turning and handing a young woman from the carriage.

Her eyes, described at one time or another by virtually every one of the countless authors who were her friends as being of every shade in the color spectrum, were a startling violet. Her full lips were painted crimson, which marked her as either an actress or a prostitute, perhaps both, for other women carefully refrained from using cosmetics of any kind. She was about five feet, seven inches tall, weighed one hundred and twenty-five pounds, and had a figure that, judged either by the standards of her own day or those of a later age, was perfect. Certainly her high breasts, supple waist, and long slender legs were those of a girl. Few people would have guessed she was twenty-six years old.

The crowd paid scant attention to her, in part because she was dressed in an old dress of faded bombazine, a combination of wool and silk, and in part because her strange haircut was considered unattractive. She was hatless, and her blue-black hair hung loosely to a point halfway between her earlobes and shoulders. Perhaps, had her tresses been waist-length as in the poster, the crowd would have recognized Adah Isaacs Menken.

But that morning, with an instinct sharpened by years of unremitting vocational failure, she had ordered a barber to cut her hair, insisting that as she was playing a man's role, she wanted to look the part. Murdoch and James had protested, and Wood had been horrified, but all of them knew her sufficiently well to have realized they should have saved their breath. Her gesture was more than that of an actress seeking authenticity in her portrayal, or even publicity. Adah, a pioneer in the age when Amelia Bloomer, Emma Willard, and other feminists were active, was the first woman on either side of the Atlantic to bob her hair.

She walked with the quick, graceful stride of a fencer down an alley to the stage door, kissed each of her escorts, and disappeared inside the theater. James, recalling the occasion in his biography, *The Life and Times of Adah Isaacs Menken,* wrote ten years later:

Adah's calm on the night that would either make her a great star or send her back to a life of squalor was monumental. Wood, Whitman and I dined with her at Pfaff's, than which no finer restaurant catering to the theatrical trade has ever existed.

There she accepted the good wishes of Edwin Booth and Ada Clare, the reigning King and Queen of our theater, as though she were monarch and they her subjects. Fitz-James O'Brien, who would have become the greatest American poet of our century had he not suffered a tragically premature death, offered her a toast in champagne. She accepted with dignity, but replied by sipping water, explaining that she preferred not to drink alcoholic spirits until later in the evening. She showed her wisdom, for the calamitous power of those spirits had marred her soul.

Her appetite was exceptional, and neither then nor on any other occasion in the many years I knew her did she eat with anything but the gusto of a workingman. She consumed a dish of raw clams, a thick soup of chicken, a hearty steak and a deep-dish pie containing, if memory does not err, a compote of fruits. Charlie Pfaff also prepared for her a roast turkey sandwich at her request, so she could eat it during one of the play's intermissions as a means of maintaining her strength.

Adah had known such great poverty that, in my belief, her hunger of past years had given her an insatiable appetite. She could eat more than anyone I ever knew, man or woman. Yet some strange quality in her nature held down her weight. When I first met her, she was hungry to the point of near-starvation, and weighed less than the one hundred and twenty-five pounds that was her normal weight. I never knew her to weigh more, even when she enjoyed a huge income and was so much in demand that wealthy citizens vied with each other in the attempt to present her with rare and delectable treats from the world over.

But I digress. At Pfaff's on the fateful night, Whitman and I had no zest for food, and found it difficult to converse. Wood, always a silent man, looked down at his plate and replied in a few words when one of us spoke to him. Adah, bless her, was the life of the party, chatting happily about a thousand and one things, yet never once mentioning the test that awaited her at the theater.

Perhaps she betrayed a trace of apprehension while smoking a cigarette in the coach whilst driving to the theater, for she extinguished it after taking only a few inhalations. She betrayed neither fear nor other nervousness when bidding us farewell at the stage door, and I later learned from Minnie, her wardrobe woman, that she sang to herself in the dressing room as she prepared for her great assault on New York.

Soon after Adah's arrival, the carriages of the first-nighters began to roll up to the theater entrance. The professional newspaper critics glumly expected the worst. Robert Henry Newell of the *Herald,* who wrote serious poetry and prose under the pseudonym of Orpheus C. Kerr, revealed some nine years later in his book, *My Life with Adah Isaacs Menken*:

My colleagues and I knew that Adah had been riotously received in Albany, of course. All of us had heard that she appeared on stage nude, lashed to a horse, and we expected some such spectacle as the climax of her performance.

That expectation did not relieve our knowledge that we faced a dreary evening. *Mazeppa* was one of the worst plays ever written, and its history had been dismal. Fanny Louise Buckingham and Fannie Herring, both ladies of charm and talent, had failed miserably when they had appeared in it, the former at Niblo's Gardens, the latter at Mike Herman's National Theater. Cora Pearl had attempted to play the role in London, and despite her great popularity there, had been hissed from the stage.

We were not comforted by the fact that the play had been revised, for none of us had heard of the playwright. I, myself, having learned something of Adah's own literary pretensions and earnest attempts to publish some of her poems, was inclined to suspect that she had rewritten *Mazeppa*.

George Wood had called on me, as well as on my colleagues, to assure us that Adah would ride the horse herself in the final, fifth act of the play. It had been customary for a horseman to take the part for those few moments when a great beast, no doubt prodded by hirelings backstage, crossed from the wings on one side to those on the other. I wondered, privately, whether tedium would propel me from my seat into the velvet air of a June night before the fifth act came.

The ladies and gentlemen who strolled through the lobby, chatting and waving to acquaintances, expected no more than did the critics. They had heard, through the mysterious grapevine of the insiders, that they would be sorry if they missed the performance. They responded accordingly.

There were nine Union generals in full uniform at the Broadway that evening, one rear admiral, and seventeen colonels. Someone kept count for Adah, who noted the figures in her *Diary*. Edwin Booth was there, surrounded by admirers, and two gentlemen of wealth escorted Ada Clare. There were Livingstons, Astors, Schuylers, the cream of New York society, and the *Post* reported the following day that the ladies exhibited even greater curiosity than the men. Everyone thought it unlikely that the star would appear onstage as a latter-day Lady Godiva, but people hoped, nevertheless, that they would be treated to such an outrageous sensation.

Promptly at eight o'clock, the house lights dimmed, then flared again. Ushers appeared with special notices, which were passed out, and the gas flames burned high so the patrons could read the small print:

The Management of the Broadway Theater wishes to announce that attacks on the patriotism of Miss Adah Isaacs Menken are without warrant. Miss Menken makes no secret of her birth in Louisiana, but proclaims no fealty to that misguided state. She is a loyal and trustworthy Citizen of the United States of North America, and joins with other patriots in the devout wish that those states which have seceded will return to the fold of the Union.

On the opposite side of the single sheet were printed several verses of "PRO PATRIA," *America, 1861,* signed in longhand by the author, Adah Isaacs Menken. One of her longer poems, it was subsequently published in full by the *Sun*. It had been written in the days immediately following the attack on Fort Sumter, according to Adah's *Diary*, when a fierce love of country had burned in the soul of the unemployed actress-poet.

The more literary members of the audience were mildly impressed, and Ed James took care to point out to Walt Whitman in a loud voice that Adah had written every word herself, which Whitman already knew. The printed verses read as follows:

God's armies of Heaven, with pinions extended,
  Spread wide their white arms to the standard of Light;
And bending far down to the great Heart of Nature,
  With kisses of love drew us up from the Night.

Proud soul of the Bondless! whose stars fleck with crimson,
  And warm dreams of gold ev'ry pillar and dome,
That strengthens and crowns the fair temples upswelling
  To glitter, far-seen, in our Liberty's home—

The spirits of Heroes and Sires of the People,
  Leaned down from the battlements guarding the world;
To breathe for your destiny omens of glory
  And Freedom eternal, in Honour impearled.

The storm-goaded mountains, and trees that had battled
  With winds sweeping angrily down through the years,
Turned red in the blood of the roses of Heaven,
  'Neath fires lit by sunset on vanishing spears.

The soft Beam of Peace bronzed the rocks of stern ages,
  And crept from the valley to burn on the spire;
And stooped from the glimmer of gems in the palace,
  To glow in the hovel a soul-heating fire.

Each turret, and terrace, and archway of grandeur,
  Its beauty up-rounded through laughs of the light;
And world-crown'd America chose for her standard
  The blush of the Day and the eyes of the Night.

Then Liberty's sceptre, its last jewel finding,
  Was waved by a God o'er the years to be born,
And far in the future there rusted and crumbled
  The chains of the centuries ne'er to be worn.

The wave-hosts patrolling the sullen Atlantic,
  With helmets of snow and broad silvery shields,
Ran clamouring up to the seed-sown embrasures,
  And fashioned new dews for the buds of the fields:

They spread their scroll shields for the breast of Columbia,
  And turned their storm-swords to the enemy's fleet;
Their glory to humble the tyrant that braved them,
  Their honor to lave fair America's feet!

The gas jets continued to burn high for at least ten
minutes so the audience would have ample opportunity
to study the somewhat less than immortal words. A few
people, who recognized Whitman and knew of his friendship with Adah, wondered whether he had been responsible for the verses. Obviously they had read none of his
poetry.

There was little to do during the long wait, and the
patrons gossiped about the actress they had come to see.
According to rumors some had heard, she was either a
mulatto or an octaroon. It was said she was Jewish, the
daughter of a distinguished Biblical scholar from New Orleans, but others declared that her first husband had been
Jewish and that she had enthusiastically adopted his faith.
Not many knew of such a marriage, but sporting buffs
stated that she had been the wife of John C. Heenan,

heavyweight prize-fighting champion of the world. Judges
and lawyers in the audience wondered if she might be the
same woman who had been involved in a lurid bigamy
case. Those who were immersed in the world of the theater
seemed to recall that she had eloped with Edwin Booth,
but were puzzled, because they had not married.

Oddly, most of the rumors were at least partly right.

A fife and drum corps came onto the stage as the house
lights dimmed again, and played "Yankee Doodle." The
audience responded with cheers, and the curtain rose on
the first scene, a Tartar mountain retreat. Declaiming
actors boomed loudly, sawing the air, and the audience
waited restlessly for another ten minutes until Prince
Cassimir appeared.

Adah, wearing skin-tight breeches, a deep-plunging
man's shirt and calf-high boots, appeared on a pasteboard
rock as one of her fellow Thespians exclaimed, "Yonder
stands the brooding Cassimir."

Friends applauded, but Adah knew only a few in the
audience, and the patter of their hands echoed weakly
though the cavern. But Adah, showing remarkable agility
as she leaped from the rock to the stage, hurried forward
to take a bow. Most of the ladies were stunned. The pale
breeches were startling, and the short hair of the slender
young woman shocked them. They were willing to believe
almost anything about her now.

It was not easy for any of the spectators to convince
himself that Adah was an actress, however. Most leading
ladies spoke in clear, bell-like sopranos. Adah's voice was
uncommonly husky, a quality that would not become
popular for another seventy-five years. Her accent was
strictly her own, and varied somewhat from scene to scene,
even from line to line. Now the audience heard a trace of
a Southern drawl, now a hint of Spanish, now the rounded

English that indicated to the initiated that she had listened long and hard to the great Edwin Booth.

Adah's acting style, too, was distinctly her own. She more than compensated for her lack of polish with an emotional intensity so ferocious that she made the stilted words of the old play come alive. If she was not Cassimir—and she was not—then she at least showed the audience that she was an unusually hot-blooded young woman masquerading as a man. Her weakest scenes were those she played as Mazeppa. Her full skirts hampered her movements, the ruffles on her sleeves seemed to annoy her, and she was singularly lacking in virtually every attribute of a lady. Feminine members of the Schuyler, Livingston, and Astor clans exchanged significant glances.

It was untrue that a lady who traced her ancestry through six generations to the patrician Killian Van Rensselaer stalked out of the theater that night. That incident occurred on the evening of the fourth performance.

Whatever the reactions of the women, the men were fascinated. When Adah stalked up and down the stage, a gentleman with side-whiskers and a gold-handled cane declared during one of the intermissions, she reminded him of a tiger stalking its prey. Ed James, leaning against a wall, wrote the observation on a slip of paper. A brigadier general of the New York militia observed that Adah was a reincarnation of Cleopatra. Again Ed James scribbled.

Newell, writing with the experience gained in a stormy marriage, declared in his book, "Adah was a symbol of Desire Awakened to every man who set eyes on her. All who saw her wanted her, immediately."

Probably no one in the audience on the opening night of *Mazeppa* realized that theatrical history was being made, that the First of the American Glamour Girls was setting a precedent that would be followed for more than one hundred years. Sex was the commodity that Adah sold best, and it sparkled across the footlights. The gentlemen didn't care about her lack of talent, her inability to read a speech convincingly. She was bold, abandoned, and daring, and they ignored the audible sniffs of their disapproving wives.

Tension mounted steadily as the play moved toward its fifth-act climax. Patrons in the cheap family-circle seats hissed when the scheming nobles decided to kill Cassimir by sending him down through the mountains tied to the back of a horse. The curtains closed, then opened again, and several ladies in the audience screamed when Black Bess cantered onto the stage, hoofs pounding. Spotlights were focused on the horse and—naturally—on the lithe figure strapped to the animal's back.

The mare cantered up the runway as people gasped. The daring feat was electrifying.

Adah Isaacs Menken was completely naked! Or was she? Perhaps she was wearing flesh-colored tights that covered her from neck to toe. No one could be certain.

Black Bess reached the runway turn at the rear of the theater, then cantered down toward the stage again. A very few in the audience realized that Adah addressed a steady stream of commands and soothing words to the horse from start to finish of the perilous ride.

The mare and her rider reached the stage, the curtains closed swiftly and the spotlights were extinguished. There was a moment of silence, then cheers rang out. Soon the entire audience was standing, applauding, and shouting wildly. Even the prim ladies were beating their hands together. What the spectators had seen was not acting, certainly, but an audacious theatrical gem that had no precedent. The young woman with the short hair and slender figure had risked her life in the presence of nearly fifteen hundred people.

Most of the men were convinced that she had appeared nude, but those who had been nearest to the runway believed she had been wearing pink tights. The difference, in an age when ladies did not display their uncovered ankles, was academic.

The roar of approval grew still louder when Adah came through the curtains, modestly covered by a scarlet and gold silk cape that completely enveloped her. Several young men raced down the aisles with huge bouquets of flowers thoughtfully provided for the occasion by George Wood. It was the first and only time that the management had to spend money for that purpose. Thereafter, the young bloods of the town bought so many flowers for Adah that the price of blossoms rose sharply.

Still composed, with a faint smile on her lips, Adah stepped down to the footlights, her arms filled with roses. The applause died away, and she started to make a little speech. "Dear friends," she said in an accent redolent of New Orleans, "I owe so much to——" Suddenly her voice broke, and she tried again. "I owe so much to—all of you."

To her horror, she discovered that she was sobbing. The audience, realizing her emotions were genuine, shouted and stomped and cheered more enthusiastically than ever.

Edwin Booth was thrust forward from his seat in the fourth row. He was lifted onto the runway, and walked with great dignity to the stage, where he embraced Adah. Then, not wanting to deprive her of the triumph that was hers alone, he disappeared into the wings.

In all, Adah took fourteen ecstatic curtain calls. Repeatedly she sank to the floorboards in a deep curtsy. She blew kisses to the audience. She bobbed her head, smiled, and bowed. People refused to leave their seats, and only the drama critics left to return to their newspaper offices. Reviews of *Mazeppa* would not appear in the morning papers for another thirty-six hours, the practice of squeezing the critics' opinions into the final editions of the morning after an opening not yet having been adopted. But the reviewers had a duty to perform as reporters, and by morning the whole city would know that a new star had received an overwhelming reception.

The lean years of obscurity and poverty had come to an end. Never again would Adah be forced to accept minor roles in foredoomed failures, to accept "lecture" engagements, dreary affairs at which she spoke to small, apathetic crowds in church parish halls. The lifelong struggle for renown had succeeded.

But only half of her ambitions were fulfilled. Later that night she wrote in her *Diary:* "It should be much easier for me, now that I have won an established place in the theater, to gain recognition for my poetry. N. [Newell] assures me that every magazine in America will be eager to print my work. I cannot share his expectations. The editors of *Harper's* will judge my work on merit. As for the *Ladies' Magazine,* I want no part of that flabby, sanctimonious collection of trash which good women read so avidly. If I had a favorite recipe, I would send it to them, and they would pay me well for it. But I have never been an accomplished cook; and now—thank the Lord—I will be rich enough to pay someone to cook for me, even my breakfast."

Several hours of the memorable evening still remained before Adah had the chance to record her reactions in the privacy of her inexpensive lodging house room at Sixth Avenue and Twenty-second Street. A score or more of prominent men sent their names to the star's dressing room, begging for the privilege of escorting her to supper. Adah thanked them, but refused.

Eventually she emerged from the alley, accompanied by Murdoch and a literary phalanx led by Whitman, O'Brien,

and James. Newell, waiting at the curb, attached himself
to the party, which repaired to Pfaff's. There a half-dozen
other writers joined them. Adah was the only woman at
the table.

She had no desire to talk about *Mazeppa,* confining
herself to the single observation that the play would enjoy
a long run, no matter what the critics thought of it and of
her. Instead she discussed a melodramatic novel that had
been published recently, *East Lynne.* Her companions
criticized the book severely, and Whitman aroused Adah's
ire when he called it "cheap."

"How can you say that?" she demanded, according to
Newell, "when it was written by a *woman?*"

For the next half-hour or more she hotly defended the
author of *East Lynne,* Mrs. Henry Wood. Apparently she
divided the members of her own sex into two categories.
There were the "good" women, whom she despised for
their domesticity. Then there were the pioneer career
women, authors and feminists and actresses among them,
for whom she had only praise. To the day of her death
she expressed great admiration for Queen Victoria, presumably on the grounds that Her Majesty was not a sit-at-
home. Certainly there could have been no other reason,
for Adah possessed none of Victoria's principles or standards, and in no way emulated her.

Hungry again after her night's work, Adah ate large
quantities of a Pfaff dish once known as New Orleans
Stew, and now hastily renamed in her honor by quick-
witted Charlie Pfaff, who knew that the Louisiana metropolis was no longer popular in the Union. Adah ate
three portions of the dish, which included prawns, oysters,
and vegetables. Then, to take the last edge off her appetite,
she finished her meal with a slab of roast beef.

The austere Horace Greeley happened to be in the
restaurant, and was persuaded to make a token appearance

at Adah's table. Countless legends sprang up after this brief encounter. According to some, the crusading editor declared that she had caused him to change his mind about the theater. This claim was sheer nonsense, for Greeley subsequently attacked Adah in a blistering series of pungent editorials, and his eventual capitulation to her was a far more dramatic incident than a chance meeting at an eating place favored by the newspaper profession and the theatrical trade.

Newell, recalling the occasion through the softening mists of time, wrote that Greeley had congratulated Adah on her success.

James said in print that the editor had offered her his best wishes.

Adah herself probably recorded the truth when she wrote in her *Diary* that the austere leader of America's moral and cultural revolution had confined himself to a stiff bow and the curt words, "How do you do, Miss Menken?"

But Horace Greeley's disapproval could not spoil the gala night. Charles Edmund Burke, the author of a collection of poetry and two successful novels, and considered by many of his contemporaries as the most promising of young writers, insisted on the ritual drinking of champagne from Adah's slipper. She protested vehemently, saying the wine would ruin her shoe. She seemed to have forgotten, for the moment, that she no longer had to be careful of her wardrobe, but could buy as many pairs of shoes as she wanted.

Burke playfully dived under the table. Adah, who had no understanding of the meaning of dignity, followed him. They scuffled, laughing and shrieking, and eventually the triumphant Burke emerged with the shoe. He filled it with champagne, drank heartily and passed it around the table. Though Adah declared she would never forgive him, it was he who escorted her home at the end of the party.

There is no verification of the story that Burke slept with her that night. In the light of Adah's background, however, there is every reason to assume that she did not send him away. Certainly they were inseparable for the next three weeks, at the end of which time they quarreled and Burke enlisted in the Union Army. On October 21 he was dead, succumbing after suffering severe wounds in the Union defeat at the Battle of Ball's Bluff in Virginia.

Adah forgot neither Burke nor the stealing of her slipper. He was only one of the many men in her life, but the scuffle at Pfaff's and Burke's untimely death only four months later were typical of the tragedy that stalked her from childhood to the grave. She was convinced it was not accidental that an indelible stain should mar her memory of the night she emerged from the shadows.

CHAPTER II

THE YEARS OF INNOCENCE

"My Heritage!" It is to live within
The marts of Pleasure and of Gain, yet be
No willing worshipper at either shrine. . . .

—"My Heritage"

AT ONE TIME or another in her publicity-conscious life, Adah Isaacs Menken made various wildly conflicting claims regarding her immediate ancestry. What she said depended on circumstances, her mood of the moment, and her audience. When she was a struggling young actress, she told people her father had been one Josiah Campbell, a successful New Orleans merchant. During the short months of her marriage to John C. Heenan, she said she was the daughter of James McCord, whom she described as a native of Dublin, an amateur poet, and the professional heavyweight champion of Europe.

She stunned her first husband, Isaac Menken, when she met his devoutly religious Jewish family in Cincinnati and confided to them that she was the daughter of Ricardo los Fuertes, a Rabbinical scholar of Portuguese ancestry. From time to time in later years she found it convenient to revive the Ricardo los Fuertes myth. When she took England

by storm, she declared that she was the daughter of
Richard Irving Spenser, a wealthy Louisiana plantation
owner, a gallant Confederate officer who had died for the
cause of states' rights fighting William Tecumseh Sher-
man's rabble at Atlanta.

The French thought her father had been Jean Paul
Henri Gautier, one of the first Frenchmen to land at New
Orleans. But for Alexandre Dumas the Elder, her ardent
admirer and himself her peer in spinning tales out of
nowhere, she generously fabricated another ancestry, making herself part Negro. Spenser came to life for her during her comic-opera interlude in Vienna. She didn't know
her fourth husband, Captain James Barkley, long enough
or well enough to fabricate a new past for him.

Newell, a trained newspaperman who was thoroughly
familiar with the techniques of investigation, made it his
business to ferret out the truth a short time before he
and Adah were married. Posterity is indebted to him for
the few facts he was able to unearth.

On April 11, 1835, Marie Theodore, the wife of Auguste
Theodore, gave birth to a daughter in the living quarters
of the family's tiny general store in Milneburg, Louisiana,
a small, drab suburb of New Orleans. The baby was
christened Adah Bertha, and the event was duly recorded
in the registry at St. Paul's, the parish church.

Virtually nothing is known of Auguste Theodore. Adah,
in one of her more expansive moods, told a group of aboli-
tionists at the time feeling was running high immediately
after the publication of President Lincoln's Emancipation
Proclamation, that her father had been "a free man of
color." There may be some substance to the claim, for
she told Newell, while married to him, that "I cannot, as
the daughter of an octaroon, sympathize with the cause of
the Confederacy."

She made no other known reference to her father's

color, either in her *Diary* or her correspondence. Ed James was inclined to think she had spun a romantic drama for the benefit of the gullible. Other friends dismissed the allegation as unimportant.

Auguste Theodore did not live long enough to influence his daughter's future, dying when the baby was only six months old. His harassed widow made an attempt to operate the business, but her baby was sickly and required most of her time and attention. So, early in 1836, Marie Theodore sold the store and moved with her child to a New Orleans rooming house. It was her intention to obtain work as a governess, which indicates that she may not have been completely lacking in education.

Even greater proof is evident in the romance that quickly blossomed between the widow and Campbell Josephs, an instructor in Latin and Greek at the St. Charles Academy for Young Gentlemen in the city. Josephs was a man who placed a high value on intellect, and it is unlikely that he would have become interested in an ignoramus. It is idle to speculate, however; let it suffice that Josephs and Mrs. Theodore were married in July, 1836, and moved to a small house in New Orleans. Adah went with them and was reared by Josephs as his daughter, although he did not formally adopt her.

Late in 1837, Mrs. Josephs gave birth to another daughter, who was called Annie Campbell. This child immediately became her mother's favorite, and until Mrs. Josephs' death in 1860, invariably received preferential treatment.

A letter written by Annie Campbell Josephs to Adah on September 18, 1860, said:

You will be grieved to learn that Ma died in her sleep last night. I am burying her in the same grave with Pa.

She knew she was mortal sick after supper, and one of her last words was to ask me to remember her kindly to you. You always treated her good, Adah, and you have no call to reproach yourself in any way for not being here at the sudden end.

I know that Ma liked me better than you ever since we was little. I hated her for it because it was not fair, but you was always a great good sport about it. Many times you must have been hurt badly enough, but you never let her see that you grieved. How I admired you for holding up your head so high! I still admire you, and wish you every success in your marriage and your work.

I think Pa liked you better than me, so you don't have to shed too many tears.

Your affec. sister,
Annie.

If Mrs. Josephs was relatively indifferent to her elder child, the instructor in Latin and Greek more than made up the difference. Adah was precocious, and it amused him to teach her to speak Latin and Greek before she could walk alone. He also instituted a strict regimen of physical exercise to overcome her weak constitution, and Adah responded to his treatment.

By the time she began school at the age of six, she was a tomboy who dismayed her mother by fighting all of the little boys in the neighborhood. Her stepfather encouraged her, and at the same time augmented her education by giving her lessons in French and Spanish, as well as Greek and Latin. Thanks to him, she could speak, read, and write all four tongues fluently.

It was Josephs, too, who was responsible for her familiarity with horses. The St. Charles Academy maintained a number of mounts for its pupils, as the education of a New Orleans gentleman would have been woefully incomplete had he been unable to ride. The faculty had access to the stable, and Josephs, as part of his physical training program for Adah, took her riding for at least an hour every afternoon.

By the time she was ten years old, she told Newell, she could ride all of the St. Charles horses, including the stallions. When she was thirteen she earned her first money exercising the animals, two dollars, and Josephs was so pleased that he added another to it. Adah never forgot the occasion. Mrs. Josephs berated her husband for squandering money, and made life miserable for him. She also tried to force Adah to return the dollar, but the girl refused, and domestic relations were strained. There are several references to this unhappy period in Adah's *Diary*, and even after her mother's death she remained indignant. The wounds inflicted by injustice did not heal.

Adah's formal education ceased when she reached the age of twelve, as she constantly reminded herself in her *Diary*. "I haven't done too poorly for one who attended no class, no school from the day I reached the beginning of my thirteenth year," was a constant refrain.

She continued to receive private tutoring from her step-father, however. Mathematics and the sciences bored her, and she turned a deaf ear to Josephs' suggestions that she follow in his footsteps. She had no desire to teach either Greek or Latin, in spite of her proficiency in both languages.

At some unspecified time in her early adolescence she discovered poetry, and plunged headlong into a wonderful new world. She read the works of every poet, major and minor, from the great literary figures of antiquity to the young artists struggling to express themselves, whose offerings were published once each week in the pages of the New Orleans *Picayune*.

Adah made strenuous efforts to join that eager, if not talented, band of amateurs. She submitted scores of poems to the *Picayune*, but was not discouraged when all were rejected. As she discovered in her studies of the lives of poets, many struggled for long years before achieving the recognition they craved. She, too, was willing to labor in the vineyards of iambic pentameter until someone, somewhere, hailed her genius.

She made good use of her knowledge of French, and devoured the works of Racine, Molière, and others in the original. She disliked Voltaire, however, and many years later confided to her good friend, George Sand, that she thought him "cruel."

Adah's thirst for learning was quenched in part by her access to one of the best private libraries in New Orleans. Her zest came to the attention of Honoré St. Eustace, an elderly, wealthy trustee of Josephs' school, who allowed the girl to borrow whatever caught her fancy in his collection of more than thirty thousand volumes. She visited his house frequently, but these calls ceased abruptly when she reached the age of fifteen.

Josephs issued an ultimatum, forbidding her to go to the St. Eustace home again. Adah delicately refrains from mentioning the cause of the disturbance in her *Diary*, but as she states elsewhere in its pages, "Men found me attractive at fifteen," it is not too hard to guess that the elderly gentleman may have overstepped the bounds of propriety.

Adah gave up riding shortly after her fourteenth birthday, too, soon after she took part in a race, apparently an annual event at the school, which she won. According to Newell, she dressed in breeches and a shirt when taking part in the races, and the parents of some of the boys found her appearance objectionable.

She won a prize, however, a gold medal that became one of her proudest possessions. This medal was not the product of her fertile imagination, for Newell saw it. James mentions it, too, saying she had refused to part with it, even when so desperately hungry that she might have been tempted to ask a pawnshop to give her, in return for the trinket, enough cash to buy herself a hearty meal.

Poetry was her first love, her abiding love, and for many years, until Murdoch suggested that she play *Mazeppa,* she sat on the back of a horse only for purposes of transportation. Her adoration of poetry—and enormous respect for poets—undoubtedly accounts in large part for her many close friendships with people in the literary world. Some of her contemporaries were unable to understand why Americans like Whitman and Bret Harte, Englishmen like Swinburne, Rossetti and Charles Dickens, and Frenchmen like Dumas and Theophile Gautier tolerated a "vulgar female mountebank," as the *Atlantic* called her in a scathing review of *Mazeppa.* Authors, like other men, were only human—perhaps all too human—and were susceptible to the flatteries of a bold young woman with enormous, violet eyes and a superb figure who sat worshiping at their feet.

Her friendship with such women as George Sand and the talented Laura Seymour (mistress of the novelist Charles Reade) is another story. Both shunned her at first and were critical of her, but were quick to appreciate her erudition, charm, and wit when they came to know her. Adah's detractors to the contrary, she had something more than sex appeal.

But in 1852, when she reached the age of seventeen, her only assets were sex, her love of poetry, and her knowledge of foreign languages. Campbell Josephs died that year, and as he left no estate, it became necessary for Adah to sell one or more of her assets. She chose tutoring, and placed a discreet advertisement in the pages of the *Picayune,* saying that a young lady in financially distressed circumstances would be pleased to teach French, Spanish, Greek, and Latin to the daughters of those willing to pay her the lordly fee of fifty cents an hour.

She obtained several pupils, and if she did not prosper, at least she, her mother, and her half sister did not starve. All that Adah earned was dutifully handed over to the frugal Mrs. Josephs, who made every penny count. The young tutor left home early each morning and, regardless of the weather, walked from house to house as she visited her young charges. Perhaps it is significant that the first entry in her *Diary* is dated August 4, 1852, and is a paraphrase of a line of seventeenth-century poetry written by Robert Herrick: "My aching feet, like snails, did creep."

Certainly Adah was totally unprepared for her abrupt emergence into the world that necessity dictated. Totally lacking in worldly experience of any kind, she had spent virtually all of her adolescence as a student in a secluded ivory tower, reading and writing poetry, daydreaming, studying the literature of France and the few Spanish works available in New Orleans.

Now, without warning, she was thrust outside. Her mother was either unable or unwilling to work, Annie was too young, and the seventeen-year-old with long, Indian-straight black hair became the family breadwinner. For the first time she became aware of the bustle and conflict in a growing, sprawling, brawling United States.

Harriet Beecher Stowe's *Uncle Tom's Cabin,* one of the most successful novels in American history, was published that year, and was extraordinarily influential in unifying Northern opposition to slavery. Adah confesses in her *Diary* that she read a few pages of the book, found it dull and threw it aside.

Hawthorne's *The Scarlet Letter* was more to her liking. The clergy of New Orleans were almost united in thundering from the pulpit that the story was salacious, and the majority demanded that the novel be banned in the city. In spite of that fact or, perhaps, because of it, Adah was eager to obtain a copy, and finally managed to borrow one from the parents of one of her pupils. She read it in two evenings, and it made a deep impression on her.

"Hester Prynne," she told her *Diary*, "was a wonderful woman. She was lovely and strong, and I wish I had that kind of strength. The people of Massachusetts tried to shame her, but she shamed them by showing such great dignity in the face of their scorn. Only the men are weak. Dimmesdale [the clergyman who committed adultery with Hester] was a poor excuse for a man. Not until he was old and feeble and dying did he have the courage to confess his sin. Even then he tried to escape to Europe with Hester. Why didn't he admit from the very start that he was the father of her child? Why didn't he take her away somewhere when they were both young? If he had done that, I could have respected him! Chillingworth [Hester's husband] was even worse. He was an evil, cruel beast, a blood relative of Beelzebub. If I had been Hester, I wouldn't have tolerated his horrible abuse. I think I would have killed him. Hester had many opportunities to kill him. There were long needles in her house that she used for sewing. One quick stab in the heart would have finished him."

She added one more comment in a separate paragraph: "Pearl [the illegitimate daughter of Hester and Dimmesdale] was a dreadful girl."

Few members of Adah's generation recognized the genius of Hawthorne or realized that *The Scarlet Letter* would be hailed in time as one of the greatest—if not the greatest —of American novels. Indeed, the young women who admired the unfortunate Hester Prynne were rare, and the parents of Adah's pupils would have discharged her instantly had they known that she regarded Hester as a woman endowed with nobility. It is useless, certainly, to wonder how many girls of the period were able to identify with Hester. It is enough, here, to note that Adah did. It

is also interesting to observe her scorn for men and indifference to children.

Her own character had already been formed, although
she did not know it. The daughter of a mother who paid
scant attention to her and of an overly strict stepfather who
hid his own inability to earn a good living behind a
façade of intellectual discipline, Adah Bertha Theodore
was ready for adventure.

In the autumn of 1852 she took her first plunge, making
speeches on behalf of the Democratic candidates for President and Vice President of the United States, Franklin
Pierce of New Hampshire and William R. King of Alabama. Both were believed to be more lenient in their attitudes toward the slaveholding states of the South than
their Whig opponents, General Winfield Scott, the hero
of the Mexican War, and his running mate, William
Graham of North Carolina.

The Pierce-King ticket was overwhelmingly popular in
New Orleans, and people cheered Adah when she appeared
at meetings in church halls. The applause was the first she
had ever known, and she loved it. There is no evidence,
either in her *Diary* or in her subsequent life, that she was
in the least interested in politics. Nor is there any indication of what impelled a girl to invade what was then
strictly a man's world.

Perhaps it is wrong to search too hard or try to dig too
deeply for her motives. She was young and unusually attractive. Men were startled when she appeared on a platform to extoll the virtues of the New Hampshire nonentity, Franklin Pierce. It is possible, even probable, that
she enjoyed the novelty for its own sake.

She mentions the campaign only once in her *Diary*. Her
shocked mother ordered her to stop making speeches, but
the rebellious, independent girl refused. As she was the
family's only source of income, she won the argument, of

course. Feminist bugles blowing a fanfare in the background, she writes triumphantly, "The woman of today
is not a slave, but free!"

The campaign meant so little to her, however, that she
did not bother to note in her *Diary* that the candidate she
supported, Franklin Pierce, was elected President of the
United States in November.

The year 1853 was an exceptionally important one in
Adah's life. She was one of the first in New Orleans to buy
a copy of an astonishingly sloppy book of poems that became one of the year's biggest sellers, much to the despair
of those who were trying to further the cause of real literature. Fanny Fern, the author, coyly called her book, *Fern
Leaves from Fanny's Portfolio,* and the modern reader
gags on verse after verse of cloying, pseudo-artistic senti-
mentality.

Adah thought Fanny Fern was the greatest of living
poets, and *Fern Leaves* a rare treasure. She memorized
long passages, quoted them at length in her *Diary,* and
redoubled her own writing efforts. The *Picayune* continued to reject her offerings, but the experience was
valuable. In later years, when her encouragement meant so
much to young authors of real talent, she could speak with
genuine sympathy and understanding of the pain and
humiliation a writer felt when his life's blood was returned to him in a self-addressed envelope.

The epidemic of yellow fever that struck New Orleans
in midyear was indirectly responsible for uprooting Adah
and changing her whole way of life. Mrs. Josephs became
seriously ill, and Annie contracted a mild case of the fever.
Adah, who had developed from a sickly child into a remarkably robust young woman, was untouched. She spent
her days tutoring her pupils and her nights nursing her
mother and half sister.

Annie recovered quickly and assumed some of the

chores, but the responsibilities that the fifteen-year-old girl could shoulder were limited, and most of the burden continued to fall on Adah. As the summer of 1853 wore on, life became more and more of a nightmare. Mrs. Josephs failed to respond to medical treatment and remained gravely ill. Adah was able to snatch only a few hours of sleep each night, and the money she paid for doctors and medicines drained away the better part of her small income.

New Orleans itself gradually succumbed to mass hysteria as the epidemic increased, spreading out through Louisiana into Mississippi. Hospitals were overcrowded, the strength of physicians was taxed, and there were too few nurses to take care of the sick. No facilities existed for keeping an accurate record of those stricken with yellow fever, but it has been estimated that between four thousand and ten thousand persons died of the disease in New Orleans and the surrounding area in the second half of 1853 and the first months of the next year.

Mrs. Josephs improved sufficiently to leave her bed, but her health was permanently impaired, and she never regained her full strength. Adah's domestic burdens were relieved, to an extent, but a new crisis deprived her of her sole source of income. The schools were closed for an indefinite period, and private tutors were ordered to suspend their operations. The three members of the Josephs family faced almost certain starvation.

Adah knew no profession other than that which she was now forbidden to practice, Mrs. Josephs was too weak to work, and no employment of any kind could be obtained by Annie, an adolescent with no training and no skills. Adah sold her late stepfather's riding boots, silver spurs, and gold-handled cane in order to obtain enough food for a few days.

Mrs. Josephs, who seemed incapable of facing reality,

protested. But Adah paid no attention to her complaints, and confided to her *Diary* that her one regret was her inability to sell anything more. The family's only remaining possessions were cheap, secondhand furniture and worn clothing. The house and the small plot of ground on which it stood had a paper value, but as thousands of citizens were trying to sell their homes and move elsewhere, the market was glutted.

Adah's future was as bleak as any faced by the heroine of a Dion Boucicault play.

Then, suddenly, salvation appeared in the portly shape of Baron Friedrich von Eberstadt, an Austrian nobleman who was spending a year in the New World and whose daughter had been one of Adah's pupils.

CHAPTER III

QUEEN OF THE PLAZA

Who hath not sent out ships to sea?
　　Who hath not toiled through light and darkness to make
　　　them strong for battle?
And how we freighted them with dust from the mountain mines!
　　And red gold, coined from the heart's blood, rich in
　　　Youth, Love and Beauty!
And we have fondly sent forth on their white decks seven times
　　a hundred souls.
Sent them out like sea-girt worlds full of hope, love, care,
　　and faith.
Oh, mariners, mariners, watch and beware!

　　　　　　　　　　　　　　—"The Ship That Went Down"

FRIEDRICH VON EBERSTADT, a man fond of wine, women, and song in the best Viennese tradition, traced his aristocratic ancestry to the Holy Roman emperors. A staunch monarchist, he had, nevertheless, found it prudent to spend a year abroad after an embarrassing incident, allegedly involving a chambermaid, that had shocked the austere young Emperor of Austria-Hungary, Franz Josef, and his conservative court.

The Baron, whose funds appeared unlimited, had taken up residence in New Orleans with his wife, Selma, and their young daughter, considering it the only sophisticated city in the United States. When the yellow fever epidemic sent the Baroness and her child hurrying to New York, the Baron remained behind to dispose of their rented house and arrange for the shipping of their furniture and other belongings to the more salubrious atmosphere of Europe.

One day in mid-October, 1853, the despairing Adah received a note asking her to call on the Baron the following morning. She speculates at length in her *Diary* on the work she hoped he would offer her, and her mind was filled with dreams of the unattainable: perhaps she would be sent to New York as a governess for the Von Eberstadt child, and would accompany the family to Europe.

She dressed carefully for the occasion in her best gown, a black bombazine purchased for her stepfather's funeral. In order to make her appearance less somber, she tied a scarlet sash around her waist and borrowed a frilly bonnet. She was dissatisfied with the effect, but could do nothing to improve it, and went off nervously to the interview.

Her *Diary* for that night contains a single, hastily scribbled line: "F. von E. loves me!"

The Baron, an old hand, moved cautiously in the next few days, and managed to persuade Adah to accept an all-expenses-paid vacation in Havana. She seems to have suffered few, if any, pangs of conscience, and happily threw herself into the role of a Southern Hester Prynne. She felt certain, however, that Von Eberstadt intended to marry her. He told her that a cousin, who was a member of the Austrian delegation to the Vatican, would obtain a Papal annulment of his marriage. Adah, in her innocence—and in her eagerness to embark on an adventure that would take care of her financial problems—accepted the story.

Mrs. Josephs, whose concern over money far exceeded her concern about right and wrong, made no objections.

She had never bothered to teach Adah either morals or principles, and now, when the cupboard was bare, was no time to start.

Adah presented her mother with a purse that would take care of her and Annie for at least two months, and sailed with the Baron on the Spanish ship *Bianca* on October 18.

New Orleans, by American standards, was a glittering metropolis, but the naïve Adah Bertha Theodore was totally unprepared for Havana, a city that combined the best and worst of both Spain and the tropics. The capital of New Spain with its two hundred thousand people was one of the largest and most cosmopolitan centers in the western hemisphere, rivaled only by New York, Buenos Aires, and Rio de Janeiro.

New Orleans had four theaters. In Havana there were twenty-seven. In New Orleans, a few wealthy families dined at circumspect inns. In Havana, there were more restaurants, inns, and taverns than a bewildered girl could count. Women, and even young ladies who never ventured abroad without chaperones, wore revealing clothes. Females who strolled down the broad avenues, smiled at strangers from tables in open-fronted cafés, and frequented the theaters were usually attired in bosom-exposing skin-tight gowns slit to the knee. Even adolescent girls appeared publicly in high-heeled silk slippers, their high-piled hair held in place by enormous combs that resembled intricately worked lace.

Adah felt dowdy. The Baron, who had engaged a luxurious suite at an inn called the Obispo, hastened to remedy the situation. He and Adah went on a shopping spree, with Friedrich supervising all purchases. He had already gained through intimate observation a keen appreciation of Adah's spectacular figure and, wanting other men to

envy his good fortune, made certain that her wardrobe
was flamboyant.

From the very beginning Adah enjoyed wearing costumes that would have made a seasoned New Orleans
harlot blush. She comments in her *Diary* again and again,
with some surprise, that men ogled her and that she found
the sensation flattering. People stared at her in restaurants
and theaters, on the boulevards and the promenades that
overlooked the warm, blue-green sea, and she soon learned
to accept their tributes to her ripening beauty.

As she was watched, so Adah observed. She found that
rouge on her lips and cheeks, powder on her nose, and
black antimony on her lashes enhanced her appearance.
The Baron, humoring her, now gave her free rein in her
purchases, and she proved that her taste in clothes was as
bold as his. "I have bought very little lingerie," she says
blithely in her *Diary*. "It is so warm and close here that
few ladies bother to wear it." She had not lost her sense of
values, however, and another night remarks that she would
be arrested in New Orleans if she dared to wear any of
her new clothes there.

One flaw made the idyll less than perfect. The Baron's
love-making disappointed Adah. She didn't know what to
expect, what she was supposed to feel, but she realized that
whatever it was, she did not experience it. Instinct, however, prompted her to conceal the truth, and she made a
pretense of being a warm and enthusiastic mistress.

It is significant that never again does Adah mention her
physical response—or the lack of such feeling—in her
Diary or elsewhere. In her poems and correspondence she
frequently refers to romantic love in accepted nineteenth-
century terms. But in her *Diary* the gates of the physical
remain firmly closed. It is impossible for the modern
reader, endowed with a greater knowledge of the human
psyche, to refrain from guessing that, in all probability,

Adah was frigid. Like so many women, throughout history and down to the present day, who took many lovers, it is likely that she was incapable of finding complete physical and emotional satisfaction and release in sex relations. She had been molded in her childhood, and for the rest of her days would seek the unattainable.

In the main, however, she relished the life she and the Baron led. They slept late, were waited on by a platoon of servants, and lazed away their days. They attended the theater frequently, and as Von Eberstadt was a man of some consequence, they often dined as the guests of high-ranking Spanish colonial officials. Adah was perturbed when she realized that on such occasions the deputy viceroy, the generals, admirals, or bureau chiefs did not invite her to their homes, but took her and the Baron to private rooms at the best restaurants. The companions of these gentlemen were not their wives, but young women whose dress was bolder than Adah's and whose manners were infinitely more audacious.

Eventually Adah became resigned to the role she was forced to play, realizing that in New Orleans, also, a man's mistress would not be welcome in the homes of his friends. Whether she knew by that time the Baron had no intention of marrying her is open to conjecture. She does not mention the subject. Neither, apparently, did Von Eberstadt.

Adah had no real cause to feel he was imposing on her, however, for he remained generous and good-natured. He doled out liberal quantities of spending money, and she —in the tradition hallowed since the dim days when the oldest profession first came into existence—was good to her mother. Every Spanish *dólar* not spent on clothes and trinkets was dutifully forwarded to Mrs. Josephs. The wages of sin insured that the invalided widow and her young daughter would not starve.

Adah was too inexperienced to know that it would have been wise to put aside an emergency fund for a rainy day, and she was too optimistic by nature to see storm clouds in the offing. Common sense should have told her that Friedrich was in a delicate position. The Baroness Selma would not be content to wait forever in New York, a strange city, giving her husband an opportunity to eat his *Linzertorte* and have it, too. Perhaps the Baroness cracked the whip, or it may be that the Baron knew that all good interludes had to end and did not want to press his luck.

In any event, he became restless, and late in January, 1854, Adah says in her *Diary,* he told her he had heard that the yellow fever epidemic in New Orleans had sub-sided. Apparently he was trying to pave the way for a break, but Adah didn't take the hint. Instead, she played into the hands of the man who had already proved himself sufficiently unscrupulous to corrupt her.

The theater fascinated Adah, and by late January she and the Baron had become acquainted with several of the leading performers, directors, and theater owners. Many of the companions of highly placed officials were girls who were trying to make second careers for them-selves on the stage, and most of them were unable to sing, dance, or recite a line. Adah became convinced that she could do far better than they, and was encouraged by people who repeated one or another version of the old saw, "You're so beautiful I thought you were an actress."

One evening early in February a crisis of volcanic pro-portions erupted suddenly at a restaurant called the Sevilla. Adah and the Baron had attended a performance of a musical play; she had enjoyed it, but he had been bored and was in an irritable mood. The stars of the play and some of their friends came to the Sevilla, and Adah made the catastrophic error of offering her warm congratulations to the leading man, whom she calls Ramon in her *Diary.*

Flattered by the attention of the attractive girl, Ramon promptly turned on the charm of a professional actor. It is conceivable that Adah flirted with him, making matters worse in the Baron's eyes. As Dante Gabriel Rossetti observed many years later, "It is as natural for The Menken to flirt with every man she meets as it is for all humans to breathe."

She must have felt something of a sense of relief when a handsome, dashing male bowed over her hand, complimented her on her appearance and made it plain that he thought her desirable. After all, she had spent several months in the company of a rotund, balding gentleman, more than twice her age, whose love-making fell flat.

Ramon brought the little farce to a logical climax by asking Adah to spend the rest of the evening with him. She refused, but by then the damage was done. The Baron had heard every word of the conversation and had been aware of every long glance, every eyelash flutter. He was furious—or pretended to be—which amounted to the same thing.

Here was his chance to achieve the break he had been seeking, and he took full advantage of it. He stalked out of the Sevilla, with Adah following, and berated her as they made their way back to their inn. His pride may have been genuinely hurt, for he ranted through the rest of the night, shouting and using what she refers to in her *Diary* as "unspeakable epithets."

She apologized and begged him to forgive her, but he refused to be placated. At last, sometime after sunrise, Adah lost her own explosive temper. In years to come her rages would be world-renowned, but Von Eberstadt was the first to feel the fury of her self-generated tornado. There is no way of determining whether she had yet

acquired the rich vocabulary that so impressed Bret Harte
when he heard her in action in San Francisco, but the
Baron could not have been comfortable as he listened to
her tirade.

She raced out of the suite, sobbing but dry-eyed, and ran
down to the waterfront. "There I wandered for hours, not
seeing the passers-by who watched me so curiously," she
relates in her *Diary,* unaware of the contradiction. Even
when upset, she was incapable of remaining oblivious to
the effect she had on others.

When her calm returned, and with it her appetite, she
decided she had punished the Baron enough and returned
to the inn, ready for a late breakfast. The first great shock
of her life awaited her.

The management of the Obispo regretted to inform the
Señorita that the Señor Baron had paid the bill and departed with his luggage. He had requested that the Señorita be informed he was sailing immediately for New York,
via Charleston and Philadelphia. And the management
sorrowfully felt compelled to inform the Señorita that the
suite had been engaged by new guests who expected to
occupy the quarters that afternoon.

Adah raced out to the balcony where she had eaten so
many leisurely meals and caught a glimpse of an American merchantman disappearing from view beyond Morro
Castle, Havana's most famous landmark.

She had no time to recover, for the management intended to have her vacate the suite immediately. Her new
wardrobe was intact in cupboards and closets, but she
was completely without funds. Only now did she realize
that Friedrich had given her no jewelry she could pawn
or sell in this moment of crisis. In fact, she had no luggage
other than the two small, battered boxes she had brought
with her from New Orleans. The proprietor of the Obispo
obligingly supplied her with several wooden crates.

A short time later she stood in the dusty road outside the inn, not knowing what to do next. But her instinct for survival, which was to prove so strong in times of trial, came to her rescue. A short time later she was ensconced in a hostelry located in the center of the theatrical district, the portion of the city that she knew and liked best. Her *Diary* does not state how she got there.

Alone behind a barred door, she took stock of her assets, which consisted of a pretty face and good figure, a flashy wardrobe and a desperation that made her reckless. She could speak Spanish, too, which helped.

Perhaps the incident with Ramon was instrumental in turning her thoughts toward the theater. But it is more likely that, having met a number of girls who played bit parts and having considered herself superior to them, she reasoned that she could find employment on the stage. She could not afford to dawdle, and started at once to make the rounds of Havana's theaters.

Everywhere she met the same resistance. Her Spanish vocabulary was good, she was told, but her accent was foreign. There was no place for her.

The next day, hungry and miserable, she tried again. Now the reactions were blunter. A girl who had no professional theatrical experience could find work only if her protector used his influence on her behalf. The Señorita had no protector? Too bad.

Adah went to the theater where Ramon was playing a matinee, and he received her eagerly in his dressing room. But his manner changed when he learned she wanted work, and he peremptorily ordered her to leave. She dragged herself into the street, too frightened to give in to the hysteria that threatened to engulf her. She had eaten nothing for thirty-six hours, and perhaps it was hunger that led to her solution of her problem.

In later years Adah described her successful Havana

career in glowing terms. She had been the toast of the town, the star of a sumptuously mounted musical play at the famous Tacon Teatro, where thousands had come to watch her dance. She had done her own choreography, and the critics had been enchanted. All Havana had been at her feet.

She had been known there as the Queen of the Plaza, and to the end of her days it pleased her to be called by that name.

In truth, Adah never danced a single step on a stage in her life. Neither the Havana newspaper critics nor anyone else ever saw her give a performance. She attended plays at the Tacon only as a member of the audience. She never earned a single *dólar* in Cuba as a dancer or actress.

What actually happened, after the disappointing interview with Ramon, was that the crushed Adah walked slowly through the streets. She had dressed with care for her meetings with producers, and her low-cut gown drew considerable attention to her well-proportioned figure.

A man looked questioningly at Adah, and she smiled. One thing led to another, and he invited her to accompany him to his bed. She agreed, provided he would buy her some food. He assumed they would eat after he took his pleasure, but soon discovered his error. Adah waded through a huge meal, then accompanied him, and suffered no pangs of conscience or remorse.

It was easier for her to think when her gnawing appetite had been assuaged, and she now took stock of her situation. It was silly to starve when all she had to do was smile at a man. And if one would buy her a hearty dinner, others would pay her rent. Without a qualm she became a professional prostitute.

Her *Diary* for the next six months is a financial ledger devoid of all comments. It was strictly a record of income and expenses, and she scrupulously noted every transaction. When she knew the name of a client, she wrote such items as, "Capt. Gonzales, three *dólars.*" When her partner was someone she didn't know, she said, "Stranger, three *dólars.*"

She gives no information regarding her dwelling places during this time, but apparently made several moves, each to a more expensive address, for her rent increased. So did the money she spent on food, and occasionally she added to her wardrobe. Twice, for periods of about ten days each, she may have been stricken with a disease that was a vocational hazard, for she lists visits to physicians during these times.

Quite possibly she enjoyed her work, for she earned more than enough to pay for her passage to New Orleans, yet remained in Havana.

Still a dutiful daughter, she continued to send the better part of her income to her mother. Any letters she may have written to Mrs. Josephs and Annie have vanished, but it seems improbable that she told them the source of the money she sent them. Annie believed she had worked as an actress in Cuba, and Adah did not disillusion her.

Suddenly, in August, 1854, the *Diary* comes to life again. Apparently Adah had made sufficient progress that she was no longer forced to roam the streets in search of clients, and the names of fashionable restaurants reappear. "To-night," she says on August 11, "at the Villarrobledo I met a Count recently arrived from Spain, who is attached to the staff of the Admiral-in-Chief. He has asked me to dine with him tomorrow, and I have accepted. He is short and swarthy, but is very earnest; I think he dislikes it here and is lonely."

She obviously helped to dispel his feeling of loneliness, for two nights later she makes the laconic entry, "Count de L., twenty *dólars.*"

Adah's sudden transformation from a modest tutor in

foreign languages to a baron's mistress was abrupt, and her move from mistress to streetwalker was equally startling. Viewed logically, however, both were dictated by necessity. She sold the one commodity that buyers in the marketplace were willing to purchase.

It is far more difficult to understand why she lingered in Havana. Her *Diary* offers no clues, no rationalizations, no excuses. She was now earning a substantial income, and apparently had found a niche that satisfied her. Although she sent money regularly to her mother, she spent a great deal more on herself. The prices of her gowns, hats, and shoes soared, and she appears to have patronized the city's most expensive dressmakers, spending as much as eighty *dólars* for a single gown. The Spanish *dólar* was worth almost as much as the American dollar at that period, and in the United States only the wives of very wealthy men spent such large sums for dresses.

If nothing else, Adah acquired an extravagant wardrobe that she used to good advantage when she finally launched her theatrical career. She continued to choose gaudy, audacious clothes, and for the rest of her life wore nothing else.

Also, she gained a deep understanding of men that was to become one of her most valuable assets. At the same time, the experience scarred her, leaving her with a contempt for males that she later seemed unable to overcome, an emotional liability that robbed her of any chance she might have had to find happiness. Or, it may be, the many months she spent living as a prostitute hardened her so much that no man appealed to her. Most of her close friends were men, the majority of them authors, but she never found a husband or lover who gave her contentment.

Whatever the reasons for her prolonged stay in Havana, there she stayed for the better part of 1855. She rose rapidly in her chosen half-world; the deputy viceroy, whom she had met when she and the Baron had first arrived, was one of her clients. She does not say whether she had any chances to become the mistress of just one man, but it must be assumed that such opportunities came her way. Other girls had protectors, and she undoubtedly could have indulged in such a relationship, too. Possibly her experience with Von Eberstadt had convinced her that it wouldn't be safe to trust any one man.

Although she seems to have found safety in numbers, there are fewer entries in her *Diary* in 1855. She was charging whatever the traffic would bear, and never had more than one client in a single day. Often there are several days in succession when the record remains blank. Her fees became increasingly high, and she now received anywhere from fifty to two hundred *dólars* from a man in return for her favors.

She was saving money, and it may have been at this time that she conceived the idea of making a determined effort to become an actress in the United States. Oddly, she makes no notation of her hopes in her *Diary*.

Neither did she write any poetry during her Havana stay. Her career was not the sort that inspired the Muse.

Finally, in September, 1855, there appears one line written in her characteristically bold, vertical slant: "I have obtained a passage home!" The line is underscored three times.

No information is available regarding the voyage itself, but she apparently entertained her last client in late September. Then, on October 14, 1855, Adah Bertha Theodore arrived in New Orleans, a wise professional prostitute at the ripe old age of twenty years.

CHAPTER IV

THE HOUSEWIFE

> Hear, O Israel! my people—to thy goodly tents do I return
> with unstained hands.
> Like as the harts for the water-brooks, in thirst, do pant and
> bray, so pants and cries my longing soul for the house of Jacob.
>
> —"Hear, O Israel!"

THE MOST UNSAVORY INTERLUDE in Adah's life was at an
end when she returned to New Orleans from Havana.
Never again did she sell her body for money, no matter
how desperate her circumstances. None of her contemporaries ever knew the sordid details of the months she
spent in Havana, and she went to great pains to prevent
anyone from discovering them. In fact, her *Diary* indicates
that even when she had sunk to the depths of depravity,
she never lost sight of her future. Many Americans visited
Cuba, and there were almost always two or three West-
Indian trading ships tied up at Havana. Yet there is no
record that she ever entertained one of her fellow country-
men while earning her living as a prostitute. Without exception, the names of her clients were Latin.

Apparently she was making certain that she would not
be recognized and embarrassed when she returned home.
On her arrival in New Orleans she held her guard high,

and thereafter never relaxed it. Both of her biographers,
James and Newell, believed the story she told about her
theatrical success in Havana. James, her enthusiastic supporter for many years, may have been easy enough to fool,
but Newell was a disillusioned and bitter former husband.
He questioned many of her claims, but it never occurred to
him to doubt her fanciful tale of this part of her life.

Mrs. Josephs and Annie accepted Adah's story at face
value, and were so gullible that Mrs. Josephs even complimented her elder daughter on her "pretty" clothes.

New Orleans had changed in the two years that Adah
had been away. Tension between the North and South was
mounting steadily, but Adah avoided controversy, con-
tenting herself with the brief statement, in her *Diary*,
that she despised the institution of slavery. President
Franklin Pierce, for whom she had campaigned, was bum-
bling along, doing nothing to heal the breach between the
two sections of the country, but Adah displayed no known
interest in him, his policies, or the state of the Union.

Her first act was the energetic reshuffling of the family's
domestic life. Annie had been happy to stay at home with
her mother and live on the money that Adah provided; but
now this situation changed abruptly. Annie was directed
to hunt for work at once, and when Mrs. Josephs protested tearfully, Adah reminded her that there had been
no objections when the elder daughter of the house had
become a wage-earner at a younger age. Annie, now seventeen and a half, was capable of bringing home money, too.

Goaded by Adah, Annie found employment as a house-
keeper. She moved from one such position to another in
the succeeding years, and was still working as a house-
keeper when she faded permanently from her celebrated
sister's life soon after the outbreak of the Civil War. There
is no record of Annie or of any contact between the two
women after that time.

Adah herself took a well-earned rest and caught up on her reading. She was thrilled by a historical novel, *The Cloister and the Hearth,* that brought great renown to its English author, Charles Reade. Henry Wadsworth Longfellow's *The Song of Hiawatha,* also published that same year, had no appeal for her, an indication that her literary tastes were maturing. She bought the newest collection of Fanny Fern's poetic jingles but had outgrown them, too, and in her *Diary* she expresses astonishment that *Fern Leaves* could have impressed her.

She was unaware of the publication in 1855 of one of the most distinguished books in all American literature, Whitman's *Leaves of Grass,* which created a stir only in artistic circles and made no impact on the general public. Adah did not read the book until she became Whitman's friend, confidante, and champion several years later. By that time her intellect had broadened, and she recognized *Leaves of Grass* as a work of genius. It is doubtful, had she encountered it in 1855, that she would have had the capacity to appreciate it.

The feminist movement had recently taken one of its unexpected leaps in a new direction, and in every major city of the United States ladies of the wealthy families were taking up horseback riding. A large stable in New Orleans became a riding academy for women, and a hurried order was sent to Philadelphia for a number of the sidesaddles that contemporary modesty made necessary.

Adah, approached to become an instructress at the academy, indignantly refused. She had learned to ride astride, thought the sidesaddle an absurd contraption and would have nothing to do with it. Once again, she was far ahead of her era. Mrs. Josephs tried to persuade her to accept the post, which offered honorable employment, but Adah says in her *Diary,* "The woman who allows herself to be placed in a sidesaddle fools herself if she thinks she is riding a horse. She could gain just as much pleasure and excitement in a rocking chair."

By December she felt sufficiently refreshed after her Havana experience to start thinking about obtaining work in the theater. First she attended each of the five plays currently running in New Orleans, paying particular attention to the reigning star of the city, an elegant brunette with a clear, sweet, speaking voice, Charlotte Crompton, whose gentle femininity appealed to both sexes.

The favorite Crompton play was *Fazio*, a third-rate drama that was popular with leading ladies because its heroine was on-stage almost constantly and was required to register a wide range of emotions. Every actress of the period wanted to play the role of Bianca, and Matilda Heron, later the mother-in-law of actor-manager Henry Miller, became famous overnight when she appeared in the part in New York.

Adah was shrewd enough to realize that she could become a star if she could persuade a producer to let her play in *Fazio*. She went to see Charlotte Crompton's performance every night for a week, then declares in her *Diary*, "I can do far better than that simpering little belle." Although Adah had never set foot on a stage or earned a penny as an actress, she was already displaying one of the most necessary attributes of stardom, complete self-confidence.

The theaters of New Orleans were preparing new plays to be presented immediately after Christmas, and Adah made the rounds with other struggling aspirants. But neither her appearance nor her manner was like that of her companions. She wore her most stunning costumes, sweeping grandly into the offices of producers to announce that the Queen of the Plaza, who had returned from the most successful engagement in the history of the Havana theater, was available for the right part and at the right salary.

The producers may not have seen through the tissue of Adah's fabrication, but nevertheless they unanimously responded with the mid-nineteenth-century version of "Don't call us, we'll call you."

Adah was, in theatrical parlance, at liberty, and at liberty she remained. Theatrical activities in New Orleans slackened during Lent, and she became bored, restless, and moody. She turned again to her adolescent love, the writing of poetry, but it failed to satisfy her now.

Material considerations made the difference. She couldn't eat her poems, and the nest egg she had brought home from Havana was dwindling. She continued to visit the offices of the producers regularly, always dressing in her most devastating gowns, and soon the theater owners knew her. But they had no work to offer her, and the future looked bleak until James S. Charles, the city's leading impresario, came to her rescue.

He had sent a company on tour through Texas, playing repertory, and had received a letter to the effect that his manager was looking for someone to replace an unreliable ingénue. The manager, Charles said, did his own hiring, but Adah could apply to him in person if she wished, armed with a note of introduction from the maestro.

Charles made the suggestion hesitantly, feeling that a "star" would not want to accept a secondary place in the company, and he warned Adah that the manager's budget would make it impossible for him to pay her more than a maximum wage of eighteen dollars per week. He didn't know Adah, who left for Texas immediately.

There are many wild tales of Adah's travels in the spring of 1856, all of them apocryphal. One of the most popular, which she herself invented, was that she toured the Southwest as the bareback-riding star of a traveling circus. She also claimed that she made a second appearance in the show shooting at moving targets with a rifle while riding bareback on a cantering horse. American and European newspapers took the bait, but the tale is totally untrue. Neither then nor at any other time in Adah's varied, turbulent career was she a member of a circus troupe. And although she had many talents, she once claimed that she did not learn how to handle firearms until she took instruction from the fourth of her husbands, "Captain" James Barkley—a lie, for her step-father taught her to shoot.

The facts are, by comparison, drab. When she found J. S. Charles' company, the letter of introduction did her no good, for the manager had already replaced the ingénue, and there was no hope of ousting the newcomer, who had made a place for herself in the manager's affections. Under the circumstances, Adah was forced to conclude that she would have to return to New Orleans, and started home.

Transportation was uncertain in those days, and the stagecoach in which she was riding broke down late one afternoon in the little east Texas town of Livingston. There was one small inn there, and Adah was given one room, the two male passengers the other. That night, while Adah was eating dinner in the taproom, one of the men approached and asked if he might join her. Adah consented, and met her destiny.

Isaac Menken, her fellow passenger, was three or four years her senior, an earnest, erudite young man whose greatest fault was his emotional instability. The son of Aaron Menken, a prosperous drygoods manufacturer in Cincinnati, Ohio, Isaac was a reluctant junior partner in the family business. Music had been his passion since childhood, and he had yearned for a career as a professional violinist.

But his father had refused to listen to such nonsense, and Isaac was currently traveling through the Southwest and South as a salesman for the Menken products. He was bored and depressed, a mood that matched Adah's. They quickly discovered they were kindred spirits, and the budding actress and would-be musician spent the evening discussing art and culture.

Isaac, of course, was not blind to Adah's beauty. Nor was she unaware of the fact that he was exceptionally handsome, with dark hair, a strong profile, and slim, elegant hands. Whatever the chemical blend, Adah and Isaac talked late into the night, then went for a walk.

"We did not speak a word as we strolled beneath the stars," Adah rhapsodizes in her *Diary*. "I love him."

It must be remembered that this was no innocent maiden, but a young woman who had spent the better part of two years living as a prostitute. A professional judge of men and the male character was suddenly behaving like a schoolgirl.

The broken axle had not been repaired the following morning, and the stagecoach was forced to remain in Livingston. Adah was pleased, and Isaac was delighted, for he, too, had fallen in love. He proposed marriage at the breakfast table, and was accepted. In the hours that followed, while waiting for the arrival of a circuit-riding judge who was expected momentarily, the couple told each other their life stories.

Adah, for perhaps the only time in her adult life, spoke the truth, except for the story of Havana, of course.

At noon, on April 3, 1856, Adah Bertha Theodore and Isaac Menken were married at the Livingston, Texas, courthouse by Circuit Judge E. R. Humphrey.

Soon thereafter, the repaired carriage became operable, and the bride and groom rode off toward New Orleans in a cloud of dust and euphoria. They did not sleep together

until they reached New Orleans, where they spent the
night at a hotel, and the following day Adah took her husband to meet her mother.

Mrs. Josephs was not surprised, and expressed neither
pleasure nor unhappiness. Her one concern was her income, and Isaac expansively promised to contribute to
her support.

For the moment, at least, Adah's theatrical career was
abandoned. She packed her belongings, and Isaac took a
cabin for them on a Mississippi River steamer that was
scheduled to leave New Orleans two days later. Neither
seemed in the least dismayed at the prospect of confronting
the Menken family, and the honeymoon voyage was idyllic. Isaac serenaded his bride with violin solos, and she
composed several impassioned poems in his honor.

It may be difficult to believe that a young woman with
Adah's background could fall in love with any man, yet
her emotions appear to have been completely sincere. A
few verses from one of her few gay poems, "Venetia," re-
flect her mood:

> Bright as the light that burns at night,
>   In the starry depths of Aiden,
> When star and moon in leafy June
>   With love and joy are laden;
> Bright as the light from moon and star,
>   Stars in glorious cluster,
> Be the lights that shine on this life of thine,
>   Be the beauty of its luster.
>
> Beneath the moon in leafy June,
>   Sweet vows are fondly spoken;
> Beneath the stars, the silvery tune
>   Of music floats unbroken.
> Beneath the sky, and moon and stars,
>   Come nestling birds of beauty,

And Love with Bliss, and Hope with Joy
Troop down the path of duty.

Aaron Menken was horrified when he met his gaudily
dressed, heavily painted daughter-in-law. Isaac's mother
had a fit of hysterics so severe that a physician had to be
sent for. Other relatives were also aghast; one of them
commented that she looked like an expensive version of
the trollops who frequented the Ohio River waterfront.
If the reaction of the Menkens surprised Adah, she
showed no signs of it. She accepted their hostility calmly,
and immediately launched a campaign to win the affections of her in-laws. Her first step, which won Aaron's
approval, was to persuade Isaac to abandon his dreams of
becoming a violinist. At her urging he spent longer hours
at his father's factory, and made a number of suggestions
that increased the efficiency and profits of the retail store
the family maintained in the commercial section of Cincinnati.

When Isaac wanted to buy a magnificent new home for
his bride, Adah put her foot down. They would live within
their means, she said, and declared herself satisfied with
a modest house and the services of a single servant. It is
impossible to gauge whether these efforts were a pose or
reflected her real feelings.

In one realm, however, Adah astonished everyone, herself included. Giving in to her mother-in-law's tearful requests, she reluctantly agreed to study Judaism. She had
grown up as a Roman Catholic, but religion had meant
little to her. She had not attended Mass in years and, with
good reason, had not gone to confession.

Judaism fascinated, delighted, and eventually absorbed
her. She threw herself into her studies with a passion that
startled her teacher, Rabbi Henry F. Grossman, and in a
short time devoured all his reading matter printed in Eng-

lish. Rabbi Grossman, in an article printed in the November, 1856, issue of the Cincinnati *Israelite*, said that Adah immediately suggested she learn Hebrew. He approved, but pointed out that it would take her some time to master a tongue with an alphabet, writing form, and pronunciation so different from her native language.

Adah rose to the challenge; the years of study she had devoted to Greek, Latin, French, and Spanish had taught her how to approach languages. Only a few members of the Jewish community in Cincinnati were familiar with Hebrew, and of these none was in Grossman's class. Adah persuaded the Rabbi to accept her as his pupil. Her zeal was matched only by her remarkable linguistic talents, and to Grossman's astonishment she was soon able to read the Old Testament in Hebrew.

That was only a beginning, however; the piece in the *Israelite* does not tell the whole story. By the early months of 1857 Adah had become so fluent that she was composing poems in Hebrew for her own pleasure and edification, then translating them into English.

In February, 1857, she wrote Rabbi Grossman a letter, telling him she wanted to become a convert to Judaism. "I have become convinced in the course of reading and our many conversations," she said, "that I have found my true spiritual home as a Jewess. The One God of Jews and Christians is the same God, but I have found that the manner in which one prays to Him differs.

"The Christian accepts Him and His teachings on faith. The Jew believes in Him because His Word is Right. One becomes a Jew with one's mind as well as with one's heart. The ethic of Judaism is the Supreme Law which all mankind obeys. Therefore, with my mind as well as my heart, my heart as well as my mind, I rejoice that I may become a Jewess. Within my own soul, which I have intrusted to the care of the One and Eternal, I have already crossed the bridge."

Adah was received into the faith in a private ceremony attended only by members of the Menken family. Her parents-in-law were elated, and only Isaac protested when she chose to wear a gown of maroon velvet with a deep-plunging neckline, a pair of long, maroon-trimmed white gloves and a hat with an enormous feather. Adah knew she was in the spotlight, and dressed accordingly.

There were skeptics, of course, who said she had accepted conversion for no other reason than to please her husband's family. The charge, heard again and again in later years, was groundless. Her conversion was one of the most honest, sincere acts of her life, and was made in the full knowledge that she would become the butt of anti-Semitic scorn. She was indifferent to prejudice, and never made a secret of her faith.

The best proof of her sincerity was her flat refusal to recant when she and Isaac separated. After she became a convert, she remained steadfast in her faith; she lived, died, and was buried a Jewess.

The last barriers that separated her from the Menken family tumbled down after Adah's conversion, and she became the pet of Isaac's parents. Her friendship with them long outlasted her marriage, and she wrote to them from New York and San Francisco, London and Paris, for many years after her divorce.

It was in 1857 that Adah, the poet, was first exposed to the light of print. A poem, "Hear, O Israel!" appeared in the March, 1857, issue of the *Israelite,* and thereafter she became a regular contributor to the bimonthly publication. Only her first poem was devoted to a religious theme; thereafter she wrote on such secular topics as the majestic sweep of the Ohio River, the joy of changing seasons, the pleasures of walking in the woods.

Adah probably knew greater contentment in Cincinnati than she experienced either earlier or later in her life. She was an established member of a comfortably situated, middle-class family, and she had no material or intellectual needs. She and Isaac lived in a small but well-furnished house, and Adah did no physical work in it, for her mother-in-law had insisted that she engage a second servant.

She and Isaac ate at home only two or three nights a week, for they went to his parents' house on Tuesdays and Fridays. They also led an active social life, attended the theater, and the concerts of which Isaac was so fond, and moved in a sedate circle of other young couples. The grim experience of life in Havana seemed far away.

Isaac, who was a graduate of a remarkable institution of higher learning, Oberlin College, the first school in the United States to grant degrees to women and the first to admit Negro students, undertook to fill in the gaps in his wife's education. Adah showed the same fierce love of learning she had displayed in mastering Hebrew, and spent hours each day devouring books of philosophy.

She absorbed much of the works of Locke and Leibniz, and from them moved logically to Immanuel Kant. The Germanic influence was strong in Cincinnati, and intellectuals there were influenced by Kant's radical approach to sense, understanding, and reason. Adah leaped into the discussions with a vigor that startled the sedate gentlemen who gathered each Thursday afternoon at the city's Alpha Society quarters. She may have looked like a Jezebel, but she quickly demonstrated that her grasp of Kant's logic was sure. Her own ability to speculate in the realm of Kantian pure reason soon surpassed Isaac's, and she established herself as a stimulating addition to the group. As a woman, however, she was barred from actual membership in the Alpha Society.

Kant's insistence that there is a moral cause and a moral effect superior to the demands of nature fitted the ethical-religious concepts Adah had formed, and she was at peace with herself. Her career as an actress was an unfulfilled, temporarily abandoned dream. She was busy, happy, and even her Southern birth was not held against her in a "border" city that was uncertain whether it sided with the North or the South in the increasingly acrimonious debate between the two sections of the nation.

It pleased Adah later, when she lived in London and Paris, to tell newspaper interviewers that she had been an active member of the "underground railway" that helped Negro slaves escape to the free North, *via* Cincinnati. On more than one occasion she helped outwit the heartless pursuers who hoped to return runaway slaves to their shackles. One such experience was particularly memorable: Adah served glasses of punch to three burly Southerners and, fooling them with her New Orleans accent, enabled her accomplices to spirit two runaway slaves away to safety.

These tales made exciting reading, but there is no valid basis for them, and Adah knew better than to spin any such yarns for the American press. It is true that Aaron Menken was an adamant foe of slavery, and contributed substantial sums of money to abolitionist causes. Isaac Menken showed no interest in the slave question and, at the time Adah lived with him in Cincinnati, neither did she.

Perhaps nothing in Adah's nature is as bewildering as her chameleonlike ability to adjust to her surroundings. In Havana, as a streetwalker, she had led a classical prostitute's existence. Now she epitomized the perfect young housewife. She did her own marketing, in the best domestic tradition, and her *Diary* is filled with such homely tidbits as, "Stewing beef very good today. Bought three pounds."

Her eagerness to acquire greater knowledge was not typical of domesticated mid-nineteenth-century women, of course, but certainly was commendable. She got along well with her in-laws, she had an established place in society, and she had acquired a deep, abiding faith in God. She was someone in her own right, too, and friends respected the talents she displayed in the poems printed in the *Israelite*.

Only in her appearance did she indicate that, like Alexander the Great, she might be yearning for fresh worlds to conquer. She continued to wear daring gowns and still used cosmetics with a heavy hand. When she and Isaac dined in the theatrical district, which they did whenever they attended a performance of a play, strangers always assumed that she was an important visiting actress.

It may have been a combination of ego demand and habit that prompted Adah to maintain a flamboyant appearance. She gives no indication in her *Diary* that she still wanted to be an actress, and for all practical purposes seemed willing to spend the rest of her days in Cincinnati.

But Isaac had other ideas, and it is possible that he, rather than Adah, provided the spur that caused her to become an actress. Perhaps it is too much to say that she would have dressed and made up more modestly had he not enjoyed the sensation she created when they appeared together in public. But the facts recorded in her *Diary* indicate that he, not she, frequently bought her new gowns, hats, and the silk stockings dyed in various shades that were supposedly the latest, naughty rage in wicked, faraway Paris.

The first hint that unseen currents were ruffling the serene air of the Cincinnati paradise appear in a poem Adah composed on her first wedding anniversary. She wrote it in her *Diary,* but did not show it to Isaac or anyone else. For the moment, at least, she grieved alone.

In the light of her background, the opening verses of "One Year Ago" are arrant nonsense, a travesty of reality:

> In feeling I was but a child,
> When first we met—one year ago,
> As free and guileless as the bird,
> That roams the dreamy woodland through.
>
> My heart was all a pleasant world
> Of sunbeams dewed with April tears:
> Life's brightest page was turned to me,
> And naught I read of doubts or fears.
>
> We met—we loved—one year ago,
> Beneath the stars of summer skies;
> Alas! I knew not then, as now,
> The darkness of life's mysteries.

There is no way of knowing whether Adah was dealing in dainty literary conceits, but surely she could not have been serious. The Havana veteran was no guileless child, and the budding actress who lost a job in Texas when her nest egg was shrinking neither lived in a world of sunbeams nor was free of doubts and fears. And if she was unaware of any dark mysteries, they must have been very dark and mysterious, indeed. In still another verse she goes from the ridiculous to the absurd, and one must admire her courage if not her abuse of poetic license:

> I gave to you—one year ago,
> The only jewel that was mine;
> My heart took off her lonely crown,
> And all her riches gave to thine.

Finally, after torrents of adolescent self-pity, in which she throbbingly recalls his love for her, she reaches her climax in three prettily climactic verses:

> Why did you fill my youthful life
>   With such wild dreams of hope and bliss?
> Why did you say you loved me then,
>   If it were all to end in this?
>
> You robbed me of my faith and trust
>   In all Life's beauty—Love and Truth,
> You left me nothing—nothing save
>   A hopeless, blighted, dreamless youth.
>
> Strike, if you will, and let the stroke
>   Be heavy as my weight of woe;
> I shall not shrink, my heart is cold,
>   'Tis broken since one year ago.

It must be remembered that these lines were not written for publication, and did not appear in print until more than a decade—and three other husbands later. Granting, as it is necessary to grant, that Adah had a tendency to exaggerate and intensify, it is still difficult to imagine the cause of the blight in Eden. What could Isaac have done to break her heart, rob her of hopes and dreams? What was "this" that all was ending in?

Outwardly, life continued to be serene. But at last, on May 29, 1857, the *Diary* reveals the dastardly crime: "I. still nags me constantly, wanting me to return to the theater."

On the surface, the picture is clear. The young husband, still hating the family business, had not given up his dream of escaping from drygoods and Cincinnati. Perhaps, if he could not have the musical career he had wanted for himself, he could find release through the lovely wife who had been, he believed, the Queen of the Plaza.

If this face-value conclusion were accepted, Adah would appear to have been happy to spend the rest of her days as an Ohio housewife. In the light of the fierce ambitions she manifested, both before and after her idyllic stay in Cincinnati, the portrait on the wall appears to hang off-center.

If there were disputes between bride and groom on subjects other than Adah's career, no mention of them appears in her *Diary* or elsewhere. On the contrary, James states in his biography, "Life on the banks of the mighty Ohio palled for the talented Adah. Her devoted spouse, well aware of her great talent, was anxious to help her find her right place on the stage, and in the affections of the American theater-going public."

James's point of view is echoed in repeated confidences that begin appearing in the *Diary* only two weeks after Adah complains that Isaac had been nagging her. The first says, "We are meeting determined family opposition to our plan, but return to the theater we will. I shall die if I am forced to remain cooped up within the walls of this little house."

Either Isaac exerted a hypnotic influence and was able to persuade Adah to change her mind almost overnight, or else she was at least as anxious as he to further her career. "One Year Ago" seems to have been the product of a squabble on some subject other than her desire to become an actress. It is possible, but improbable, that the poem did not refer to their relationship, but, since it was written on their wedding anniversary, Adah's melodramatic expression of her feelings was unlikely to have been an art-for-art's-sake coincidence.

The mystery is compounded by the many *Diary* references to her *return* to the theater. Isaac and his family, Adah's own mother and half sister and the theatrical producers of New Orleans believed she had been an actress in

Havana. She herself knew better, but found it convenient
to pretend otherwise, even to herself. She had never acted
in public or private, as either professional or amateur, yet
insists, through the rest of 1857, that she wanted to "return" to the stage.

An obvious solution would have been to seek work in
Cincinnati, but neither Adah nor Isaac seriously considered the idea. There were two theaters in the city, each
of them presenting semiprofessional companies for no
more than six months of the year. Concerts, lectures, and
a variety of other entertainments filled the halls when
the two locally recruited groups of actors were not working. Judged by the real professional standards of the time,
the theater in Cincinnati was second-rate. Stars of national and international standing worked in New York,
Philadelphia, Baltimore, Washington, New Orleans, and
San Francisco, but nowhere else. Chicago was just beginning to emerge as a theatrical center of standing; Boston
frowned on the theater; and the rest of the country was—
in the eyes of the pros—a cultural desert.

Adah could have spent the rest of her days starring in
Cincinnati, and no one would have heard of her if he
lived any farther from the city than Covington, Kentucky,
directly across the river. Money, in 1857, was not a motive.
Had the young couple remained in Cincinnati, their financial future would have been assured. In time Isaac would
have become a senior partner in his father's company, and
eventually, as the only son, he would have inherited the
entire business.

The inescapable conclusion is that Adah sought fame,
and that Isaac wanted to bask, vicariously, in her reflected glory.

Aaron Menken resisted strenuously, and his wife took to
her bed again. Their fond hopes were shattered, but their
son and daughter-in-law adamantly refused to heed the

voice of reason. "We will go to New York in October,"
Adah says in a July notation in the *Diary,* "and I shall be
starred at the Astor Opera House before Christmas."

Her father-in-law, an eminently sensible man, countered with a suggestion that was too practical for the young
people to refute. Let Isaac go to New York, he said, and
see what roles might be available for Adah. In August,
Isaac packed his bags and made the journey. He returned
four weeks later to report that no producers were clamoring for the services of an actress who now called herself
Adah Bertha Theodore Menken.

His report was so discouraging that their plans were
abandoned, at least temporarily. But Adah says, on September 21, "I swear by the Eternal, Omnipotent and Al-
mighty Lord, I *will* be a great actress!"

If she realized that this attitude was inconsistent with
the petulant declaration that Isaac was nagging her to
return to the theater, she does not mention it.

Isaac recovered his optimism by October, and opened
a spirited correspondence with the theater owners of
New Orleans. At least they were acquainted with Adah,
even though she had not worked for them.

Newell, who had no reason to write charitably of a
woman who caused him distress and humiliation, says,
"J. S. Charles indicated a willingness to give Miss Menken
employment, and the owners of the smaller theaters followed his lead. Unfortunately, no roles suitable for the
talents of a star were open at the time, so Miss Menken
was forced to await a more propitious moment."

The girl who had been willing to travel across Texas
in the remote hope that she might be hired as an ingénue
was now unwilling to accept any part that did not befit
the dignity of a star. This change in attitude may have
been due to Isaac's influence, for he thought of his wife
as a leading lady, and he was now in charge of her career.

His assumption of power may have been a natural outgrowth of his marriage to Adah. They had no formal agreement, as she proved conclusively in 1863 when he filed suit against her in New York City demanding a share of her earnings. That suit was dismissed when he could produce no contract, letter, or other document giving him either a voice in the direction of her career or a percentage of her salary.

But a far different situation existed in 1857, when the couple had been married for only a year and a half. Isaac was his wife's personal manager and business agent, and when she began to earn money in the theater, both considered it joint income. Certainly Isaac deserved every penny he received. His energy was unflagging, and he bombarded the New Orleans producers with so many letters that both J. S. Charles and Alexander Sweeney, the owner of the Théâtre de Paris—which presented plays in English—finally capitulated.

If Miss Menken came to New Orleans and read for them, both said in letters received during the course of a single week in late November, perhaps satisfactory arrangements could be made for her appearance.

The servants were dismissed, Isaac resigned his position with his father's company, and the little house was closed. Adah now called herself Adah Isaacs Menken, a name she used for the rest of her life. Whether she or Isaac originated the name remains an enigma. There is no record that either discussed the subject, nor is it mentioned in Adah's *Diary* or in her biographies. It can only be said that her in-laws were very unhappy.

In 1864, Adah wrote to her former father-in-law, telling him, "Would that it were possible for me to spare you embarrassment. My fondness for you and Mother Menken is such that I would gladly do all in my power to relieve you of pain. Alas! The price of fame is great. The world

knows me now as Adah Isaacs Menken, and it is too late
for me to adopt another [name]."

ADAH ISAACS MENKEN was emblazoned on twenty-four
pieces of new luggage, and the star who had never set foot
on a stage set out for New Orleans with her husband-
manager. The girl who had been a tutor, a prostitute, and
a housewife was at last traveling the road to worldwide renown, enormous influence in literary circles—and unprecedented notoriety.

CHAPTER V

THE ACTRESS

Now I gloss my pale face with laughter, and sail my
   voice on with the tide,
Decked in jewels and lace, I laugh beneath the gaslight's
   glare, and quaff the purple wine.

—"Myself"

"Miss Adah Isaacs Menken, the stage star," said the New
Orleans *Picayune* a few days before Christmas, 1857, "has
returned to the city of her birth. It is hoped that she will
grace our theater with her presence."

Isaac had done his work well—Adah, who had yet to
speak a line of dialogue or earn a single day's wages as an
actress, was hailed by the leading newspaper of New Orleans as a star. His achievement was a public-relations
triumph whose magnitude not even he suspected. Adah,
the untried neophyte, carried off her role with style and
great dignity, arriving at the Orleans Parish Inn wearing
a green velvet gown with a matching feathered hat and
cloak with a fur collar.

There her husband established her in a suite of rooms,
and had the temerity to invite the theatrical producers to
call on her. That they actually did is a tribute to Isaac's
persuasive powers, for the managers remembered when

the girl with violet eyes and black hair had been coming daily to their offices. Adah received her all-important guests graciously, and the shrewd J. S. Charles—who could not have been fooled by the performance put on for his benefit—decided to take a chance. Any woman who played the aristocrat with her finesse and self-assurance obviously had talent.

He did not intend to expose her to New Orleans' audiences, however, until he saw for himself whether her personality was strong enough for a star's role. Therefore he offered her an engagement in Shreveport, where he also owned a theater, promising that if she did well there, he would bring her to New Orleans.

Adah would have accepted her first bona fide offer instantly, but Isaac preferred to settle contract terms and other details before committing his wife. What salary was Charles prepared to pay? How many weeks of work in Shreveport would he guarantee? Was he willing to insert a clause in the contract guaranteeing a New Orleans engagement if business in Shreveport exceeded sixty percent of the theater's capacity? And above all, what vehicle did he have in mind for Miss Menken?

Adah, listening to Isaac, learned a lesson she never forgot. It did not pay to be too eager; an actress who claimed to be a star had to behave as one in her business relationships.

Remembering Charlotte Crompton's performance in *Fazio,* she demanded the right to do that part. Charles had her read it for him, and diplomatically suggested that she try something lighter. *The Lady of Lyons,* a comedy of the type that a few decades later would be known as a French bedroom farce, might be more appropriate for her debut, he thought.

Adah's talents were not taxed, and she read the part satisfactorily, so the vehicle was settled. Salary proved to be a major snag, however, as Isaac had learned that Charlotte Crompton was paid two hundred and fifty dollars a week. He demanded the same sum for his wife.

The astonished Charles pointed out that Miss Crompton had a large and loyal following. Audiences came to see her in any play she chose, and she was therefore worth her huge fee. He could not afford to give Miss Menken more than one hundred dollars a week until she proved that she could fill a theater. Isaac countered with a demand for one hundred and fifty dollars, and a compromise was reached at one hundred and twenty-five. It was also agreed that Adah would play in Shreveport for four weeks, and if box-office receipts justified the move, she would then be brought to New Orleans. A contract was drawn, stipulating that she would open in Shreveport on the Tuesday following Easter Sunday.

Adah immediately went into seclusion to study the part of Pauline in *The Lady of Lyons,* a role that was longer and more intricate than she had suspected. She locked herself in the bedroom of the hotel suite for the better part of each day to study her lines. Isaac appreciated her zeal, but with nothing to occupy his own time, went every day to visit Adah's mother. Certainly Mrs. Josephs needed soothing, as she was disturbed because her daughter had chosen to live at a hotel rather than with her family. The diplomatic Isaac managed, by means unknown, to smooth the invalid's ruffled feelings.

Every evening Adah emerged from seclusion to appear with Isaac at one or another of the city's hostelries and taverns, always wearing a stunning gown. Some of the town's gay blades were attracted to her, and Isaac had a foretaste of what it meant to be married to a theatrical star who possessed a magnetic sex appeal. Apparently he had not realized this aspect of his plans, nor that his domestic tranquillity would be disrupted.

"I. becomes unpleasant every time a gentleman bends over my hand," she complains to her *Diary* on February 3, 1858. "His jealous scenes become tiresome."

J. S. Charles observed the effect Adah had on members of the opposite sex, too, and thoughtfully turned her obvious assets to his financial advantage. It was customary for stars to provide their own costumes, and he was delighted when he learned Adah owned a large and varied wardrobe. He went over it with her, and selected the most daring and revealing gowns for her appearances on stage. In one scene Pauline, the heroine, was required to appear in a negligee. Oddly enough, Adah owned none that Charles considered suitable.

So the producer suggested that one be made for her. Isaac promptly reentered the picture, insisting that Adah's salary was too small for her to make new purchases. Charles agreed to buy the negligee, and when he came to the hotel with it, Isaac understood why he had been so agreeable. The negligee, which was made of white silk, was semitransparent; by the standards of a later era it was demure, but in its own time it was shockingly revealing.

Isaac declared that he would not permit his wife to appear in such a costume. Adah quietly but firmly overruled him. She was not in the least shy about showing her charms in public, and Isaac was unable to force her to obey him. The domestic rift widened.

The play went into rehearsal in late February. Not even the most enthusiastic of Adah's admirers ever claimed that she could speak a line convincingly, but no one paid much attention to what she said on stage. Her manner was bold and uninhibited, and in some unexplained way she projected her enormous sex appeal across the gas-jet footlights. Charles began to realize that he had signed up a woman who had the potential of becoming a real star.

Before the opening, word seeped out through the ranks

of those "in the know" that the girl who had been the talk of the town in recent weeks would be well worth seeing, and scores came from New Orleans to Shreveport for the first-night performance. Most of them were men.

On April 4, 1858, just one week before her twenty-third birthday, Adah Isaacs Menken, who had never before performed publicly in her life, became a star. She was received enthusiastically at each entrance, appearing in one dazzling gown after another. When she came on-stage in the negligee, after a moment of stunned silence, the applause and cheers stopped the performance.

The night of Adah's first triumph was one of despair for her husband. The audience was not saluting her acting ability, but commending her figure. After the performance, while Adah was being toasted in the taproom of the Shreve's Landing Hotel, Isaac sulked alone in their room on the second floor.

"Isaac Menken," James later wrote, "was not a real showman. He could not accustom himself to his wife's appearance before large audiences, wearing what other ladies dared to wear only in the privacy of their own boudoirs."

If Adah knew or cared, she makes no mention of it in her *Diary*. "I have always known that I am an actress," is her only comment on the night of her first opening.

Plantation owners and other members of the gentry flocked to the theater, and all seats were sold out for the first two weeks. The new star was a complete success, and Charles immediately extended the engagement one week, later adding an additional two weeks. Isaac did not share his wife's happiness, but observed bitterly that the audiences were composed almost exclusively of men.

Late in May the play was transferred to the J. S. Charles Theater in New Orleans, and there Adah enjoyed an even greater triumph. There were ladies in the cosmopolitan audience, and their gasps were as audible as the male cheers when Adah appeared in her negligee. The next morning there was a line at the box office. The play was assured a run.

Adah received her first press notice two days after the opening, the *Picayune* commenting, "Miss Adah Menken has treated this city to the sight of a feminine shape of great beauty. She has used *The Lady of Lyons,* long an amusing and serviceable comedy that has pleased many an audience, as a means of exhibiting her form. Many who saw her at the J. S. Charles Theater admired her courage while deploring her lack of taste." The review did not mention her talents as an actress.

Mrs. Josephs declined to attend a performance, claiming that her frail health did not permit her to go to the theater. Annie saw the play, and was mortified, but apparently realized that her half sister was no ordinary mortal, for she remained on friendly terms with Adah.

Crowds of men waited at the stage door after every performance, and Isaac was driven to distraction because his wife smiled impartially at her admirers, patted their cheeks, and allowed them to escort her to restaurants in large groups. Apparently it did not cross his mind that he had no need to worry unless and until she began to go out alone with one man.

In spite of his emotional problems, he was still a good business manager, and went to Charles hoping to renegotiate Adah's contract. The manager refused, and his relations with both the star and her husband cooled. Adah, playing to packed houses, agreed with Isaac that she should be earning more money. But the most Charles would promise was that he would think in terms of an increase for her next play.

A decision had to be made soon, as it was unusual for

any one play to run more than eight to twelve weeks. Adah promptly insisted that she do Bianca in *Fazio*.

Charles flatly refused. Not only did he consider her incapable of playing the part, but he had Charlotte Crompton under contract to do *Fazio* in the autumn. Adah stuck to her guns, in spite of Charles's attempt to persuade her that she should follow *The Lady of Lyons* with another vehicle in which she could show off her figure. But the applause Adah heard every night had convinced her that she was an actress, and she threatened to leave Charles for another management if he would not agree to her demand.

Obviously he remained firm, for Adah signed a contract to do Bianca in *Fazio* at Crisp's Gaiety Theater. Apparently persuading both the producer and Isaac that it would be wise to open before Miss Crompton appeared in the same play, she went into rehearsal at once, while continuing her part in *The Lady of Lyons*. When the Crompton opening was announced for September 15, Adah cut short her successful run and opened in *Fazio* on August 29.

The results were painful and embarrassing. "Miss Crompton," the *Picayune* said, "need fear no competition from the lovely Miss Menken."

Adah bravely continued to perform, but the audiences who had flocked to see *The Lady of Lyons* were unimpressed by Bianca and the play closed in two weeks. Chastened, she returned to the management of J. S. Charles and for the better part of a year played almost continuously under his management.

Isaac obtained a salary increase to one hundred and fifty dollars a week for her, and she appeared in a number of plays that displayed her beauty but made no untoward demands on her talents. Charles and Isaac worked together to choose her roles and the ones they selected were perfect for her. She played the wanton Lady Freelove in a light comedy, *A Wife's First Lesson,* in which she wore two negligees. Her next was *A Day in Paris,* an undistinguished comedy-melodrama, in which she took six different parts. In one she wore a remarkably low-cut evening gown, and in two others she masqueraded as a man, giving her the opportunity to wear skin-tight breeches. *A Day in Paris* was an unqualified success.

Audiences demanded novelty, and Charles, aided by Isaac, tried to give it to them in the other two plays that were added to Adah's repertory, *The Maid of Munster* and *The Unprotected Female.* Both were very weak plays whose chief virtue lay in the constant presence on-stage of the star. Ways were found for Adah to wear strapless evening gowns and to give the audience flashlike glimpses of her long legs. Someone decided she had a singing voice, and songs were interpolated. Adah wrote her own lyrics, and even the drama critic of the *Picayune* was impressed.

"Miss Menken," he declared, "shows a surprising talent for writing verse." He did not compliment her acting ability, however.

Isaac, remembering his wife's glowing accounts of her success as the Queen of the Plaza in Havana, tried to urge her to include some dances in her performance, too. But Adah, not wanting to push her luck, refused. Apparently there was some confusion on the subject, for a handbill announcing *The Unprotected Female* said: "Additional Attraction! ADAH ISAACS MENKEN will sing and dance!" These advertisements were withdrawn, and others, hastily substituted, merely announced that she would sing.

Adah later claimed that she toured through the Southwest under J. S. Charles's banner, but the records indicate that she played in New Orleans except for a two-week period in June, 1859, when municipal riots forced the temporary closing of all theaters.

In any event, she was a changed person as the result of constant employment. She was a professional actress now, with a list of substantial credits to her name, and had acquired considerable stage presence. Even if her reading of a line still made some of her fellow actors shudder, she had proved conclusively that she had the strength to draw audiences into the most prominent theater in New Orleans. No one could deny that she was a genuine star.

She developed other interests during the year, too, returning again to poetry. Every issue of the Cincinnati *Israelite* printed at least one of her poems, and there were four in the February, 1859, issue. A French sculptor of some note, Andre de Beauville, visiting in New Orleans, moved in the same artistic circle in which Adah had become a leader. De Beauville was sufficiently attracted to Adah to give Isaac some anxious moments, but too little is known for the modern reader to determine whether the young husband's fears were justified.

Regardless of whether Adah became romantically involved with De Beauville, he aroused her interest in sculpture, and she tried her own hand at the medium, molding figures out of clay, then working them in stone. Two of her first attempts, statues approximately eighteen inches high—both of attractive young women who bear a striking resemblance to Adah Isaacs Menken—are extant in private New Orleans collections.

It might be added that she retained her enthusiasm for sculpture as long as she lived, working in stone statues of comely, nude females, of proud cats and strong-backed dogs. Her greatest years of productivity began in 1864, when she no longer had to worry about money, and from that time forward she turned out an average of four or five pieces a year. Her efforts were sufficiently good to attract the attention of Antoine Barye, whose marble cats, horses, dogs, and other animals are among the most realistic ever done in stone. Barye was a recognized master when Adah first came to Paris, and although he was then an old man, impatient with students and unwilling to let anyone waste the time he wanted to devote to his work, he became interested in Adah after seeing several of her sculptures.

Under his tutelage she improved enormously, and was producing competent statues at the time of her death. Barye was her only instructor; until she began going to his Paris studio she had learned all she knew from trial and error.

De Beauville was said to have created some of her earlier marble figures, but in his *Memoirs,* published a few years after Adah's death, he says, "I wish I could claim credit for the sculpture of the talented Adah Isaacs Menken, but she did all of her own work. Although I knew her in the United States for a short period of time and, again, in France, later, I never visited her studio nor did she come to mine. Her figurines were her own."

Adah worked very quickly with chisel and mallet and, apparently, showed the same self-confidence that marked everything she did. There was no market for her work when she first took up sculpture as a hobby; later, after she became famous, she could have sold her animal and human figures for almost any price, but instead she chose to give her statues to her friends. George Sand received two, a splendid horse's head and a somewhat less-well-executed female nude, both done in alabaster. She gave Rossetti a marble kitten. She did a bust of Swinburne, not a very good likeness, but she refused to give it to him, precipitating one of the many quarrels that marked their stormy affair. She later presented it to John Thompson, his secretary.

Adah's sculpture, like the mature poetry she wrote in her last years, was, at best, second-rate. What is surprising is that, with no training, she showed any talent at all. Perhaps it was her creative urge, her flair, that made her so sympathetic to other, greater artists. Walt Whitman may not have realized he was writing her literary epitaph when he said to her, in a note written from Washington in 1864, "Would that I had your facility, and would you had my tenacity. I am a boor to complain, for I would be so much the poorer without your constant, sweet encouragement."

Whatever enduring place Adah achieved for herself as poet or sculptress was due to the help she gave others, not to her own efforts.

In 1858 and 1859, she thought of herself as neither, although active in both fields. She was a successful actress, and the people of New Orleans gave her no chance to forget it. A crowd waited to cheer her when she emerged from her hotel each day, the curious gathered outside any restaurant where she was known to be dining, and there was a throng outside the stage door of the J. S. Charles Theater before and after every performance.

Adah loved the attention, and craved still more. Perhaps she failed to realize that her fame was ruining her marriage, or it may be that she no longer cared. The gallants of New Orleans offered her jewels and other gifts of value, and she realized—as only a former streetwalker could—that scores of men found her enormously attractive and desirable.

If Adah was indifferent to the effect all this attention was having on her marriage, Isaac was miserable. Late in February, 1859, he said in a portion of a long letter to his father, "I would gladly return home, if I could, but Adah will not hear of it. She is determined to make a success of her stage work in New York and the other great cities where she is not yet known, and I can not dissuade her.

For myself, I am heartily sick of the life we lead, and I acknowledge that the fault is mine, for without me she would be nothing."

He did not resent being pushed into the background, as Newell did when he was married to her. But the constant attention of ardent swains tortured Isaac, and he made several feeble attempts to persuade her to give up her career. It is doubtful that Adah bothered to listen to him. The world had become her oyster, and now she wanted the pearl—the adulation of New York, then, as later, the theatrical capital of the United States.

A wedge even stronger than the career conflict driving her and Isaac apart was a personal habit she acquired in 1858 or 1859. Among her many distinctions was a somewhat dubious one: she was the first woman, anywhere, to smoke cigarettes in public.

Cigarette smoking was a new fad among the sophisticated. British soldiers brought the habit home with them from Turkey in 1856, at the end of the Crimean War, and some French troops had become addicts, too. Bohemians in London quickly took up smoking, and were soon followed by the artists of Paris. The fad leaped across the Atlantic, and young gentlemen in the major cities of the United States began to puff on cigarettes, too. Pipes were now considered too cumbersome by the cosmopolitan, and snuff was old-fashioned.

It is probable that other women experimented with cigarettes, as Adah did, but no lady would let herself be seen smoking in public, a taboo that persisted well into the twentieth century. Adah, the militant feminist who broke the rules of convention because she loved to shock people, began to smoke in the restaurants of New Orleans, and created a sensation.

"We do not approve of cigarette smoking by ladies," the *Picayune* said in a stern editorial printed on March 10,

1859. "We agree with Mr. Isaac Menken of this city and Cincinnati, Ohio, that the habit destroys the delicate fabric of femininity, a lady's most precious possession."

The editorial could not have been published without Isaac's knowledge and consent. Obviously he made it his business to convey his views to one or another member of the newspaper's staff, and the mere use of his name constituted a rebuke to Adah, the only woman in New Orleans who dared to smoke in public.

She reacted furiously, and states in her *Diary* three days later: "I have told Isaac I will leave him if he does not stop badgering me with his sermons on cigarettes. I do not criticize him for smoking segaros, and he owes me the same courtesy. I will not submit to the dictation of any man."

Isaac did not heed the storm signals, and continued to lecture her. He was disgusted by Adah's cigarette smoking, but there was even more involved, a principle. From the moment the first contract with J. S. Charles had been signed, Adah had stopped leaning on her husband. She had acted contrary to his demands when she had appeared on-stage in a negligee. She was pleased to accept the invitations of companies of gentlemen after her evening performances, and went with large groups to restaurants for midnight suppers. Apparently she did not object if Isaac chose to go along, but if he refused, she blithely went without him.

Now, at a time when she was hoping to storm the citadel of New York, her husband chose to make an issue of her cigarette smoking in an attempt to assert his ultimate authority. He believed that Adah needed his help if she intended to conquer New York. How a man could have been married to a girl of Adah's temperament and misjudge her so badly is difficult to understand. She continued to smoke, and told him he could accompany her to New York or not, as he pleased.

Isaac discovered he needed Adah more than she needed him, and swallowed his pride, along with clouds of her cigarette smoke. They would conduct a joint assault on New York, and although the domestic tie was badly frayed, they optimistically assumed that Adah would enjoy another overnight success.

It is unlikely that Adah would have evaded the challenge, even if she had known what was ahead.

CHAPTER VI

FAILURE

Where shall I lead the flocks today?
Is there no Horeb for me beyond this desert?
Is there no rod with which I can divide this sea of blood
    to escape mine enemies?
Must I pine in bondage and drag these heavy chains through
    the rocky paths of my unrecompensed toil?

             —"Where the Flocks Shall Be Led"

NEW YORK was the fastest-growing city in a country of more than thirty million inhabitants when Adah Isaacs Menken and her disgruntled husband arrived there in the spring of 1859. The young couple stared at the horsecars on Third Avenue and on Sixth, stood with the crowds that gathered to watch the construction of St. Patrick's Cathedral, a huge structure on upper Fifth Avenue, and like scores of others, scrambled for safety when cattle were driven down lower Fifth Avenue to the city's stockyards.

The most popular song in the country was a new tune, "I Wish I Was in Dixie's Land," and Adah quickly wrote a set of her own lyrics to use at auditions for theatrical producers. A new novel by Charles Dickens, already recognized as the greatest of living English fiction writers, had just been published in the United States, and Adah hastened to buy a copy of *A Tale of Two Cities*.

"How I wish," she says in her *Diary*, "that I had the imagination and talent of Mr. Dickens!"

Isaac was concerned with the more prosaic matter of finding work for his actress wife. He was diligent and conscientious, as always, but soon discovered that stardom in New Orleans meant nothing to the hard-bitten theater owners of New York. He made the rounds each day, but had nothing to show for his efforts, even though the theaters of the city were prospering.

A variety bill was playing to capacity audiences at the Astor Place Opera House, and occasionally new acts were introduced there, a singer or dancer replacing someone to whom audiences had become accustomed. There was no place, however, for a girl who had been a local favorite in New Orleans, but was completely unknown in New York.

Joseph Jefferson was the reigning favorite of the moment, starring in *A Pretty Piece of Business* at Wallack's Theater. It was almost impossible to obtain seats for any performance, and Jefferson's friends usually formed a ring around him to protect him from overly enthusiastic well-wishers when he went to Pfaff's for a meal. On the distaff side, Julia Dean Hayne, who was appearing in *Antony and Cleopatra* at Niblo's Gardens, was highly regarded by both critics and audiences. According to rumors not yet substantiated, she had agreed to play opposite Edwin Booth in *Macbeth* at the Winter Garden later in the year.

A comedy-melodrama, *The Gun Maker of Moscow*, which featured no stars, was a hit at the Bowery, and an exciting play, *La Grâce de Dieu*, was unexpectedly drawing English-speaking patrons to the French Theater. George Wood was doing a fair business at the Broadway, where he shuffled several plays in repertory, and Mike Heenan, the owner of the National, announced plans to present *Fazio* in the immediate future with the incomparable Ada Clare as his star.

In spite of the bustle, the doors of New York theaters seemed to be closed tight to outsiders. Adah, who spent most of her days sightseeing and window-shopping, reading the latest fiction and writing poetry, became restless. Not even the newest novel by Mrs. E. D. E. N. Southworth, *The Hidden Hand,* could hold her attention, and one day she went job hunting on her own.

The Astor had been her idea of the most important theater in New York, and it was her first stop. There, an assistant manager, conscious of her strong appeal, agreed to hear her sing, but stopped her after she had completed only one chorus of her version of "I Wish I Was in Dixie's Land." The man told her he had no work for her, but invited her to dine with him.

Adah rejected the advance, and then made the mistake of telling Isaac about it that evening. They quarreled for hours, and were still on bad terms the following morning, when they finally decided to make use of a letter of introduction that J. S. Charles had given them to Ed James, editor of the New York *Clipper.* They had refrained from using the letter sooner because of Isaac's reluctance to deal with a newspaper that he believed to be devoted primarily to sports.

James describes the meeting in detail. "I have never forgotten the day Adah first came into my office. I don't recall what she wore, but I know it was a costume that caught my eye, as she had perfect taste and an infallible sense of the dramatic. She was the most beautiful girl I had ever seen, so beautiful that I could scarcely believe I was seeing aright."

Apparently afraid that his readers would leap to the wrong conclusion, he hastens to add, "Mrs. James agreed with me when she also met Adah. We have always been proud of our friendship with her, and we are very happy that our eldest grandchild has been named Adah."

He expresses a less enthusiastic opinion of Isaac. "Menken was a surly fellow who sat in a corner, glaring at the lovely Adah and tapping his gloves on the arm of his chair. I knew their marriage was a bad one, for he addressed no civil word to her and she rightly ignored him.

"I was surprised when she showed a great interest in the *Clipper,* and I was pleased to take her on a tour of discovery around our small offices. She showed me some of her poetry, which had been published by a magazine in Cincinnati, and I agreed to pay her five dollars for a new poem, 'The Great Heart of the City.' As readers of the *Clipper* know, Adah became a regular contributor to the *Clipper.* There was a period when the small, five-dollar fees I paid her helped to ward off starvation, paying for her food and humble lodgings. Later, after she became the most famous woman in America and Europe, she continued to send me poems, and refused to accept more than the same small fee, even though other editors would have paid a fortune for the privilege of printing anything she penned."

Five days after the initial visit of the couple to the *Clipper* office, James reports, Adah and Isaac Menken came to an abrupt parting of the ways. He was heartily tired of the tinsel and insecurity of show business, and was ready to return to the drygoods business in Cincinnati. She was more determined than ever to become a star.

Her only acquaintance in New York was Ed James, and Adah returned at once to his office, telling him she had no prospects and a rapidly vanishing bankroll. Her delusions of grandeur remained undiminished, however, and he found it difficult to persuade her that there was no chance she might be hired to do *Fazio* at the National Theater.

At the *Clipper* office she met the burly giant, John C.

Heenan, a towering six-foot, two-inch prize fighter who weighed two hundred and twenty-five pounds. John Morrissey, the world's heavyweight champion, had retired the previous December, and Heenan now claimed the crown. Others, among them the aggressive Joe Coburn, disputed his right to call himself the champion, but Heenan challenged all comers in the columns of the *Clipper,* and even Coburn was afraid to meet him in the ring.

A gregarious, heavy-drinking extrovert, Heenan took an immediate fancy to Adah. She, alone and friendless, returned his interest, and was flattered to be in the spotlight when he took her to Pfaff's for dinner. But the attention of the prize fighter did not pay her bills, and James finally secured a small part for her in a forthcoming play, *The Soldier's Daughter,* which was going into rehearsal at Purdy's Theater.

Adah's role was that of a young widow, and was perfect for her purposes: it was small, required little acting ability, and won the sympathy of the audience. The play opened late in May, and a claque led by John C. Heenan gave the unknown actress from New Orleans a standing ovation.

A romance quickly blossomed, and the *Clipper* scooped its competitors by reporting that Champion Heenan would soon marry the most beautiful actress currently gracing the Manhattan boards. Adah's domestic situation at this moment was clouded, but not in her opinion. When Isaac had returned to Cincinnati, she assumed he would get an immediate divorce, saying in her *Diary,* "I. wants a divorce as soon as possible, and will obtain one. I prefer to let him bear the expense, and want no more to do with him."

She assumed he had already obtained the divorce, when in fact he had taken no legal action whatever, apparently still entertaining the remote hope that she might find the theatrical situation hopeless and rejoin him at the house he had bought for her. Isaac later claimed that his help in

the family business had been urgently needed on his return
to Cincinnati, and that he had intended to file suit for the
divorce at his first opportunity. The facts indicate that he
did not take legal action until a national scandal forced
him to sue in 1860.

Adah, the eternal optimist, could not be bothered with
trivial legal details. *The Soldier's Daughter* closed after a
brief, unsuccessful run, and she obtained a larger role in
another play, *The French Spy,* presented at the same
theater. In it she played the title part, that of a sweet, innocent ingénue, and although somewhat miscast, made a
good impression on the critics because she spoke a number
of her lines in faultless French.

She was earning enough money to maintain the small
suite of rooms at Fifth Avenue and Eighteenth Street that
she and Isaac had taken when they had arrived in New
York, and John C. Heenan was now a nightly visitor.
Adah's moral standards were completely elastic, and she
made no secret of the fact that she and Heenan were living
together.

The arrangement suited Heenan, but Adah had learned
the difference between the lot of the mistress and the
protection that marriage gave a woman. So, when negotiations were opened for Heenan to fight the English heavyweight champion, Tom Sayers, in London, Adah demanded that Heenan marry her.

He agreed, meekly and without argument. Walt Whitman, who first met Adah during this period, observed in a
note to Ed James, "I am amazed that this frail wisp of a girl
can force a brute like Heenan to do what she pleases, when
she pleases. She dominates him, body and soul."

The marriage ceremony was performed on September 3,
1859, by Alderman Joe Brice, and the newlyweds retired
to a farm in New Jersey for their honeymoon. There,
James relates, the groom taught his bride the manly art of

boxing. Newell offers an explanation for this startling turn of events. "Miss Menken," he says stiffly, "was so charming and radiated such warmth that men constantly pressed their attentions on her. Being small and delicate, she felt the need to defend herself against unwelcome advances of strangers, and persuaded Heenan to give her instruction in self-defense."

Each day the heavyweight champion of the world and the young woman whom he outweighed by one hundred pounds sparred in the farmyard. "My wife's footwork is as good as any man's in the ring," Heenan told the New York *Daily News* when a reporter learned of the bizarre honeymoon. "Her left is weak, but she has a solid right and is very quick."

After spending an idyllic two or three weeks absorbing the Marquess of Queensbury rules, Adah returned to New York with her new husband and set up housekeeping in a small, rented home at the corner of Broome Street and Sixth Avenue. She was hired for a part in a new farce, *The Three-Foot Man,* at Purdy's and went into rehearsal at once. Heenan's fight with Sayers was postponed, and the champion immediately broke training.

While Adah spent her days at the theater, her husband sat in saloons with his cronies, and by nightfall was drunk. He became belligerent when he drank too much, and some of Adah's new literary friends, among them Fitz-James O'Brien and Emily Rebecca Page, the young Vermont poet who was making her first visit to New York, feared for Adah's safety.

Miss Page said to a group at Pfaff's, in the hearing of a New York *Mercury* reporter, who duly noted the statement for the edification of the newspaper's readers on October 9, 1859, "I fear for her life!"

Adah soon demonstrated, in the most conclusive manner possible, that such fears were unwarranted. One evening in mid-October she appeared at Pfaff's unescorted, and sat down at the "authors' table." There she and Emily Page became deeply involved in a spirited discussion of free verse, Adah upholding it, Emily insisting that it was not poetry. Their talk, the *Mercury* reported, was interrupted when Emily saw a bruise on the back of Adah's right hand. The knuckles were skinned, but Adah made light of the injury and insisted on returning to the discussion of poetry.

An anonymous representative of the *Mercury* sensed a story, and went looking for John C. Heenan, finally finding him at a small saloon located near the Bowery Theater and favored by the sporting crowd. Heenan had been drinking, and liquor had made him garrulous.

The reporter saw that the heavyweight champion of the world was nursing a very black eye, and dared to ask the question that everyone else had been afraid to put into words. John C. Heenan replied in words of classical simplicity. "My wife hit me."

Overnight Adah became a celebrity, and the management of the Astor Place Opera House offered her a place in its variety bill, singing a number while standing in a replica of a boxing ring. She remained loyal to Heenan, and refused.

Her loyalty did not prevent her from attacking him with her fists whenever he became abusive, however. Thereafter her knuckles were often skinned, and Heenan appeared with bruises on various parts of his face. When he was sober—which was seldom—he and Adah seemed to get along well. When he was drunk, he avoided going home and slept at the apartments and houses of friends rather than face another drubbing from his wife.

Even Ed James, the friend of both, could not refrain from calling Adah "the battling Mrs. Heenan" in the columns of the *Clipper*. As a result of the publicity, *The Three-Foot Man* was sold out on opening night, and Adah

was applauded on her first entrance. Later that evening she
and other members of the cast went to Pfaff's, but Heenan
did not join her there.

His fight with Sayers was rescheduled, and domestic
peace returned when he again went into training. Adah
faded from the limelight, and was virtually forgotten when
her play, an inept farce, closed after a brief run. She spent
the rest of the year being Mrs. John C. Heenan, but her
existence was a lonely one.

Heenan came into New York only on weekends, living
on the New Jersey farm through the week, which he devoted to rigorous physical exercise. Adah searched for
work, but finding none, became discouraged. She had won
a place for herself as a professional actress by now, and
could even claim, on the basis of the *Clipper* publishing
an occasional poem, that she was an author, too. So she
was always welcome at Pfaff's, which became her headquarters, and she went there daily, hoping to see producers, just as actresses of later generations have haunted
Sardi's.

It was during this period that Adah first demonstrated
her real genius, that of helping, encouraging, and sustain-
ing struggling authors of merit. Her own literary efforts
improved as she grew older, but by no stretch of a critic's
imagination could they be considered lasting. Yet, in spite
of her inability to produce a body of work that had stature,
her taste was impeccable, and she repeatedly demonstrated
an instinct for recognizing genuine talent.

The sensitive Emily Page, a poet of some standing, was
bewildered by the pace of life in Manhattan, and would
have retired to the obscurity of the Vermont countryside,
where her father earned his living as the toll-taker at a
bridge, if Adah had not helped her through a trying time.
Emily, three years the older girl's junior, was Adah's constant companion, and wrote to her father in November,

1859: "Were it not for the sensitive understanding of the *best friend I have ever known,* I would not write another line of poetry in my life. I grieve that I cannot do more to improve the nature of her work, as she has improved mine. We sometimes sit for a half-day debating the use of a single word in one of my verses. I marvel that I have found such a friend in this maelstrom."

Whitman, too, became Adah's close friend. Bohemian in his living, he knew many men and a few women on the fringe of New York's artistic circles, but was too shy to permit himself any degree of intellectual intimacy with anyone. In Adah he found a kindred spirit, and gave her a copy of his *Leaves of Grass.* She spent all of one night reading it, and the following day did not appear at Pfaff's for an appointment with him.

The retiring Whitman immediately jumped to the conclusion that she disapproved of his work, and made no attempt to get in touch with her. But by the next day, he began to worry about her health, and paid a visit to the house on Broome Street. "I was overwhelmed when I saw W. W. at the door," Adah says in her *Diary.* "It made me feel very humble that a man of his extraordinary genius should seek my companionship and solicit my poor opinions. Alas for the souls of artists! He is afraid, as I am, that his work is mere scribbling, but he is mistaken, and I must help him to see that he is a great poet."

Ethel Lynn Beers, who was considered a major poet during her own lifetime (1827–1879), but who has since faded into the ranks of lesser literary figures, was another who numbered Adah among her close associates and supporters. A frail Southerner who wrote sentimental, nostalgic verse, she drifted into the Pfaff's "set" during her one prolonged visit to New York in 1859 and 1860, and although the editors of the periodicals that published her work were kind to her, she felt very lonely in the city.

Adah soon became her protectress, shielded her, and

gave her advice on her writing, which Ethel ignored. The
two women apparently felt something of a sense of rivalry,
for Adah says in her *Diary,* "I hesitate to show E.L.B. my
poems, past and present, for fear she will snatch at some
of the ideas she rejects when I mention them in connection
with her own poor scribblings. Why is it, I wonder, that
editors are so blind to my verse, which is superior in
every way to hers?"

A relationship of a different sort existed between Adah
and O'Brien, a dashing young man with black curly hair
who dressed in the Lord Byron tradition and, after meeting Adah, tried to emulate Byron as a lover, too. Unafraid
of the heavyweight champion of the world, O'Brien composed verses to Adah and made innumerable attempts to
persuade her to have an affair with him. He failed, and
their friendship became less intimate, but in time they
drew together again.

O'Brien was intense and romantic, almost a stage cari-
cature of a poet, but his work was solid and he was well on
the way toward his goal of becoming one of America's
leading literary figures when he met his tragic death in
the second year of the Civil War. "When I loved you as a
man naturally loves a woman," he wrote to Adah early in
1862, "I could not think clearly, and a blight settled on my
work. Then you taught me to be your friend, and the skies
cleared. If my poems endure, I have you to thank for teach-
ing me tranquillity of soul."

Perhaps Adah was able to teach serenity to others, but
she was unable to practice what she preached. Shortly before Christmas, Heenan sailed to England for his fight
with Sayers, leaving Adah penniless and, as she discovered
a few weeks later, pregnant.

The couple never spoke again, although their paths
subsequently crossed in New York on a number of occasions. Heenan's fight with Tom Sayers was to give him
additional fame and, at the same time, make him some-

thing of a laughingstock. His marriage would add to his notoriety in the months ahead, and cause him grief that he found unbearable.

The fight itself brought out the largest crowd in the history of prize fighting, and Sayers, the local champion, was the favorite of the English crowds. Heenan proved in the opening rounds that those who had wagered on him could not lose their money; a slightly built young woman might blacken his eye, but another fighter could not touch him. He slashed Sayers mercilessly, and by the twenty-eighth round—or thereabouts—the Englishman was groggy.

Heenan knocked his opponent across the ring, and he flew into the ropes. In some inexplicable manner the two top ropes became entangled with his head and neck, and the referee, Tom Dowling, saw that he was strangling. Dowling took a knife from his hip pocket and cut the ropes, thus saving Sayers' life.

Then the referee went to Heenan and raised the American's right hand over his head, proclaiming him the winner of the bout. But no one saw the move, for the irate crowd, believing itself cheated, poured into the ring. Heenan was extricated from the mob with great difficulty and spirited away to safety. The next day Sayers' supporters claimed that a freakish accident had stopped the encounter, and denied that Heenan was the winner. Heenan's admirers retorted that he had won fairly and was now the undisputed champion. But others were quick to take advantage of the confusion. Coburn in New York promptly renewed his claims, and several fighters on the European Continent also demanded the crown.

Heenan went off to France, Denmark, and Belgium to fight the contenders in those lands before returning home. He was thriving on controversy, making more money than ever before in his life, and the wife he had left behind in New York was forgotten.

"After the departure of John C. Heenan for England," Newell says, "he addressed no letters or other communications to his wife."

James was blunter. "Heenan was too busy to send Adah any money," he declared.

Adah badly needed money. Work was scarce, and she was forced to live on crumbs. The house was too expensive for her to maintain, and she moved to a tiny room in a lodging house at Third Avenue and Fourteenth Street. She continued to frequent Pfaff's, but ate frugally. Charlie Pfaff won her lifelong friendship by extending her credit during the worst of the drought.

She was unable to find work of any kind in the first months of 1860, and the nightmare gradually became worse. Her figure began to swell and, since it was impossible for her to obtain employment as an actress, she advertised "Selections from Shakespeare" in handbills that James printed for her. At Hope Chapel she read various passages from his plays and passed the hat. Some income was better than none, and she gave several repeat readings.

Some of her friends believed there was a growing interest in poetry, so she gave a series of three lectures on "The Age of the Irrepressibles" at Clinton Hall on Eighth Street. The talks were sparsely attended, and her profits, after paying for the hall, were slim.

Suddenly, one night late in April, 1860, she felt violently ill, and in the early hours of the morning suffered a miscarriage. She fell unconscious, and was found later in the morning by her landlady, who notified James. The editor and Whitman hurried to her room, and took her in a carriage to the charity ward at the Jews' Hospital, which later became Mt. Sinai.

Two days later Adah returned to her room. She was in a weakened physical condition, but her financial plight was desperate, and she had to find work. At least she was no longer carrying the baby, and could now return to the theater if any of the managers would hire her. She made the rounds, but there were no openings.

In her agony, she wrote the moving poem "A Fragment," later included in her only volume of published poetry, *Infelicia*. A few lines indicate her mood:

> Oh, I am sick of what I am. Of all
> Which I in life can ever hope to be.
> Angels of light be pitiful to me.

Every day she continued her ceaseless search for a job, but found no one willing or able to make her an honorable offer. To her credit, she refused to become a prostitute again. But the pressures were too great for her, and at night she wrote:

> Oh, rest for thee, my weary soul,
> The coil is round thee all too fast.
> Too close to earth thy pinions clasp:
> A trance-like death hath o'er thee past.
>
> Oh, soul! oh, broken soul, arise,
> And plume thee for a prouder flight.
> In vain, in vain—'tis sinking now
> And dying in eternal night.

Her friends bought meals for her at Pfaff's and less expensive restaurants. James printed several of her poems so she could pay the rent on her room and carry a little money in her purse as she looked for work. There were few openings in the city for unskilled laborers, as immigrants were pouring into the United States from Europe, and there was on the market a glut of waitresses, housekeepers, serving maids, and cleaning women.

Adah realized that her one hope was to remain in the

theater. At last her persistence was rewarded, and she played the part of "Bones" in a minstrel show for a men's club, her figure hidden beneath a flapping swallow-tailed coat and a pair of trousers several sizes too large, her facial beauty concealed beneath a coating of burnt cork. The show was a success, and was repeated several times each week, providing her with rent and eating money through the long, hot summer of 1860.

In the autumn she haunted the offices of the producers again, but had no luck. Once more she rented a hall, and gave imitations of Edwin Booth and Charlotte Cushman. "My performance was dreadful," she wrote to Whitman, who was out of town, "but at least I fooled enough people to give another show next week. Please don't come to see it. I would be too conscious of myself. I pray that Booth does not come."

In October she moved a tiny step up the scale. Charles Blondin, the French acrobat who had crossed Niagara Falls four times the previous year, performing stunts on a tightrope, was capitalizing on his feat by going into vaudeville. At the climax of his act he planned to cross the stage on a high wire, blindfolded and walking on stilts, with a girl standing on his shoulders. The requirements for the part were pulchritude, a sense of physical balance and enough courage to wear a very short, thigh-length skirt and black net stockings, a costume common in Paris but virtually unknown in the United States.

The Bowery Theater advertised the role in several newspapers, among them the *Mercury* and *Daily News,* for the management was well aware of the publicity value of such an ad. Dozens of hopefuls appeared on the appointed day, and a large crowd gathered outside the theater to watch them.

At least half of the girls stalked out when shown the brief costume. Adah, the former Queen of the Plaza, who had dared to wear a negligee on-stage in New Orleans, re-

mained. Blondin was one of three judges who inspected
the candidates, and ordered Adah to take the pins out of
her hair. It tumbled down her back to her waist, and the
judges went into a huddle.

Blondin asked her if she thought she could balance on
his shoulders. Instead of replying, she hoisted her skirts,
vaulted onto his shoulders and stood there triumphantly,
almost smothering him with her petticoats. She was hired
instantly, and the others were dismissed.

For the first time in many months Adah now had steady
employment, and could look forward to eight or more un-
interrupted weeks of work. Blondin was a success, and
four times each day audiences filled the theater to ap-
plaud him, gasp at his daring—and ogle the long-limbed
girl who provided dressing for his act.

Adah had no time to visit other managers during the
engagement, but wrote invitations to every producer in
the city, saying, "I hope you will visit the Bowery whilst
I am playing there." Inasmuch as she spoke not a word of
dialogue, sang not one note of a song and, in fact, did
nothing but perch on the shoulders of Blondin as the acrobat made his way across the high wire, she could hope to
gain little. But some recognition was better than none,
and she had reason to believe that her luck had finally
changed.

She could afford to pay for her suppers at Pfaff's again,
and went every night to the literary table there, immersing
herself in hectic talk about poetry and fiction. None of
her friends thought any less of her because she appeared
onstage in a scanty costume. She had a living to earn,
and they did not sit in judgment on her.

But a judgment on a far graver issue was not far distant.
Adah, in her innocence, thought that her problems had
been solved for the moment, but she was about to learn
that financial woes were the least of her worries.

CHAPTER VII

THE SCANDAL

The stars that are trembling forth their silent messages
to the hills have none for thee!
The mother-moon that so lovingly reacheth down her
arms of light heedeth not thy Love!

—"Hemlock in the Furrows"

NEWSPAPERS of the mid-nineteenth century were published in a day when the gossip column had not yet been
developed, and editors, aware that their product went into
readers' homes, exercised caution when discussing the
personal problems of celebrities. Modesty prevailed, and
virtually none of the sensational exploits of the great, near-
great, and neurotic ever saw the light of print. The New
York *Clipper,* which was something of a trade paper in
the theatrical and sports worlds, did, however, occasionally
deal in relatively intimate terms with persons whose names
appeared in its news columns.

On November 2, 1860, a remarkable editorial appeared
in the *Clipper* with the signature of Frank Queen, the assistant editor. Writing at the instigation and under the
direction of Ed James, Queen said:

The short time Adah Menken has been before the public, no actress has been more talked about, vilified, and misrepresented.

Systematic efforts have been made by certain persons to injure her in the estimation of the public, and thus deprive her of the means of earning an honest living in the trade she has adopted.

She came to this city friendless, with nothing to rely upon but her own energetic spirit. There seems to be a conspiracy afoot to deprive her of that matchless spirit.

The association of her name with that of John C. Heenan has made her the target of nearly every newspaper scribbler in the country, who has severally married her to Tom Thumb, President James Buchanan and the King of the Cannibal Islands. She has at times been compelled to answer these calumnies, but her letters have been altered to suit the purpose of the editors, who pervert the real intent and meaning of the writer, and wilfully misrepresent her in every way they can.

Miss Menken is no longer friendless. This newspaper has the honor of calling itself her friend, and those who oppose her also oppose us. Let her calumniators take heed.

We trust the scribblers have got to the end of their tether and that they will hereafter assist (as they have hitherto endeavored to retard) her efforts to support herself in a legitimate and honorable calling.

The editorial made no sense to the vast majority of the *Clipper*'s readers. Some, who understood, snickered; a very few realized that James, with Queen's help, was trying to batten down the hatches before a storm blew up. They had good cause to expect a hurricane that could totally destroy Adah.

What had happened was, in essence, quite simple. John C. Heenan, an exponent of the love-them-and-leave-them school of romanticists, had become enamored of a young woman who frequently visited his training camp outside

Brussels. It now became important to him that he free himself of previous encumbrances.

Heenan, indifferent to Adah's fate since he sailed to England, donned his snug-fitting thinking cap. It is not clear whether he corresponded with friends who then got in touch with Isaac Menken in Cincinnati, whether he wrote direct to Menken, or whether he had suspected from the first that Adah's marital status was cloudy. Whatever the methods of his investigation, he determined that Adah was not divorced from Isaac Menken.

In brief, she was a bigamist.

Ten days after the publication of Queen's editorial, a small letter to the editor appeared inconspicuously on an inside page of the *Clipper*, signed by Heenan. In it he denounced Adah for being married simultaneously to two men, and declared that his own marriage to her was, as a consequence, null and void.

The letter created a minor sensation in the theater and in the ranks of sporting buffs. Of all the city's newspapers, however, none reprinted it, and only the *Sun* and *Daily News* said, in small fillers, that Heenan was no longer married. The name of his wife was not mentioned.

Adah took the news in her stride, continuing to dine nightly with Walt Whitman and Fitz-James O'Brien. She wanted no more to do with Heenan after his callous treatment of her, and she assumed, quite rightly, that the men concerned would take the necessary action to settle the unsavory business. "She acted in good faith when she married Heenan," James says in his biography, "and so she believed she had nothing to fear."

Her sanguinity was misplaced, as she could have been arrested and sentenced to a five-year prison term had either of her "husbands" chosen to bring charges against her. Ironically, her best protection was her relative anonymity. The overworked authorities of New York, trying to cope with anti-Southern riots, abolitionist demonstrations, and the manifold problems growing out of the tidal waves of immigration from Europe—not to mention the wild release of emotions attending the election of the controversial Abraham Lincoln as President of the United States—had their hands full. Unless someone complained, they had no intention of persecuting an obscure actress.

Isaac Menken, however, was spurred to sudden activity. It is impossible to determine whether he was unaware of Adah's quick marriage to Heenan so soon after his own separation from her, or whether he had entertained hopes that she would return to him, following an affair with Heenan. Now that her remarriage had been made public, he had to clear his own name as rapidly as possible, and on December 1, 1860, filed for a divorce in Cincinnati. Apparently Adah was not served with papers of any kind in the case, for she expressed surprise when informed, two weeks later, by the busy Ed James that Isaac had divorced her.

"When a man disappeared from Miss Menken's life," Newell wrote with understandable bitterness, "he also disappeared from her mind and heart. She cared not one whit that Menken had tarnished her reputation. I was told by Charles Pfaff, Jr., son of the noted tavern keeper, that Miss Menken reacted with pleasure when notified that Menken had divorced her, saying in the hearing of many, 'Now, thank the Lord, I am free.' "

Attorneys hired by Heenan believed otherwise and, taking no legal chances, filed a suit on his behalf for a divorce in the Circuit Court of his native McHenry County, Illinois. The court demanded that he be present in person, a complication that upset his romance. He remained in Brussels for some months, and did not actually obtain the divorce until October, 1861, by which time Adah had become the most notorious woman in the United States as a result of her performance in *Mazeppa*. Heenan liked publicity as much as many and more than most, but saw nothing to be gained by remaining linked to a woman whose very name meant wickedness and debauchery.

Adah was astonished when a number of her acquaintances reacted strongly to the revelation that she was a bigamist. Mrs. E. D. E. N. Southworth, the most popular and successful of women novelists, cut the bigamist-actress-poet dead in Pfaff's. Horace Greeley walked past Adah's table without seeing her. Wendell Phillips, the distinguished antislavery leader and enthusiastic exponent of women's rights, came to New York from Boston to address a meeting and, invariably, later found himself at Pfaff's. Someone brought Adah to his table, intending to present her to him, but a member of Phillips' party whispered in the great man's ear, and he made a point of snubbing her.

Even Blondin wondered whether to terminate Adah's employment in his act, a development that alarmed her. She had been receiving complaints from Mrs. Josephs in New Orleans, and had been hoping she would soon resume her payments to her mother, but it appeared that she would soon be pounding the cobblestones again. Whitman came to Adah's help, persuading the owners of the Bowery Theater that she would be a drawing card that would attract the curious rather than a liability, and she remained in Blondin's act. In fact, when his run ended, she stayed on at the Bowery briefly, wearing her same abbreviated costume, as window-dressing for a team of jugglers.

Adah maintained a cheerful, firm façade through this trying period, but her real suffering was intense. Repeated entries in her *Diary* say she could neither sleep nor eat— and when Adah had no interest in food, she was not herself. A poem, "Dying," which was her gloomiest literary effort and, perhaps, one of her strongest, indicates her

bleak desperation. The opening verse completely expressed
her mood of emptiness and shame:

> Leave me; oh, leave me,
>   Lest I find this low earth sweeter than the skies.
> Leave me lest I deem Faith's white bosom bared to the
> betraying arms of Death.
> Hush your fond voice, lest it shut out the angel
> trumpet-call.
> See my o'er-wearied feet bleed for rest.
> Loose the clinging and the clasping of my clammy
> fingers.
> Your soft hand of Love may press back the dark,
> awful shadows of Death, but the soul faints in the strife
> and struggles of nights that have no days.
> I am so weary with this climbing up the smooth steep
> sides of the grave wall.
> My dimmed eyes can no longer strain up through the
> darkness to the temples and palaces that you have built for
> me upon Life's summit.
> God is folding up the white tent of my youth.
> My name is enrolled for the pallid army of the dead.

The "you" to whom she refers appears to have been a
poetic figure of speech. She was not engaged in a romance
at that period, which is no wonder, as any sensible man
would have run from a woman married to two husbands.
It is unlikely that she was thinking of either Menken or
Heenan, and her friendships with Whitman, James, and
others were platonic. Perhaps she was grieving because
she felt she had been branded as a tainted creature in the
eyes of all men.

Her engagement at the Bowery was terminated on New
Year's Day, 1861, and on January 3 she was again a patient
at Jews' Hospital, suffering from what later generations
would call nervous exhaustion. Not even her brave front

could hide from her friends that she felt keenly the disgrace of having been publicly called a bigamist. At her written request, Whitman sent her a copy of *The Scarlet Letter*, which she expressed a desire to read again, "so I may draw strength and inspiration from it, if there be any of these qualities left in my poor, tired soul."

Her self-pity was obvious, but she did not forget that her friends needed encouragement, too. The better part of her letter was devoted to unstinted praise for what has subsequently been recognized as one of Whitman's greatest poems—"Out of the Cradle Endlessly Rocking." It had been written in 1859, and there is no explanation for Adah's unfamiliarity with it until her hospitalization.

"You have broken free of the fetters of convention," she told the poet, recognizing his genius. "You are doing for American letters what Samuel Taylor Coleridge, poor tortured soul, did for poetry in England. Let nothing deter you. Let your voice forever be raised high, 'Out of the cradle endlessly rocking,/ Out of the mockingbird's throat, the musical shuttle.'"

Edwin Booth formed a committee to take up a collection for the distraught young woman, and when Adah was released from the hospital in mid-February, her friends presented her with three hundred and twenty-seven dollars in cash. "Miss Menken was always gallant in the face of adversity," Newell says in his biography, "but on this occasion, so Mr. Edwin Booth has himself informed me, she could not contain her tears. She always gave to others, and was so startled when those whom she had befriended showed kindness to her in her hour of need that she took refuge in feminine weakness to which she but rarely resorted."

Adah and her friends repaired to the Bowery Restaurant for a festive dinner, and the atmosphere was dampened only momentarily when Mrs. Miriam Harris—an author who liked to think of herself as a serious novelist—whose books usually sold well because of their concentration on romantic themes, made it a point to snub Adah.

"If I am a sinner, let a large 'B' be placed on my chest, and I will take my stand with Hester Prynne," Adah is supposed to have said on that occasion, teasing Booth. The remark was later repeated endlessly, and allegedly was made on any one of a dozen or more evenings. If Adah actually said it—she does not refer to it in her own writings, nor do her biographers—the night of the dinner following her release from the hospital was probably the time.

Certainly she would have wanted to shock Miriam Harris and others like her. Adah had a lifelong contempt for members of her own sex and developed a bitter antipathy toward female authors. Fanny Fern was the only second-rater she ever admired, and she was happy to forget Mrs. Fern when she learned to appreciate good poetry. Then there was Harriet Beecher Stowe, whose writing Adah found dull.

The two are alleged to have met in a Fifth Avenue restaurant at some unspecified time during the Civil War, but the occasion was not a memorable one. The timid Mrs. Stowe, whose *Uncle Tom's Cabin* had done so much to solidify antislavery sentiments in the North, may not have recognized the gaudily attired Jezebel who was presented to her. According to a story that should be accepted with a dose of large-grained salt, Adah eagerly grasped the author's hands.

"Mrs. Stowe," she supposedly gushed, "I have dreamed of this moment, for I am a great admirer of your work."

"I do not admire yours, Mrs. Menken," Harriet Beecher Stowe is said to have replied.

Mrs. Stowe was too much of a lady and far too timid to express such blunt disapproval of another woman in public. It may be, of course, that she was seething with

righteous New England indignation, but no authentic
source can be found for the often-repeated tale, which did
not begin appearing in print until a year or two after
Adah's death.

In any event, the dinner at the Bowery Restaurant was
a smashing success. Until this time, most of Adah's associa-
tions in New York had been primarily literary, but now
members of her own profession began to take an interest
in her career. The pendulum of public opinion, at least
within the theatrical industry, had swung in her favor
following her illness.

Edwin Booth was already recognized as one of the foremost of American stars, and his productions of Shake-
spearean tragedies at the Winter Garden, beginning in
the following year, would bring him even greater renown.
Joseph Jefferson was not yet "the beloved Joe Jefferson,"
but he had a large, loyal following. Charlotte Cushman
was, by all odds, the first lady of the American theater,
having already enjoyed enormously successful careers as an
opera singer, theater owner-producer, and tragedienne.

It was she who took over the direction of Adah's career
and, for a short time, the girl became her protégé. Thanks
to her influence, Adah played Lady Teazle at Niblo's Gardens, but the enthusiasm of Miss Cushman was misplaced
and the venture a total failure.

Booth, who had a sharp eye for publicity, pretended to
elope with Adah, renting a carriage and driving with her
to White Plains after leaking the word that they would
be married. The newspapers were wary of such antics, and
only the *Mercury*, which fell for the stunt, recorded it for
posterity.

The practical-minded Joe Jefferson suggested Adah for
the leading role in a new play, based on the life of the ad-
venturess, Lola Montez. Adah bore at least a vague resemblance to what the notorious Lola supposedly looked

like in her prime, and was hired. The character of the woman fascinated Adah, and she read all she could find on the Irish-born wanton who had been a king's mistress, caused a revolution, and had been the direct cause of at least four authenticated duels.

"Adah has found the perfect role at last!" Fitz-James O'Brien wrote enthusiastically after seeing a rehearsal of *Lola Montez, or, The Proud Courtesan.* "Not even those who know her best can recognize her own individuality, so perfectly does she submerge herself in the part of Lola."

It appeared that Adah was in her right element at last, and she was teased unmercifully at Pfaff's literary table, as Lola Montez had been an off-again, on-again actress during her tempestuous life, and had sometimes horse-whipped drama reviewers who had dared to criticize her in print.

Charlotte Cushman attended a rehearsal, and later advised Adah in detail how to make the role more effective. The energetic first lady of the theater seldom paid anyone that great a compliment, and Adah was flattered.

There were rumors that *Lola Montez* would be a hit, but the play was in unexpected difficulty before it opened. The producers, one of whom was reputedly a cousin of John C. Heenan's, had been rehearsing in church halls and lofts while they negotiated for a theater. They were earnest young men, but unfortunately were penniless, and therefore could not conclude a rental deal with any theater owner. The cast, which had been working without pay, was dismissed with thanks and regrets, and Adah was again at liberty, having wasted the better part of a month on a venture that had not jelled.

James Murdoch, the liveliest of New York's theatrical directors, who was not averse to acting when he found the right part, had seen one of the rehearsals. What he thought of Adah's acting ability is unknown, but he was

impressed by her beauty and vitality. Adah had known
him casually, but Murdoch reputedly traveled only with
the highest-ranking stars and she was surprised when he
invited her to dine with him at one of lower Fifth Avenue's
more elegant restaurants.

An unemployed actress always accepted offered meals,
and Adah went with Murdoch, expecting him to propo-
sition her. Instead, he asked her to put her career in his
hands. "J.M. believes," Adah tells her *Diary* on her
twenty-sixth birthday, "that there is, in my individuality, a
quality that will make me a leading star!"

Twenty-four hours later she was employed again, working at one of the cheapest theatrical establishments in the
city, the Canterbury Melodeon, located at 663 Broadway.
Performances were continuous from noon to midnight,
and the audience was made up almost exclusively of men
who paid from twenty-five to fifty cents a seat in order to
ogle the girls who sang and danced on the little stage.
The man who hired Adah was Murdoch's friend, orchestra
leader Dave Braham, at that time just starting his climb to
the top. He later became the father-in-law of Ned Harrigan, a member of the renowned vaudeville team of
Harrigan and Hart, and composed hundreds of H. and H.
songs.

The Civil War was just beginning, New York was fever-
ishly excited, and young men by the thousands were already joining the Union Army. At least half of the audiences at the Canterbury were made up of recruits on leave
from training camps, and they whistled and shouted when
they approved, hissed and jeered when they did not like
a performer.

Adah, who had no real experience in the rough-and-
ready world of the musical theater, was frightened, knowing that the audience would pelt her with rotten fruit and
eggs if she gave an inferior performance. Braham im-

mediately took her under his wing, and spent two hectic hours with her, rehearsing, before the day's shows began at noon.

The act in which Adah appeared was called "Turn in Tights," and she was given a pair of sequin-spangled tights that had belonged to her predecessor in the role and were a half-size too small. Her duties consisted of standing at one side of the stage and singing several ditties while four other girls, also in sequined tights, did a listless acrobatic dance. Hurrying frantically onto the stage, Adah was still trying to learn her lyrics.

Braham covered for her, and for two days the orchestra played loudly, brasses blaring and drums rolling, whenever she sang. The audience couldn't hear a word, but appreciated her figure and she became a fixture of the act. Thereafter she sang the lyrics in a husky but almost childlike voice, a combination that fascinated Braham.

"Adah was a grand girl," James reports him as saying, "even though she couldn't sing. But it didn't matter. She was the only one out of all the hundreds of girls who got up onto the Canterbury stage who didn't need talent. The applause rocked the house every time she stood on the stage."

As Murdoch had realized, she projected a quality, an aura of "something," across the footlights. The something was sex appeal, and Murdoch, who was determined to use it to advantage, watched many of Adah's nine daily performances. He was present one night in mid-April when an unexpected crisis erupted.

The act which preceded "Turn in Tights" was one called "Ha-Ha, Horsie." In it several girls cavorted about the stage in imitation horses' heads, and at the climax a girl rode out onto the stage on the back of a live horse to sing a song. The young woman knew nothing about animals, and became panicky when the normally tired horse suddenly became frisky. She screamed, and Braham frantically directed his musicians to play as loudly as they could.

The girl was in imminent danger of being thrown, but the audience, unaware that a real drama was taking place, applauded enthusiastically, and the stage manager did not order the curtain rung down. Adah, who was waiting in the wings, ready to go on next, dashed onto the stage and helped the young woman to dismount. Then she leaped onto the horse's back, quieted him and rode off to the wild applause of the male audience.

That night Braham accompanied Murdoch and Adah to a nearby Broadway restaurant, and told the story of the occasion many times in following years. "Jim was very thoughtful," he said, "and kept asking questions. He didn't stop until he was convinced he hadn't seen a freak accident. Adah swore she could ride any horse on earth, and he took her word.

"He suggested that she play in a revised version of *Mazeppa*. She had never heard of the play, so he told her about it, and suggested that at the end she ride out through the audience on a steep, spiral runway built so everyone could see her. She agreed at once, not hestitating one minute. That's how *Mazeppa* was born."

Braham was unaware of what happened in the following frantic days. It was Murdoch's idea that Adah ride tied to the back of a horse, but he was afraid she couldn't manage. She swore she could, and he took her to the Third Avenue Livery Stable to prove her boast. There, at nine o'clock in the morning, grooms and ostlers watched, round-eyed, as a comely young woman in full-skirted street attire was strapped to the back of a gelding that cantered five times around the ring.

Murdoch was satisfied, and produced a contract—a document that was to make him a wealthy man—for in it Adah agreed that he should receive 10 percent of the profits earned at every performance of *Mazeppa*.

At noon she went off to the day's grind at the Canterbury, and Murdoch, digging up a copy of the ancient vehicle, *Mazeppa*, started to work rubbing some of the rust off its wheels. He was conscious of Adah's limitations as an actress, and gave her short, simple speeches. Other parts were rewritten, too, so that competent actors could carry the burden of the drama.

He did enough in three days to convince himself that the entire play could be reshaped satisfactorily, and then started making the rounds of the theater owners. The producers knew and respected Murdoch, but the venture he was suggesting was so unorthodox that they hesitated. Several were interested, but only George Wood made a specific offer. If the play could be presented elsewhere, so he could see for himself that the production was feasible, he would be willing to book it into the Broadway.

Murdoch wasted no time, and immediately made a trip to Albany. There his friend, Captain John P. Smith, managed the Green Street Theater, and had worked with him in the presentation of many hits. The Captain listened, and the next day accompanied Murdoch to New York. There he watched Adah perform at the Canterbury, and was not impressed. He felt even less inclined to have any part of the undertaking after he met her that evening, as Adah's cigarette smoking shocked him. Smith was in show business, it was true, but as a resident of Albany he was less sophisticated than New Yorkers.

Murdoch talked for hours, and Smith finally agreed to present *Mazeppa*, stipulating that if the play should prove successful, it would return to his theater after the New York run. Everyone concerned shook hands on the deal, Smith went back to Albany and Adah, released from the drudgery of the Canterbury Melodeon, hoped her funds would last until *Mazeppa* opened.

The entire production was put together in the incredibly short span of one month. Murdoch was known as a man of action, but not even he had ever shown such great energy. He hired his cast, continued his polishing and rewriting of the old play, and, using funds that Smith and Wood had advanced him, ordered his sets and costumes. *Mazeppa* went into rehearsal, and Murdoch, in his "spare" time, made several quick trips to Albany to supervise the building of the all-important spiral runway.

Adah accompanied him on these journeys, as Murdoch wanted to make certain that she was satisfied with the runway. Making every minute count, he rehearsed her in her part while they rode on the train. It was on one of these trips that Adah conceived the revolutionary idea of wearing flesh-colored tights in the climactic scene. She had made her first acquaintance with tights at the Canterbury, and believed that for her purposes, in *Mazeppa* at least, the illusion she wanted to create would be spoiled by the costume she was scheduled to wear.

Till then, no one had ever worn flesh-colored tights, but Murdoch was willing to be convinced they would be effective, and ordered a set made for Adah. When he saw her in the tights several days later, he knew instantly that she had hit on something so sensational that the costume alone would guarantee the play's success. He ordered her never to answer when asked if she appeared in the nude or wore tights, and he swore the play's wardrobe mistress, Emma Hazeltine, to strict secrecy.

The company went to Albany on May 20, and Adah started daily practice with the horse, Black Bess, that she had selected from at least a score she had ridden and inspected. The runway was completed, and she spent at least an hour each day working on it, gradually increasing the mare's pace. Everything was proceeding smoothly until Adrian Murphy, the first-billed featured actor, who played the villainous leader of the Polish nobility, invited Adah to have supper with him one night after the rehearsals.

Murdoch came upon them at three o'clock in the morning in the taproom of the old Beverwyck Tavern, and threatened to punch Murphy in the nose if he "molested" the star again. The incident started rumors to the effect that Murdoch was romantically interested in Adah, but the stories were untrue. He had seen disaster strike other troupes when his leading ladies and leading men had become involved in affairs, and he wanted nothing to interfere with the success of *Mazeppa.*

Adah learned a lesson from the brief flurry, and thereafter made it her policy never to accept invitations from fellow members of a cast. She and her colleagues frequently ate together, but she never permitted herself to go anywhere alone with one of the men.

In spite of Murdoch's attempts to protect Adah, the accident he dreaded took place three days before the opening. Black Bess had become accustomed to her routine, and nonchalantly cantered up one side of the horseshoe-shaped spiral, then down the other, with the sophisticated ease of a veteran. But she had not yet appeared before an audience, and Murdoch was afraid she might react violently when facing a mass of applauding men and women. So, at his suggestion, Captain Smith invited a large number of friends to attend the rehearsal, and seated them on either side of the runway.

The people were told to make themselves at home, and perhaps responded too enthusiastically, standing and cheering when Black Bess and Adah started up the runway. The horse became frightened at the sight of a lady's feathered hat, lost her footing and slipped from the runway. The horrified crowd scattered, and several women shrieked.

But Adah was ready for the emergency. Breaking her bonds of light, paper tape, she leaped out of the path of the terrified Bess, caught the reins, and began to speak soothingly to the animal. Two seats were broken, but Black Bess was unhurt, and Adah suffered nothing worse than a minor bruise on her arm.

Murdoch wondered aloud whether the ride should be eliminated or, perhaps, shortened to a brief appearance across the stage. Adah laughed at his fears, led Black Bess to the foot of the runway and, after having herself lashed to the mare's back, made another run. The audience, naturally, was in a subdued mood, but Adah asked the guests to behave more noisily, and in all made five rides up the runway before she was satisfied.

"Show people," she says confidently in her *Diary,* "fear their own shadows. None of them has ever taken a tumble from a horse, and I'll not be spilled again. I know Black Bess now, and she knows me."

It might be noted that not one riding accident marred the many hundreds of performances Adah gave in *Mazeppa.* Through the years she used three different horses in theaters from San Francisco to Vienna, and handled all of them with disciplined perfection. The lessons her stepfather had given her in New Orleans paid handsome if unexpected dividends.

In the days immediately prior to the opening of the play in Albany, however, she had no idea she had found a vehicle that would bring her everything a woman could want—except happiness. There had been so many unpleasant experiences since she had gone to New York from New Orleans that she could not really believe her luck might change.

"If you hear of any new plays being cast in the next few

weeks, please let me know," she wrote to Ed James. "Our run here is limited to two weeks, and I don't think we'll bring the play into New York. George Wood arrived last night, and watched today's rehearsal. He said very little, but he looked sad. I can't blame him.

"C.C. [Charlotte Cushman] has said I should have been born a princess or the daughter of the rich rather than live as a slave of ambition, which was her way of saying I'm not a very good actress. I'm afraid I agree with her, but it is too late at my age to change. I can't promise you much if you come up for the opening here, but the beef and kidney pies at the Beverwyck are tasty. They do something special to the sauce.

"Do you suppose I'll ever earn enough to publish a volume of my verse? W.W. knows a printer who is reasonable, but I must put aside enough to insure that I can keep a roof over my head before I dream of immortality."

She signed this letter "Infelix Menken."

Here she used the name Infelix for the first time, and thereafter was to call herself nothing else when writing to her friends. She had formed the word from the noun infelicity, which means unhappiness or misfortune. It is easy enough to understand her attitude prior to the opening of *Mazeppa*, but it seems a trifle strange that she should have chosen to cling to the name after becoming one of the most celebrated, sought-after and highly paid women on earth. Her poetry indicates that she frequently suffered from depressed moods, of course, and modern medical scientists might have called her a depressive with masochistic tendencies. It is idle, however, to speculate at length on the character of someone seen only through letters, diaries, and poems, the written words of contemporaries, and the record she created.

It must suffice that Adah thought of herself as Infelix, and that she titled her book *Infelicia*.

Apparently she felt certain that *Mazeppa* would be a failure and that she would soon be job hunting again. But she had become a professional trouper by now, and gave the part her best. Customers would be paying for seats at the Green Street Theater, and she intended to give them a performance worth their money.

The opening night in Albany far exceeded Murdoch's highest hopes, and Adah's ride almost brought down the roof. She had carefully refrained from wearing her flesh-colored tights until the actual opening performance, and stunned the fellow members of the cast. As experienced a showman as George Wood believed she had been nude when strapped to the horse's back, and protested to Murdoch that she would need more decent attire if they expected to play in his theater.

Most of the New Yorkers who had gone to Albany for the opening were convinced that *Mazeppa* was a hit, but Adah and Murdoch awaited the verdict of the public, and did not relax until a line formed at the box office the following day. By sundown every seat was sold for the entire engagement, and the pessimistically cautious Adah sent a short, careful note to Fitz-James O'Brien.

"Tastes differ, and Albany isn't New York. So we can't guess whether they'll like me at the Broadway. If not, J.M. [Murdoch] thinks we can spend the rest of the year touring such towns as Baltimore, Toledo and Chicago. It may be possible that I'll be solvent for a few months. Who can say?" It was signed "Infelix Menken."

Wood did not share her apprehension, and spread the word, as soon as he returned to New York, that the hit of the century would open at the Broadway Theater in two weeks. Word spread through the grapevine of those-in-the-know, and tickets for the Manhattan opening disappeared as if by magic.

Adah, in spite of her caution, was already displaying

the characteristics of a star, and demanded a bloc of one hundred seats for the New York opening. Wood promised her fifty, and she sulked, believing herself the victim of injustice. In the meantime she was officially elevated to stardom. New posters appeared outside the Green Street Theater, and new handbills were printed. Captain Smith promised local theatergoers that those unable to see the play now would have ample opportunity when Miss Menken returned after her New York engagement.

The young aristocrats of Albany, whose ancestors had lived in the town when it was a Dutch possession bearing the name of Fort Orange, flocked to the stage door every night. But, at Murdoch's insistence, Adah refused to accept invitations from any of them. She was a valuable property, and had to be protected accordingly. It must be added that Adah herself cared nothing for the company of patricians. Perhaps her experience in Havana had soured her on men, or it may be that she felt she had nothing in common with bluebloods, for only rarely—in New York, London, Paris, or anywhere else—did she associate with great names or great wealth. Her friends were authors. She was drawn to them and they to her. None of her lovers had titles or bulging bank accounts, and although some of the offers she received were dazzling almost beyond belief, she rejected all of them.

Murdoch added the final touch of stardom by sending for a personal maid and dresser from New York. This young woman, a mulatto named Minerva, had been a slave who had escaped to the North with the aid of the underground railway. She and Adah immediately became friends, and Minnie, who had no surname, took the name of Menken. This led, eventually, to the belief in some quarters that she was Adah's sister or cousin, and that Adah had Negro blood. The truth of the matter is that the two had never heard of each other until two days after the opening of *Mazeppa* in Albany.

Adah wanted to cut her long hair, saying that the demands of realism required it, as she was playing the role of a man when thundering up the runway. Murdoch protested vehemently on the valid ground that her hair was one of her greatest physical attributes. Perhaps, as has been suggested in more recent times, there was a Lesbian streak in Adah, as there is in many prostitutes. On the other hand, a simpler explanation might be that she was a stubborn girl who refused to change her mind after she formed an opinion.

Regardless of the cause, she clung to the idea, but did nothing about it in Albany, waiting until the day of the opening in New York, when it would be too late for Murdoch to have a switch made for her. The instinctive publicity sense which had prompted her to suggest that she appear in flesh-colored tights, combined with the genuine desire to shock people that manifested itself in her public cigarette smoking, may have been factors in her decision to cut her hair.

Cut it she did, and wore it short for the rest of her life. Over the years it became shorter, and eventually was cut like a man's, with sideburns and a close trim at the back of the neck, and only a mass of curls on the crown and over the forehead to let the world know she was really a woman.

The *Mazeppa* company was jubilant on its return journey to New York after the Albany engagement, but Adah sat quietly on the train, reading poetry. Whitman, Burke, O'Brien, and James met her at the station, and conducted her to her mean lodgings on Third Avenue. Murdoch had tried to persuade her to find another, more suitable place to live, but she had been disappointed too often, and refused to consider the idea until she found out whether the play would succeed in the city. Never again, as long as she lived, did she display such good financial common sense.

Two days were spent preparing for the all-important opening, and Adah practiced for hours with Black Bess on the runway built at the huge Broadway Theater. Again there was a near-catastrophe when the horse momentarily lost her footing, but no harm was done, and the accident was not repeated.

Adah stayed away from Pfaff's and the Bowery Restaurant before the opening, preferring to eat in obscure restaurants. Her reason, which appears in her *Diary*, was a simple one: "If we fail, I don't want anyone to say I was trying to behave like a star when I had no right."

Her humility on the eve of what everyone else—with the possible exception of the superstitious, perpetually gloomy Murdoch—believed to be an inevitable triumph was a remarkable quality. She, who had suffered so much, took success in her stride. It may be that she endeared herself to novelists, poets, and newspaper writers because, like them, she was sufficiently introspective to retain the ability to laugh at herself.

On the day of *Mazeppa's* opening, however, she was not in a laughing mood. She ate a late breakfast with Dave Braham and Murdoch, and then disappeared—to sit before a mirror while a barber and Minnie cut her hair. When she joined Wood, Whitman, and James at Pfaff's, she was ready for her rendezvous with fame.

CHAPTER VIII

THE SENSATION!

Genius is power.
The power that grasps in the universe, that dives out
beyond space, and grapples with the starry worlds of heaven.
If genius achieves nothing, shows us no results, it is so much
the less genius.

—"Genius"

ADAH'S RECEPTION at the Broadway Theater on the night
of her opening in *Mazeppa* guaranteed the play's success
and made her a personage of consequence overnight. But,
even as today, the reaction of the press was awaited with
a mixture of eagerness and fear. Adah had broken the
code of propriety, her costume and hair were the talk of
the town, and it was feared—with good cause—that if the
press protested too violently, New York City officialdom
might demand more modesty and less flamboyance.

The *Times*, even in its early days an organ of great dignity and impeccable taste, confined itself to a brief, factual
announcement, informing its readers that Miss Adah
Isaacs Menken had opened an engagement at the Broadway Theater in a revised version of *Mazeppa*. That much,
and no more, seemed to be all the news fit to print.

Horace Greeley's hard-hitting *Tribune* was frank, fair,

and pulled no punches. "Miss Adah Menken wants tam-
ing down," the *Tribune's* critic wrote. "Her talent is like
gold in quartz veins—all in the rough; and so must un-
dergo the refining process of intelligent and critical audiences. . . . I will have to see her in other parts before
I can determine what is her real 'line.' Based on what I
have already seen, I feel certain it is not the 'clothes line.' "

The *Post,* owned and edited by William Cullen Bryant,
one of America's most distinguished poets and leading
intellectuals, tried to restrain itself. "The verses of Miss
Adah Isaacs Menken have not appeared in the columns of
this newspaper," the *Post* critic wrote, "but our devotion
to poetry is recognized throughout the United States and
we have no wish to dim the luster of one whose verses show
promise. We are tempted to urge the shoemaker to stick
to her last, but if she followed our advice, she would, more
would be the pity, deprive New Yorkers and guests who
visit our city of a rare and diverting spectacle. . . . It will
be necessary to view Miss Menken on another occasion before a fair judgment of her performance can be rendered.
. . . Miss Menken places the male in her audience at a
disadvantage. She is so lovely that she numbs the mind,
and the senses reel. . . . It will be a pleasure as well as a
duty to see her in *Mazeppa* once again, although, one must
confess, the play is itself a dreary excuse for a theatrical
entertainment."

The penny press pulled out all the stops, and the
Mercury used huge, bold type in a headline that shouted:

THE SENSATION!

The body of the review was equally excited. "Adah
Menken is the sensation of New York. Her rare beauty and
the tantalizing audacity of her performance defy description. She must be seen to be believed, and anyone who

misses her at the Broadway Theater will be denying himself the rarest of exhilarating treats."

The *Sun's* critic made an unsuccessful attempt to bridle his enthusiasm. "Miss Adah Menken's style is dashing, and her performance is full of promise," he said primly, then revealed his true feelings. "She is Aphrodite and Diana, a marble statue of exquisitely molded perfection come miraculously to life."

The *Daily News* positively bubbled. "May a lady be naked?" the reviewer asked. "The naked lady lives and breathes, and may be seen in *Mazeppa*. Nothing like her beauty has ever been seen on our stages, and many years will pass before any actress displays the courage shown by the doughty Miss Adah Isaacs Menken, who performs a feat of breathtaking daredeviltry. We salute the Naked Lady of New York!"

A new poster appeared in front of the Broadway Theater, advertising the appearance of The Naked Lady. The name stuck, and was used frequently throughout the rest of Adah's career. She acquired many names through the years, the majority self-devised:

The Menken
Cleopatra in Crinolines
La Menken
The Royal Bengal Tiger
The Fiery Centauress
La Belle Menken

Apparently she did not particularly care to be known as The Naked Lady, but theater owners knew the name was good for business, and gave her no choice. Once, when asked by *L'Express* of Paris what she thought of the title, she said diplomatically, "It is often used." The reporter asked for an opinion, and Adah shrugged Christendom's shapeliest and best-known shoulders.

Ed James paid tribute to his friend by printing excerpts of the other reviews in the *Clipper*. Writing none himself, he confined himself to the simple, happy statement, "This paper is proud to be the friend of Miss Adah Isaacs Menken, the toast of the town."

A great many people wanted to be Adah's friend now, including scores of men and women she had never met. She soon learned that stardom in New York was not at all the same as being a leading lady in New Orleans. She was subjected to constant pressure from people who knew her, claimed to know her, or wanted to know her. Dozens of letters arrived at the theater each day, huge crowds awaited her everywhere she went, and she found it impossible to escape from the limelight she had sought—and into which she had now been thrust so suddenly.

Ed and Hannah James gave her sanctuary in their Brooklyn home until she could straighten out her life. Her possessions, aside from several trunks filled with clothes, consisted of about two hundred books and a collection of other belongings that fitted easily into a small box. O'Brien acted as a volunteer secretary to answer the letters that required replies, and Adah tried to catch her breath. She was deluged with financial offers, people wanted to borrow money from her, and she received several proposals of marriage each day from men she had never met.

Pfaff's named a dish after her, a plebeian lamb stew that she particularly liked, and the Bowery Restaurant advertised "Soup Adah Menken." The chef did not disclose his recipe. Several prominent dressmakers offered Adah new wardrobes if they could advertise that she was their patron. In this she was interested. She listened to their ideas, told them several of her own, and finally came to terms with a Madame Marguerite, whose cards thereafter bore the legend, "Dressmaker to Miss Adah Isaacs Menken." This, of course, led wits to observe that "Madame Marguerite has an easy time dressing The Naked Lady."

Adah's salary was doubled, then doubled again within the first month of *Mazeppa's* run. She was now making the fabulous sum of five hundred dollars a week. Crowds stormed the box office, and George Wood ordered tickets printed for a run of six months, which no theater owner in his right mind had ever done. The *Mercury* was mistaken when it printed an article in July, 1861, to the effect that Adah was now making one thousand dollars a week. Eventually, when she played in London and Paris, she would earn that sum, but her maximum income in the United States—except for her incredible western tour—remained five hundred a week, which was as much as the highest-paid business executives in the country were making.

It was now her duty to herself and her public to start living like a star, and for the first time she began to think of buying her own home, a luxury she had never enjoyed. Ed James shrewdly advised her not to hunt for a house in person, as property owners would be sure to raise their prices if they knew her identity. So all of her friends went looking on her behalf, and no one was more devoted to the task than Robert Henry Newell of the *Mercury*.

Newell's reputation in his own day was enormous, and the decline that his fame has suffered in the past century makes it difficult to understand how much he was admired and respected by his contemporaries. He was in his mid-thirties, had achieved recognition on the *Post* before transferring to the *Mercury*, and was considered a topnotch newswriter. He was also the author of an impressively large number of books, many of them for children, which he wrote under a pseudonym, Orpheus C. Kerr.

Talented, financially secure, and a success in two fields of the writing profession, Newell was unlike any other man who had figured prominently in Adah's romantic life to date. He had his own opinions, did not hesitate to express them either in person or in print, and was regarded as an authority on many subjects. When he talked, people listened, and no one listened more avidly than Adah. The facile, handsome author fascinated her.

The feeling was mutual. Newell, by his own admission, fell in love with Adah during the winter of 1860–61, the most trying period of her life. He could have been under few illusions, for this was the time when, as he undoubtedly knew, two men were making simultaneous efforts to terminate their marriages to her. He could not have been unaware of her brief affair with Burke, either, and he saw her at her dismal worst when she was out of work, hospitalized, and playing in the cheapest of vaudeville at the Canterbury Melodeon.

Isaac Menken had been a young idealist; John C. Heenan had been a drunken, callous egocentric; but Newell was highly intelligent, sensitive, and realistic. In his case love was not blind, though he certainly was wearing rose-tinted glasses.

"Miss Menken," he states unequivocally in his biography, "had the keenest mind I ever encountered in a member of her sex. Indeed, few men were her mental equals, and she could discourse fluently on matters pertaining to literature, the sciences and the latest news of the world in which we live. She was a learned theologian, and I have heard her hold long, erudite talks with Dr. Henry Ward Beecher, the Rev. Jonathan Flaherty and other divines of note, in which she more than held up her end of the conversation. Her erudition, coupled with her great beauty, made her the rarest of her sex."

Newell's opinion of Adah's intellect was shared, in later years, by such people of consequence as George Sand and Theophile Gautier in France, Dante Gabriel Rossetti, Charles Reade, and the great novelist Charles Dickens in

England. It is unfortunate that a later generation must accept their opinions at face value, but Adah wrote no body of prose work and her sentimentally self-conscious, severely stylized poetry unfortunately only hints at the depths of her thinking.

Charles Stoddard, a poet of considerable talent who became Mark Twain's secretary and assistant, sat in wonder at Adah's feet in San Francisco and called her "brilliant." Stoddard was very young, so his judgment may have been immature. But Newell was a man equipped with a trained, adult mind.

He was very busy in the summer of 1861, writing a book for children, another of whimsy, and turning out a series of articles for the *Mercury* on the preparations for war being made in New York. His was the most important name on the newspaper's staff; he was given the best available space and the largest by-lines, and every manufacturer, munitions maker, and merchant in the state inundated him with requests to be included in the articles.

Newell nevertheless found time to go house hunting for Adah, and found precisely what he thought she needed at 458 Seventh Avenue. It was a thirty- to forty-year-old brick house with a large living room and equally handsome dining room, a kitchen equipped to prepare banquets, and six bedrooms, besides the servants' quarters and a stable. It also had two libraries, which may have influenced Newell's thinking, as he undoubtedly visualized Adah composing poetry in one while he wrote prose in the other.

The price was six thousand dollars, payable in two installments, one immediately, the rest within the following year. Adah heard Newell's enthusiastic report, and, "incognito," went with him to see the house. The proprietor, who showed them through the place, could scarcely have been unaware of Adah's identity, as she was the only woman in New York who wore her hair short, and her idea of inconspicuous clothes would have been wildly flamboyant by anyone else's standards.

Fortunately a price had already been quoted, and when the owner tried to raise it, Newell resisted. Adah's friends soon learned that his firmness on this occasion impressed her, and it may have been then that she began to regard him as a potential husband. She had told James and Whitman that she had no intention of marrying again.

Newell, however, was unique in her experience. He was someone of stature in the vocation she admired above all others. He was as handsome as Isaac, almost as husky as Heenan, and he had a strong, masculine business mind as well. Her *Diary* remains silent on the subject of Newell until the eve of their marriage the following year, but in late August, 1861, he became her most frequent and devoted escort, so she could not have been unaware of him as a man.

He gave her little opportunity to forget him. Adah accepted his recommendation that she buy the house, but a hitch developed. She had not yet had the chance to save the sum of three thousand dollars from her salary. Newell, presumably knowing what he was doing, advanced her the money. It was never repaid, as he goes to some lengths to explain in his biography, so he considered himself co-owner of the house when he married Adah. When they were divorced, he was so anxious to wash his hands of her that he voluntarily relinquished the promissory note she had given him. That, however, is another story.

Adah moved into the house in late August or early September of 1861, and beginning at that time surrounded herself with a staff befitting her new, exalted state. In addition to her personal maid, Minnie, she had a cook, two housemaids, and a man-of-all-work who doubled as her coachman. At Newell's suggestion she did not buy a carriage, but rented one, together with a team of horses, from a nearby stable. The economy was unique in her new era of heavy spending.

Adah went on a prolonged buying spree, completely furnishing the house from attic to cellar with the most expensive furniture, rugs, draperies, and bric-a-brac she could find. Her taste, as many visitors to her home were surprised to discover, was excellent, and in no way resembled her gaudy wardrobe. Tables and chairs were of polished oak, the fabrics covering sofas and other pieces of heavy furniture were of good quality and subdued colors, and her rugs were quietly elegant. The bedrooms were done soberly, too, but had feminine appeal, and only in her own chamber was she unable to resist the temptation of placing a very long vanity table with a large mirror. On the table, as Newell observes in his biography, were "lotions, pomades, perfumes and cosmetic aids of every description, too numerous to count and too varied to categorize."

Perhaps Newell was in part responsible for the taste Adah displayed. He claims credit for dissuading her from buying an ornate four-poster with a cloth-of-gold canopy. It is unlikely that he imagined the gaudy piece, and Adah appeared satisfied with a featherbed of the sort used by lesser mortals.

The first guests were, appropriately, Ed and Hannah James and Walt Whitman and his mother, whom Adah entertained at a gala little dinner party on a Sunday evening, the Broadway Theater being closed on Sundays. Newell was conspicuous by his absence, and Adah apparently was holding him at arm's length, for he says rather stiffly, "I was not invited to dine at Miss Menken's mansion until the evening of October 17, 1861."

He made up for lost time through the remainder of the autumn and early winter, while Adah presided over her first salon. The literary table at Pfaff's moved to 458

Seventh Avenue, and there were long discussions, debates, and disagreements on the relative standings of the more prominent authors of the period who were writing in English. Newell summarizes the results of these talks.

Dickens was conceded to be the great master of prose fiction. Adah greatly admired Reade, and persuaded others that he was worth their serious attention. Hawthorne ranked first among the American writers of prose fiction. No one, it appeared, had heard of Herman Melville. The group expressed a reluctant, almost grudging admiration for Ralph Waldo Emerson. Thoreau appears to have remained in the shadows.

Adah, herself so offbeat, enjoyed the poetry of the mysterious, alcoholic literary critic Edgar A. Poe, who had died a sodden, tragic death in Baltimore twelve years earlier. Her friends believed his criticism sound and were not averse to his fiction, but were unable to accept his poetry as serious work. Adah, it would seem, was one of the first to recognize his genius and had, in fact, spoken at length on his poetry in her lectures on "The Age of the Irrepressibles."

She had ample time to read now, as she had no lover and *Mazeppa* had settled down to one of the longest runs in the history of the New York Theater. It had been customary, up to that time, to present even the greatest successes in repertory of a sort, withdrawing them after several weeks, then presenting them again. But George Wood chose to change the pattern, and *Mazeppa* played continuously until early January, 1862.

Then the patient Captain Smith had his chance to reap a profit, and Adah played to capacity audiences at the Green Street Theater in Albany for six weeks. Her triumph was as great as her initial reception had been, and she was Albany's darling. Her suite at the Beverwyck became the cultural and social center of the town, and she impressed people with her erudition and wit while shocking them with her barely decent attire, short hair, and cigarette smoking.

A less successful period followed. *Mazeppa* went on tour, and although business everywhere was good, there were empty seats in the theaters, and audiences were less than rapturous. Hartford looked calmly down its long New England nose and gave The Naked Lady a cool reception. Philadelphia was even more restrained. She did not play in Boston.

The theatrical industry was not prospering in the winter and spring of 1862, as citizens of the North were in no mood for entertainment. Union forces were being beaten and harassed repeatedly in the Virginia area of operations by smaller but better-led and better-disciplined Confederate troops. Early in April the largest and most bitter engagement yet fought took place at Pittsburg Landing, Tennessee, and was thereafter known as the Battle of Shiloh. The Union Army under General Ulysses S. Grant suffered severe losses, the Confederates took an equally frightful pounding, and their brilliant commander, General Albert Sidney Johnston, was killed. Shiloh was believed to have been a victory for neither side, the pattern of Grant's triumph not yet having emerged, and no one felt like celebrating at the theater.

In mid-April, 1862, *Mazeppa* returned to the Broadway Theater. Again Adah played to capacity houses, but the audiences were restrained. News of the capture of New Orleans on May 1 by Admiral David G. Farragut of the Union Navy produced a curious reaction. Adah was known to be a Southerner, a native of New Orleans, but her loyalty to the Union cause had been established—or so her managers believed—the night in 1861 that *Mazeppa* had opened at the Broadway. The New Yorkers who listened to the rumors about Adah or knew her even indirectly knew that Adah had consistently opposed the institution of slavery. Her friends pointed to her devotion to Minnie as well as to her patriotic poems as proof of her feelings.

The audience that came to the Broadway on the night of May 3 was in a peculiar mood, however, and hisses greeted Adah from various parts of the auditorium. Someone shouted, "Hang the Reb!" when she made her second appearance. The incident upset her, and she forgot some of her lines.

The audience, aware of her discomfort, proceeded to bait her. There were catcalls throughout the performance, and people laughed at the wrong times. Adah's mood changed to one of defiance, and she became violently declamatory, trying to prove that she couldn't be frightened. At the climax, when she rode through the auditorium strapped to the back of Black Bess, there was a polite spattering of applause, but most of the audience sat on its hands. Not even Hartford and Philadelphia had failed to give her an ovation at that electrifying moment.

Adah was bewildered and heartsick, and by the time she reached home, she was running a high fever. A physician was summoned, and she remained in bed the following day. That evening she said she was too sick to go to the theater, and the performance was canceled.

Murdoch and George Wood were alarmed. Obviously something had to be done quickly to counteract the impression that the star from New Orleans had wilted under pressure and was grieving because her native city was now in Union possession. A brief advertisement was placed in the newspapers:

"Miss Adah Isaacs Menken wishes to announce that she is a faithful citizen of the United States of America, and swears fidelity to its aims."

Below it appeared a verse from her poem, "Pro Patria":

Columbia! My Country! My Mother! thy glory
  Was born in a spirit immortal, divine;
And when from God's lips passed the nectar of heaven,
  Thy current baptismal was deified wine!

That evening a rejuvenated Adah went on-stage. Every seat was taken and the audience was tense, anticipating an incident. Adah did not disappoint the throng. With the house lights still burning high, she appeared before the curtain in her street clothes, a gown of plum-colored velvet with matching hat, gloves, and shoes, and made a brief announcement. Newell, who was present, reported the speech in full in the *Mercury:*

"Ladies and gentlemen. If any among you doubt my patriotism, stand forward to be branded as a liar. If any man denies that I love this, my land, I challenge him to a duel and will fight it here and now, on this stage, with swords or pistols, as he prefers. Most of you have come here believing in my sincerity, as I believe in yours. It is my intention and that of my supporting cast to give you a good performance of a play that has been acclaimed by many thousands.

"This we cannot do if there are interruptions. If anyone feels the need to disturb us on the stage and his neighbors who are seated near him, let him stand now. I will gladly refund the money paid for his tickets out of my own purse. I thank you."

The audience applauded warmly, and the star received a standing ovation at the end of the play. There was no more trouble at the Broadway Theater, and the question of Adah's patriotism was settled—for the moment.

Her offer to fight a duel created a fresh sensation, of course, as she undoubtedly knew it would. Scoffers thought she had thrown down the gauntlet for the sake of publicity, so Murdoch invited doubters and anyone else interested to attend a "public exhibition of the use of firearms and fencing weapons, to be given by Miss Adah Isaacs Menken at the Bowery Academy on May 9th at 2:00 in the afternoon."

A huge crowd appeared, of course, eager to see a free show. The Bowery Academy was a large hall that had been used, in prewar years, as a practice ring by young men taking instruction in the ancient art of self-defense with a sword. It had clearly seen better days, but was spruced up with bunting for the great event. On one wall were five targets, each the size of a man's fist.

Promptly at two o'clock Adah appeared, dressed in tight-fitting men's breeches, a pair of knee-high boots and an open-throated man's shirt. Murdoch silenced the crowd, and announced that Miss Menken would demonstrate her skill with the pistol. An attendant approached her, carrying five pistols. She took each in turn and, at a distance of more than fifty feet, fired at the targets.

Her first shot was wide of the mark, and the bullet imbedded itself in the wooden wall. She later said that a trace of nervousness had spoiled her aim. The other four shots pierced the four remaining targets. The lessons she had been given as a child by her stepfather, who had tried so hard to bring her up as a boy, were paying dividends that neither had imagined.

A committee selected at random from the crowd was invited to inspect the targets. The gentlemen were duly impressed, as they well should have been. Few sharpshooters in either of the armies taking part in the vicious fighting south of Washington were her equal.

Before the stunned spectators had a chance to recover, another attendant appeared with two exceptionally long, double-edged swords. These ancient, murderous antiques had probably been made early in the seventeenth century, judging by their description, and perhaps had been found in some dusty theater cellar. They were so heavy and cumbersome that a strong man would have had trouble wielding one, and it is doubtful that Adah could have lifted a blade over her head.

There was no need for her to go that far. She seized one by the hilt, and drove the point into the soft wood of the Academy floor. Then she made an announcement. She was prepared, she said, to fight a duel to the death against any man in the house. There was a dead silence, she was the victor by default, and her admirers cheered themselves hoarse. It is useless to guess what might have happened had some man been foolish enough to accept the challenge. No one was that stupid, the gentlemen having taken the target-shooting exhibition to heart.

The stunt was the most successful that the resourceful Adah had yet conceived. She was the talk of the town again, and it was rumored that, when she had lived in Ohio, she had been Honorary Captain of the Governor's Life Guards, often putting the company through complicated drills. Posters depicting her in a hussar's uniform soon appeared outside the Broadway Theater, and the legend—which she took care neither to confirm nor deny—followed her to the grave. In actual fact, she held no commission from the Governor of Ohio, honorary or otherwise, and there was no company of Life Guards.

But the myth persisted. And on two occasions, once while playing in Baltimore and again, some years later, while visiting Vienna, "Captain" Adah Isaacs Menken reviewed honor guards and put the men through their paces. Always careful to give at least the semblance of substance to the fiction she created, she had made it her business to learn the rudiments of the manual of arms and close order drill in the Union Army. How she achieved the same effect with royal Austro-Hungarian troops is something of a mystery, but the Vienna *Zeitung* hinted that an obliging staff officer stood beside her and whispered the commands, one by one, before she bawled them aloud.

Adah's skill with a pistol would have made headlines in any age, of course, but was perfect grist for the suffragettes' mills of her own time. She, who had been more or less ignored by the good ladies, was now hailed by them, much to the delight of the newspapers. The *Sun* printed a cartoon depicting several bloomer-clad women charging across a battlefield, with the intrepid Adah in the lead. And the *Daily News,* which was critical of President Lincoln's conduct of the war, suggested in an editorial that she be commissioned to replace the inept generals who were unable to win a decisive victory in Virginia.

It is not surprising that the emotional Adah was carried away by her own publicity, and a few weeks later, through Newell's intercession, the *Mercury* published one of her better poems, which she called "Judith." It began:

Ashkelon is not cut off with the remnant of a valley.
Baldness dwells not upon Gaza.
The field of the valley is mine, and is clothed in verdure.
The steepness of Baal-perazim is mine;
And the Philistines spread themselves in the valley of
Rephaim.
They shall yet be delivered into my hands.
For the God of Battles has gone before me!
The sword of the mouth shall smite them to dust.
I have slept in the darkness—
But the seventh angel awoke me, and giving me a sword
of flame, points to the blue-ribbed cloud, that lifts his
reeking head above the mountain.
Thus am I the prophet.
I see the dawn that heralds to my waiting soul the advent
of power.
Power that will unseal the thunders!

    Power that will give voice to graves!
        Graves of the living;
        Graves of the dying;
        Graves of the sinning;
        Graves of the loving;
        Graves of despairing;
And oh! graves of the deserted!
These shall speak, each as their voices shall be loosed.
And the day is dawning.

"Judith" created a stir in literary circles, and won for
Adah a respect from people who had previously ignored
her. It also recalled her to the attention of the peripatetic
Horace Greeley, who wrote a short, scathing editorial in
the *Tribune*. "It is to be deplored," he said, "that a
woman whose sole claim to questionable fame is her
nightly appearance in the nude before depraved audiences
should be hailed as an artist. Her poetry has no more
merit than her theatrical performance."

Manager George Wood promptly composed a rebuttal,
which was printed as an advertisement in those newspapers which were less than fond of the publisher-politi-
cian-abolitionist. The owner of the Broadway Theater
declared passionately, "Miss Adah dresses the part very
prettily and displays a leg, or rather two legs, in silk flesh-
ings of such delicate proportions that they would have
made a Saint Anthony lift his eyes from the prayer book.
To see Miss Adah in the matured beauty of her woman-
hood, costumed as she is costumed, is alone worth the
price of admission."

The battle was joined. Greeley paused sufficiently long
in dispensing advice to the President, members of Congress, and the Union Army to snort, "Pericles observed
that a nation's moral standards become corrupted in a
time of war. This decline in our own day is to be seen on

every side, and is deplored by all decent citizens, who believe that even debauchery has limits which must not be transgressed. An actress who uses her naked body to entice audiences into a theater should be barred, by legislation, from the stage."

Wood was pleased, as was Murdoch, for the publicity was priceless, and seats for a performance of *Mazeppa* again became difficult to obtain. But Adah was furious, and entered the fray in person. "Mr. Greeley," she said indignantly in a paid advertisement, "has not deigned to see a performance of *Mazeppa*, yet he criticizes me on gossip and rumor. Is he afraid to judge for himself?"

This sally bounced off a wall of Olympian silence. Greeley had no more to say, and returned to the more serious business of telling the Government what to do and what not to do. But he grossly misjudged his adversary, to whom oblivion was an even worse fate than abuse.

"Mr. Greeley," Adah said in another ad, addressing him directly, "are you so lacking in the essence of fairness and justice that you refuse to make your own judgments? I challenge you to pay an evening's visit to the Broadway Theater. See me in my notoriety! Then say about me what you will, and I will abase myself at your feet, heeding your wisdom and accepting in silence your rebukes, if rebukes there be."

Greeley paid no attention to the generous offer, but Adah had maneuvered him into a difficult spot, and he must have known it. Her gesture was sporting, courteous and, above all, fair. By the standards of many people she was no lady, but Greeley was a gentleman, and could not refuse her terms without seeming to be a boor.

The advertisement having produced no results, Adah launched a noisy private campaign of harassment. Greeley dined in public at his peril, for his meals were certain to be interrupted by acquaintances who inquired, at the top of their lungs, when he was going to see *Mazeppa*. He received daily letters, at the *Tribune* office and at home, urging him to spend an evening at the Broadway. His friends joined in the game with almost as much enthusiasm as his enemies were displaying, and he knew no peace.

He did not budge, however, until he finally realized that people were laughing at him. Greeley's skin was as leathery as that of any other newspaperman, but he couldn't tolerate the knowledge that people were snickering behind his back because of his discourtesy to a gaudy actress and would-be poet. A staff member was sent to the office of George Wood for tickets, and although Greeley may have hoped to attend a performance incognito, Wood saw through the ruse.

Adah's performance on the night that Greeley sat in the audience was typical, neither better nor worse than usual. In no way did she indicate an awareness of his presence, brusquely rejecting Wood's suggestion that she greet the editor in a curtain speech. She had no intention of making overtures to Horace Greeley. If he wanted peace, he would have to come to her.

He did. Immediately after the final curtain he went backstage to her dressing room and, in the presence of a half-dozen witnesses, congratulated her on her daring as a horsewoman. If he damned her with faint praise, he had nevertheless praised her, and Adah was jubilant. An editorial in the *Tribune* would not only vindicate her, but would give her the increased stature she sought.

But each day Adah searched the editorial columns of the *Tribune* in vain. She waited for two weeks, and with the second New York run of the play drawing to a close, she knew she would have to act quickly if she wanted vindication. So she wrote a letter, which she sent to the publisher by private messenger.

Nothing maddens a biographer more than the frustration suffered when he follows a trail promising great excitement, only to have it disappear in the mists of the past. James and Newell both refer to the letter, and it was common knowledge in New York's newspaper and theatrical circles in 1862 that Adah had written and dispatched such a communication. What she said, however, remains a mystery, and if she confided in anyone, he kept his mouth shut. Certainly discretion was the better part of valor in dealing with an editor as vigorous and outspoken as Horace Greeley. Adah could not have been foolish enough to adopt a threatening tone, for she had no real weapons in her arsenal. And if she taunted him, it was best to keep that fact to herself.

Whatever her tactics, they succeeded. Greeley's capitulation, when it came, was dignified, graceful—and complete. Only George Wood had reason to cavil, for the long-awaited editorial in the *Tribune* did not appear until the issue of August 10, the day *Mazeppa* was scheduled to close. "The New York Theater will not be the same," the *Tribune* said, "without Miss Adah Menken, whose talents as a horsewoman have delighted large audiences, and whose beauty has been admired by all. Her many friends hope she will return to the local stage after audiences elsewhere have heard the thunder of her mare's hooves."

Adah's nudity was not mentioned, which was a victory, and if there was no word of her talents as an actress, she did not care. Greeley had gone out of his way to be friendly, and she could not ask for more. Two nights later he received his just reward, a public embrace from Adah in Pfaff's, a carefree gesture of camaraderie that must have mortified him to the depths of his New Hampshire soul.

But if Adah went too far, she suffered no unpleasant consequences. She usually knew how far she could go when dealing with a man—other than one of her husbands. Greeley shrugged off his embarrassment, and thereafter became one of Adah's friends. They were never close, as the fiery editor was capable of forming an attachment only for those who shared his political convictions, and Adah had no interest in politics.

She did have a quality possessed by few other women in her age, an understanding of authors, including newspapermen. Greeley paid her a deep and sincere compliment in a brief editorial written soon after her death, when he said, "Newspaper writers have lost a dear friend. Miss Adah Menken was one of the most renowned theatrical stars of our century, but we do not mourn her as do her audiences, which have included kings and governors. We shall miss a kindly woman who possessed a rare talent, that of listening intelligently and sympathetically to the men who gather, write and edit news."

Greeley, in his editorial obituary, may have put his finger on the secret of Adah's literary friendships. She, who dominated most social gatherings and was almost compulsively flamboyant in manner, dress, and speech, became another person in the company of writers.

Horace Greeley's opinion seems to match that of Charles Dickens, whose celebrated comment on Adah was long believed to have been a quip. Someone remarked in Dickens' presence that she was disreputable, and the great novelist roared, "I don't know and don't care whether Miss Menken is a jade. She is a sensitive poet who, unfortunately, cannot write."

CHAPTER IX

THE UNBLUSHING BRIDE

Speak to me tenderly.
Think of me lovingly.
Let your soft hands smooth back my hair.
Take my cold, tear-stained face up to yours.
Let my lonely life creep into your warm bosom, knowing no
other rest but this.
Let me question you, while sweet Faith and Trust are folding
their white arms around me.

—"Answer Me"

THE TECHNIQUE employed in his wooing by Robert Henry
Newell, the most persistent of Adah's swains, was unique.
By his own admission, he made no attempt to sleep with
her prior to the marriage that he offered her daily. He
should have known that Adah would have unhesitatingly
gone to bed with him, as she did with others whose work
she admired. It was simply her way of expressing her appreciation of an author's writing talent.

But Newell wanted her as his wife, not his mistress, and
followed her to Philadelphia in August, 1862, when she
went there for a second engagement in *Mazeppa*. Her
failure was abysmal; not only did Philadelphians stay
away from the play in droves, but Adah was pointedly
snubbed. She received so few supper invitations that she

made it her habit to return to her hotel suite for a late meal before retiring.

The cold reception chilled her soul. Perhaps that is why she finally accepted Newell's proposal, if one assumes she really didn't love him. She was alone, she was undoubtedly depressed, and the offer of marriage from a personable, talented writer a few years her senior must have sounded like a good idea—at the time. No other explanation makes sense, as she had said, "No," to him on many occasions in New York. His attentive persistence, combined with Philadelphia's indifference to The Naked Lady, finally won Newell the dubious victory.

Adah returned to New York after spending a miserable four weeks in Philadelphia, and on September 24, less than forty-eight hours after her arrival, she and Newell were married in the living room of her house. Whitman postponed a trip into the field to visit his brother, an officer in the Union Army, in order to act as best man, and Mrs. James was the matron of honor. A large group of friends attended the ceremony, which was performed by Alderman Joseph Brice, a theater buff who had become one of Adah's friends.

A riotous wedding feast was held at Pfaff's, with the owners of the restaurant footing the bill for their celebrated customer. Everyone, the bride excluded, drank vast quantities of champagne, and the enthusiastic guests insisted on hauling the happy couple back to the house at 458 Seventh Avenue in a carriage to which they harnessed themselves. There the party continued until the small hours of the morning, and Murdoch became so drunk that his wife had to appeal for help to get him home.

At last the bride and groom were alone, and Adah made a discovery that delighted her. "N.," she exclaims in her *Diary* the following day, "is a wonderful, gentle lover!"

Apparently he, too, thought the marriage was off to a perfect start, for he comments in his biography, "Our first days together were filled with a bliss we were to know but once again."

The honeymoon was brief. Murdoch, sober again and smarting from the losses *Mazeppa* had sustained in Philadelphia, concluded hasty arrangements to send the play on tour. Adah went to Trenton for a week's engagement scheduled to begin on October 6. Newell was unable to accompany her. The unexpected booking caught him completely off guard, as he had set up a number of interviews with Government officials in Washington, where he hoped to learn why the war was progressing so badly. He had intended to take Adah with him, and quarreled with her before they parted.

Both were professionals and, in spite of the sudden strain on the recently knotted family tie, both earned their salaries. Newell's findings appeared in a penetrating series of articles published in the *Mercury,* and in the meantime Adah enjoyed a round of dazzling triumphs in cities from Wilmington to Pittsburgh.

She was in her element again, flourishing in the limelight and the effervescent excitement of success. Crowds gaped at her at hotel entrances, stage doors, and restaurants. Wealthy gentlemen made vain attempts to entertain her at supper, which she usually ate in the company of local literati and newspapermen. Good ladies sniffed at her spectacular costumes, and even the Bohemians were shocked by her short hair and the clouds of cigarette smoke in which she was wreathed.

The conservative Pittsburgh *Dispatch* reported breathlessly: "The artistry of Miss Adah Isaacs Menken is debatable, and we think that no actress from New York has ever shown less genuine talent. We are pained when she recites, but she offers us an elixir that makes us forget she

is no Charlotte Cushman. Miss Menken came to us advertised as a sensation, and surely no one can begrudge her
lack of refinement. She is beauteous to behold, and every
man who sees her falls madly in love with her.

"If the ladies turn their backs to her, let them look to
their own limbs. Let those who whisper behind gloved
hands offer us, as she does, surcease from our daily cares.
Let those who malign her help us, as she does, to forget the
War for a little while.

"We are a brighter, happier place because she is a visitor
here, and we can ask no more of any guest. We are proud
that she is our friend, and think her husband is much to
be envied."

Newell held a contrary opinion. He wrote daily letters
to Adah, but she was a negligent correspondent, and he
complained bitterly because he rarely heard from her. By
late November, when she arrived in Baltimore for an extended run, he had received only two short notes from
her, and he was furious.

Adah added insult to injury in an incident that not only
threatened to break up her marriage but almost ended her
career. She had, from the time of *Mazeppa's* first opening
in New York, calmly ignored the gentlemen who sent her
notes, flowers, and invitations, but a Baltimore eccentric,
a middle-aged bachelor who bore the striking name of
John C. Calhoun Beaumont, tried a new technique.

He sent her a diamond and emerald bracelet so glittering that she took it to a jeweler the following day and had
it appraised. It was worth fifteen hundred dollars, a small
fortune. No strings had been attached to the gift, so, with
no qualms of conscience, Adah decided to keep it. That
evening Beaumont sent his card backstage, and she agreed
that the least she could do would be to go to supper with
him after the performance.

They dined at the "Ann McKim," an inn named after

one of the city's most famous clipper ships, and there, in a crowded room, Beaumont confided to the New Orleans belle that he was a Confederate sympathizer. There were many in the city who felt as he did, so his announcement had no visible effect on people at neighboring tables.

All would have been well had Adah been content to let the subject drop. But her love of the dramatic got the better of her, and in a Louisiana accent that became thicker by the minute, she replied at length that she, too, loved the South. She had known President Davis of the Confederate States, she said, when he had visited New Orleans, and thought him a great and wise man. It didn't matter that she had never set eyes on Jefferson Davis and probably would not have recognized him had they passed each other in the street. She was not only enjoying herself, but was giving her one-man audience something in return for his expensive bracelet.

The evening ended on a decorous, proper note. Beaumont escorted Adah to her hotel, and several witnesses later swore that they parted company in the lobby. Adah promptly went to her suite, where she forgot all about the incident as she dropped off to sleep, the gem-encrusted bracelet warming her wrist.

The next morning there was hell to pay. Maryland, an ambivalent border state, was one of President Lincoln's principal worries, and Federal authorities were having an exceedingly difficult time keeping the state in the Union ranks. Citizens loyal to the North were sensitive to the slightest hint of treason, and a half-dozen indignant men hurried to Army headquarters to report the conversation they had overheard at the inn.

Colonel T. E. Radford, the assistant provost, immediately sent a squad to arrest Beaumont. A man who bore the name of John C. Calhoun, the patron saint of Secession, was automatically suspected of the worst, but the in-

genuous Beaumont astonished his captors by making no
secret of his sympathies. He made a long speech to Colonel
Radford, defending the Confederacy, and succeeded in
convincing the assistant provost that he was of unstable
mind.

Radford's trouble was that he was a conscientious officer, completely lacking a sense of humor, who knew nothing about the temperament of actresses. It was his job to
protect Baltimore, and when he confirmed that Beaumont
had given an expensive bracelet to a young woman from
New Orleans who had publicly announced her own love
for the South, he jumped to the logical conclusion that
Adah was Beaumont's mistress. The mind of a military
bureaucrat being rather simple, he also assumed that she
was a Confederate agent.

Adah was awakened at the exceptionally early hour of
10:30 A.M. by a terrified Minnie, who informed her that a
squad of soldiers armed with muskets was waiting in the
living room of the suite, and intended to come in for her if
she did not present herself at once.

Adah spent no more than thirty minutes or so on her
toilet while the young lieutenant in command of the
squad impatiently paced up and down the living room.
When she finally made her entrance, her face glowing with
cosmetics, her body encased in one of her more flamboyant
negligees, she was placed under arrest in the name of the
Government of the United States of America. The lieutenant, acting under orders, refused to specify the charges
against her.

Adah, considerably sobered, dressed hurriedly and was
taken to headquarters under escort, with a crowd of curious newspapermen and anguished theater representatives
trailing behind. Colonel Radford interrogated her behind
closed doors, and Adah apparently tried to charm him,
but to no avail. She later referred to him as a "surly fel-

low, who is so unpleasant that he will never be promoted to General."

She spent the entire afternoon at headquarters, and the alarmed management of the theater hired an attorney to represent her. But the lawyer was barred from the inquisition chambers, and the representatives of the press began to wonder if they had stumbled onto a real spy case. It was almost too good to be true that the spectacular Adah Isaacs Menken was a genuine, dyed-in-the-wool espionage agent for the Confederacy.

Wheels turned and churned. Huge crowds gathering outside the provost's headquarters were twice dispersed, but each time reassembled. Someone sent a telegram to Newell, in New York, and he caught the first train for Baltimore, accompanied by Murdoch, who had returned to Manhattan for a brief visit with his family. The New York newspapers cautiously printed nothing, suspecting a publicity stunt. And Adah's friends just laughed.

But the young woman undergoing a thorough grilling in the office of the assistant provost in Baltimore was not amused. Adah was alarmed, then angry, and finally lost her temper. Colonel Radford is alleged to have said that she cursed at him, using a colorful vocabulary that would have shamed a cavalryman, but no authority for his supposed statement can be found.

Common sense prevailed in the end. Adah's record was good, she had done nothing treasonable or seditious, and about one hour before she was due at the theater, she was released—on parole. The manager of the theater announced that she would appear in *Mazeppa,* as scheduled, and thereafter every seat in the house was sold for the remaining four weeks of the run. Newspaper stories about the incident were just big enough to make Adah wonder what might have been printed had she really been a spy.

The luckless Beaumont prudently took himself elsewhere, and that was the end of the public side of the incident. Late that night a haggard Newell arrived, and was no doubt overjoyed to find his wife free and safe. But his relief and pleasure were tempered by the sight of the bauble that sparkled at her wrist.

The argument that raged until daybreak was the first serious quarrel that marred the happiness of the newlyweds. Newell, not unreasonably, insisted that Adah return the bracelet to its donor. She refused, insisting that it had been freely given, that she had done nothing dishonorable, and that she saw no good reason why she should have to part with such an expensive trinket. Newell begged, pleaded, reasoned, and finally commanded. But when the smoke of battle had cleared away and the weary couple retired for a few hours of sleep, Adah had emerged the victor. She kept the bracelet, wearing it frequently until, years later, she impulsively gave it to her principal rival in Paris, Hortense Schneider of the Opéra Bouffe. She had won a battle, it was true, but had lost a war, for her relationship with Newell suffered a blow from which the marriage never recovered.

"N," she writes in her *Diary*, "revealed that he has a mean and craven nature."

"Any husband will understand the feelings I suffered on that unhappy occasion," Newell declares righteously in his biography. It was improbable that his male readers could imagine themselves in his boots, none of their wives ever having been given diamonds and emeralds by a total stranger.

After spending only a day or two in Baltimore, Newell returned to New York. Adah, of course, remained in Baltimore, playing to capacity audiences. She kept her mouth shut on anything even remotely concerned with the war, and instead impressed her local acquaintances with her encyclopaedic knowledge of the city's late, great

Edgar Allan Poe, who, posthumously, was just achieving recognition as one of America's foremost men of letters. When she talked about literature she was not shamming. Claude Murphy, a distinguished Baltimore critic who wrote for such publications as *Harper's,* said in a letter to Walt Whitman, "You are right about Adah Menken. She is remarkable! I have heard her quote from memory the stories, poetry and prose of Poe for as long as an hour at a time, scarcely pausing for breath. She neither falters nor misplaces a word.

"Her logic is compelling. She argued that Poe was both a romantic and a macabre cynic. When I protested that no man can carry such buckets of water on both shoulders, Adah destroyed my defenses. It is her contention that all authors of substance have such a dual nature, and she cited chapter and verse from Shakespeare to Coleridge to prove her point.

"She is willing to admit that Poe belongs in a somewhat special category, the weird and loathesome often o'erbalancing the romantic. But I had no ready reply when she presented the thesis that the eerie quality of Poe's work, so like a nightmare, strikes a responsive note in all of us. We are romantics, too, she believes, yet there are nights when we cannot sleep, and are afflicted by dreams not unlike those that tortured Poe.

"She has made me see a new unity in his work, and if I am unable to accept her contention without reservation, I am nonetheless grateful to her for an interesting idea that makes Poe one man rather than two writing under the one name. Her theories are original, which I did not find surprising. But I was indeed surprised, as you said I would be, at the sound logic that shores up her claims.

"What a pity that she wastes her substance in vulgar displays when she should spend all her time at her desk. But I stand corrected. I have not tired of watching her performance, though I have seen it many times now, and go again to the theater tonight. Her beauty is not vulgar; the lewd stares of the prurient make it so."

Baltimore having been duly conquered, Adah resumed her tour early in January, 1863. Wartime conditions made travel less than a joy, but she was a trouper who never complained, either in public or private. Chicago gave her a thunderous welcome, as did Detroit and a dozen smaller cities, and everywhere the theaters were filled to overflowing. Adah wrote to Isaac Menken's parents that she was anxious to see them again and was eagerly looking forward to spending a week in Cincinnati, but perhaps she was just being polite. *Mazeppa* was not booked into Cincinnati, and the loyal *Israelite* expressed its regret in an editorial. Isaac, now remarried and a senior partner in his father's business, probably did not share the newspaper's sense of disappointment. To the end of his days he remained sensitive, with good cause, resenting the use of his name by the most scandalous woman of the age.

In April, Adah finally returned to New York and Newell. Both took the reunion in their stride, without fanfare. Adah says in her *Diary,* "N. met me on my arrival." Newell remarks in his biography, "The successful tour of *Mazeppa* having been concluded, Miss Menken disbanded her company and came back to her home." They appear to have been still in love. If there were differences between them, they were forgotten in a new, exciting project in which both were involved.

Tom McGuire, owner of the glittering new Opera House in San Francisco, the fastest-growing, wildest, and bawdiest city in the United States, had been corresponding with Murdoch, and now made a dazzling offer. He would pay Adah the fabulous, unprecedented sum of fifteen hundred dollars a week to play *Mazeppa* at his theater for eight weeks.

Ladies didn't visit San Francisco, but Adah was no lady. The salary McGuire offered her was so large she couldn't believe he meant it, and insisted that Murdoch obtain confirmation in another exchange of telegrams. Murdoch obediently sent a long wire, which the San Francisco impresario misunderstood. He thought Adah was holding out for still more money, and replied that the seating capacity of his theater prevented him from raising her salary, but he was willing to compromise by guaranteeing her twelve weeks instead of eight.

The dazed Adah quickly accepted, and made frantic efforts to prepare for the long journey. Minnie would go with her, of course, and so would Black Bess. She also thought it would be pleasant if Newell accompanied her, and he was still sufficiently in love with her to arrange with the editors of the *Mercury* to do a series of articles on San Francisco, and Adah's reception there.

It was far more difficult to transport a horse than a husband.

There were three routes to California, all of them complicated and tedious. The least exhausting, but by far the longest, was by ship, down the Atlantic coastlines of North and South America, around Cape Horn, and then north in the Pacific. Navigation companies offered their passengers halfhearted promises that they would arrive in San Francisco eight weeks after leaving New York—provided no major storms were encountered on the voyage.

The shortest and most dangerous route was the overland one across the United States. Travelers could now go west by rail as far as Kansas City, where they transferred to stage coaches. An aura of glamour and excitement still surrounded such a journey, as, occasionally, a coach was attacked by Indians on the vast plains or in the Rocky Mountains. More frequently, bands of armed men masquerading as Indians halted a coach and robbed the passengers. In the years immediately prior to the war, passengers had been given a measure of protection by cavalry patrols, but no troops could be spared for the purpose when every fighting man was needed in the struggle against the most brilliant strategist and tactician in American history, Confederate General Robert E. Lee. Anyone who made a journey by stage coach took his chances.

The so-called sea-and-land route was by far the most hazardous. Those who chose it went by ship to Panama—this was in the days before the Panama Canal was constructed. There they disembarked, then made their way through a dense tropical jungle infested with snakes, insects, and the wildest of primitive natives, who shot poisoned arrows out of blowguns at strangers. This journey through the jungle on what the navigation companies called the Balboa trail, after the explorer who discovered the Pacific, was made under heavy guard. Depending on the weather, the Indians, a passenger's resistance to tropical diseases, and his ability to avoid stepping on a deadly reptile, this portion of the trip lasted anywhere from two or three days to a week. Once on the Pacific side, another vessel was boarded, and the travelers were carried north through the seldom benign waters of the Pacific to San Francisco.

The challenge of violently hostile pygmies armed with blowguns, mysterious diseases that could prove fatal within a few hours, and an assortment of the most dangerous reptiles on earth proved irresistible to Adah—she would go by the Atlantic-Panama-Pacific route. A suite of cabins on the *São Jorge,* a Portuguese ship, was engaged for an early summer voyage, and Adah concentrated on the purchase of a new wardrobe. She discarded virtually everything she owned, including clothes she had bought in Havana so many years earlier.

Newell was irritated by the extravagant splurge, but was

in no position to complain too loudly, as Adah was spending her own money. The fact that she hadn't earned it yet, that she was buying on credit extended to her by eager dressmakers and shopkeepers, was beside the point.

Murdoch and the members of the supporting cast, preferring comfort and safety to adventure, sailed on a ship that would take them to San Francisco by way of Cape Horn. With them went a carpenter Murdoch had engaged to build the runway for Adah's horse.

That horse, it developed soon after the director had departed, would not be Black Bess. The navigation company that was happy to give Adah and her husband a royal suite of cabins drew the line at transporting the mare. Conditions in the Panama jungle made it impossible to guarantee the safety of an animal unaccustomed to the tropics, and the company, afraid of a lawsuit, decreed that Black Bess would have to remain behind.

This sudden crisis almost ruined the entire deal. Adah stormed and wept, threatened and cajoled, but to no avail. Corporations were not men who could be persuaded to change their minds. Adah was sorry now that she hadn't gone with Murdoch and the rest of the company, but it was too late for her to change her plans. Shipping was scarce, and no other vessel was scheduled to make the long voyage around Cape Horn in time for her to reach San Francisco in mid-August. She considered making the overland journey, but once again faced obstacles. The owners of the stagecoach companies could not object if she chose to ride her own horse halfway across the North American continent, but refused to consider Black Bess as part of a theatrical star's baggage.

Thwarted on every side, Adah made the best of the situation, and sent a telegram to McGuire, asking him to procure her another horse. "I want a mare," she told him, "gentle but spirited. She must be accustomed to noise and excitement. Murdoch must approve final selection."

McGuire replied by telegram, saying he would present a half-dozen mounts for Murdoch's inspection, and Adah was reassured. She resumed her clothes buying, and by the time she was finished, had to crowd her purchases into eight trunks, too many to carry in her suite on the steamer. A week before the *São Jorge* sailed, an additional fee had to be paid for the luggage, as transporting so many cases across the Isthmus of Panama presented the travel authorities with a major problem.

Adah's departure was given little attention. Her friends gave no farewell parties for her; she was, after all, merely making a journey to a far-distant part of the United States. Although ordinary citizens considered such long jaunts major adventures, people in the theatrical and literary worlds were then, as later, somewhat more sophisticated.

Another reason for Adah's quiet leave-taking may have been the somber mood of the nation. The armies of generals Lee and Meade had just met at Gettysburg, and both the Union and the Confederacy were horrified by the carnage in the gentle, rolling hills of Pennsylvania. The battle ended on July 4, and that same day another Confederate force, thirty thousand strong, surrendered at Vicksburg, Mississippi, to General Grant.

The following day, at noon, Adah left New York on the *São Jorge,* accompanied by her husband and personal maid. The Portuguese flag fluttering at the fantail was the ship's best protection from Confederate raiders, but some of the passengers were nervous and carried firearms. Newell, whose writing had established him as an ardent Union supporter, undoubtedly would have been taken off to prison if captured by the Confederates, but his only weapon was a small pistol he had bought to shoot snakes in the Panama jungles. A sober realist, he took his risks calmly.

Adah was less serene. Deeply shaken by the newspaper accounts she had read of the Battle of Gettysburg, she spent her first few hours at sea writing some of her most lugubrious poetry. Then her mood changed, and that evening she and Newell dined alone in their suite. They had seldom spent so much time together since their marriage, and the enforced privacy imposed on them by the voyage had a remarkably soothing effect.

Newell found his wife as lovely, charming, and intelligent as he had believed her to be in the days when he had courted her. Adah discovered anew that her husband was wise, witty, and strong. The interlude at sea proved to be the happiest period they had ever known in each other's company.

Newell writes, "The voyage was pleasant, as cares drop away at sea."

Adah expresses herself with greater candor in her *Diary,* scribbling, "N. makes love beautifully."

The idyll ended abruptly at the steaming, dilapidated town of Porto Bello. There mules were supplied, armed guards and guides were provided, and the couple, trailed by Minnie and a string of pack animals, started off toward the Pacific.

Adah later claimed that the jungle had enchanted her. In an interview with members of the British press soon after she arrived in London, she told an exciting story of having witnessed savage head-hunters' rites, and her description of the event was a tribute to her almost unlimited powers of imagination.

Newell, however, was prosaically factual in the first account he wrote for the *Mercury.* "Rain fell constantly, and the party was always soaked to the skin. Tents erected at night provided little protection, as the rain fell in such great quantities that it soon soaked the canvas and poured through it. Those who have never visited tropical places cannot imagine the density of the rain nor the discomfort it causes.

"There is a disagreeable, sickly-sweet odor in the tropical forest caused, I believe, by rotting vegetation. Swarms of mosquitos, flies, gnats and an infinite host of other flying and crawling creatures make these forests no place for the fastidious.

"We saw no persons other than members of our own party on the journey. Nor, contrary to what we had been warned, did we encounter any vipers. The greatest discomfort was encountered at the City of Panama, on the shores of the Pacific, which we reached after an overland march of more than fifty miles through the rain forest.

"This city, believed to be one of the oldest in our Hemisphere, lacks every modern convenience. We were quartered in an ancient hostelry much used by the adventurers seeking gold in California and silver in Nevada. The food is inedible, a combination of Spanish and local Indian dishes which are boiled for long periods in the greases of tropical plants and lose all individuality and flavor. Streets in the City of Panama are narrow, winding and filled with a stench of decay less tolerable than the odors of the forest.

"Spanish is the only language spoken in the City of Panama. Miss Menken is fluent in the tongue, and was greeted everywhere with warmth. But there are few divertissements in the City of Panama, and the wait for the *Palace Queen,* the steamer that was to take the party to San Francisco, became tedious. The *Palace Queen* arrived at the harbor eight days behind the date scheduled for her arrival, her Master offering no excuses for his tardiness nor apologies for the inconveniences suffered during the interim by his passengers."

Newell's understatement concealed the fact that he and Adah found the stay in Panama intolerable. Rough, tough

Americans using the few hotels of the city for more than a decade had caused so much damage that rooms were stripped to their bare essentials, and only beds were provided. Guests were required to furnish all other necessary furniture and conveniences, including slop jars.

The stench in the streets was one of Panama's most noticeable characteristics, and other travelers commented at length on the powerful smells. This condition prevailed, it might be noted, until much of the city was reconstructed at the time the Panama Canal was built.

Adah used her fluent Spanish in the few dingy shops and restaurants in the City of Panama, and, long accustomed to accepting what was placed before her at a dining table, she ate with gusto, as usual. Newell, on the other hand, was as hungry as he was irritated, and the couple began to bicker.

The heat and rain added to their misery, the squalor of living conditions did not improve their mood, and the tension created by the failure, day after day, of the Pacific steamer to appear caused their tempers to soar. On top of everything else, they were bored. Aside from visiting a few churches, there was literally nothing to do. The heat and dirt drove them out of their hotel room, and the stench in the streets sent them scurrying back to it. They did not dare go into the interior again for fear the *Palace Queen* might arrive and depart again during their absence.

In brief, the stay of almost two weeks in the dreary City of Panama stamped the final seal of doom on their ill-fated marriage. The author could not cope with a wife whose mercurial moods drove him to distraction and whose intellectual perspicacity, easily as great as his own, was used to his disparagement. As for Adah, it is dubious that any man could have made her happy for more than a brief period. Her childhood—and Havana—had left scars that could not be healed.

"I've never been so miserable," she wrote to Ed James

from the luxurious Presidential suite on board the *Palace Queen*, calmly forgetting the agony she had known when she had been poverty-stricken. "I have made many sacrifices for Rob, but he is a boor and can't recognize all that I've done for him."

She didn't outline these sacrifices, so there is no way of knowing what she meant. A record, pieced together from scraps after a lapse of one hundred years, is necessarily incomplete and inadequate, but no data can be found to substantiate Adah's claim. Therefore, it is not illogical to assume that, if she mentioned sacrifices to Newell, he stared at her in blank amazement.

A prominent San Franciscan, Colonel Benjamin H. Jefferson, gave a colorful account of the stormy voyage on the *Palace Queen*. Writing to his wife, who was visiting relatives in Springfield, Illinois, he revealed that Adah and Newell had reached the breaking point. "At some meals," he said, "Miss Menken enlivened the saloon with her presence, and all found her a jolly companion, full of salty wit. Mr. Newell never came to the table with her. At other times he came to the saloon alone, and was a gloomy fellow, speaking no more than civility demanded. I saw Miss Menken with reddened eyes walking alone on the deck two or three evenings, and felt sorry for her.

"Perhaps, as is said, she is no better than she should be, but I felt sorry for her. Newell is a surly brute, and must have been overbearing and cruel, or why else would such a gallant woman weep? Her frequent displays of good spirits were remarkable, when one thinks of the harsh treatment she was forced to endure."

The courtly colonel, being a man, placed all the blame squarely on Newell's shoulders. By no stretch of even the most feverish imagination was Adah a damsel in distress, but Jefferson sounds as though she used him as a confidant on the voyage.

"Minnie has moved into my cabin," she says in an undated line scribbled in her *Diary* on board the *Palace Queen*, "and N. has moved into hers."

Husband and wife were on the verge of a separation, and the decks were being cleared for Adah's almost delirious reception in the preponderantly male Far West.

CHAPTER X

GIRL OF THE GOLDEN WEST

Ah! When I am a cloud—a pliant, floating cloud—
I will haunt the Sun-God for some eternal ray of Beauty.
I will wind my soft arms around the wheels of his blazing
chariot, till he robes me in gorgeous trains of gold!
I will sing to the stars till they crown me with their
richest jewels!
—"In Vain"

SAN FRANCISCO and Adah were made for each other, soul
mates brought together by destiny, luck, and the acumen
of Tom McGuire, who extensively advertised the forthcoming opening of *Mazeppa*.

Six great fires had raged through San Francisco between
Christmas Eve, 1849, and Adah's arrival in the late summer of 1863. The city had survived each of these holo-
causts, rising Phoenixlike from the ashes to become
stronger, more vigorous, larger and—if possible—more
flamboyantly alive. Then Adah appeared, blazing with her
own special brand of fire, and neither she nor San Francisco was ever the same again.

The breathtakingly beautiful Golden Gate site had
been discovered in 1769 by Spaniards, who had built a
small garrison and a mission to found the town. A village

grew around the fort, called the Presidio, but San Francisco languished until gold was discovered nearby in 1848. Then began one of the wildest, most hectic periods in the development of any community on the face of the earth.

Men heeded Horace Greeley's instructions by the thousands and tens of thousands. Such vast hordes of fortune seekers went West that no accurate population figures could be estimated, and only semieducated guesses tell the story of the city's growth. No one knew San Francisco's size, and few cared. She was big, growing bigger every day, and even her most conservative, respectable citizens were proud of her bulging muscles.

Perhaps no town anywhere had ever known the violence that marked San Francisco's early years of mushrooming expansion. Few of the aggressive, brawling newcomers were women, virtually none were ladies, and men lived by the guns that everyone carried. According to the ablest historian of the era, George Bancroft, there were more than four thousand murders committed between 1848 and 1854, and one thousand despairing gold seekers took their own lives. In 1855 the reign of the pistol reached an all-time high, and there were nearly six hundred killings.

Respectable citizens, many of them men who had made fortunes in the gold fields and now wanted to settle down, were compelled to take the law, if any, into their own hands, and met anarchy with controlled violence. A Vigilance Committee, organized in 1851, solved the problem of dealing with desperadoes by stringing them from trees or riding them out of town on rails after applying liberal coatings of tar and feathers. The Committee formed and reformed sporadically, conducting its last major drive in 1856.

Those who preyed on the treasure seekers, trying to separate them from their precious gold dust, were legion. Owners of rooming houses, shops selling supplies, and dining establishments charged outrageous fees. As the vast sea of huts, shanties, and tents gave way to more permanent structures, saloons sprang up more rapidly than any other type of building. The demand for liquor was insatiable and the supply limited, so a number of enterprising amateur chemists made their own alcoholic beverages, some of them poisonous. The majority of saloons encouraged gambling on the premises, and females of questionable standards were everywhere. Those who preferred gambling without liquor could find establishments that suited their needs, and those who wanted a little solace from members of the opposite sex had no difficulty in locating houses that were not bashful in advertising their merchandise.

Beginning in 1855 or thereabouts, San Francisco developed an articulate hard core of conservative gentlemen who wanted to make it possible for their wives to travel through the streets without molestation, who wanted to be neither robbed nor beaten, and thought it important that their children receive a good education. The Gold Rush having subsided, the city turned to other interests, and the ranks of the respectable multiplied. Shipping became a major industry, as did lumbering and fishing. Men invested their profits in huge ranches, and became even wealthier.

Schools were built, and libraries and hospitals. There were comfortable, respectable hotels, restaurants that served palatable food, and the nucleus of an intelligentsia was formed. For five relatively tranquil years San Francisco succumbed to the blandishments of civilization, and old sourdoughs sadly shook their heads.

Then silver was discovered in next-door Nevada, and again man-made earthquakes shook San Francisco. New treasure hunters appeared from the East, and were joined by brethren from rapidly growing California. San Francisco was the hub of the search for silver. Men used it as their base, starting from it to climb into the Sierra Nevada Mountains and returning to it in triumph or hopeless defeat. There were fresh orgies, new killings, and whiskey flowed as freely as the waters of the blue-green Pacific.

Vast new fortunes were accumulated, powerful recruits joined the ranks of the respectable and this time the regiments of the righteous held firm. The police force was doubled, then doubled again, a new wing was added to the already large jail, and every householder carried a loaded pistol in the tail pocket of his frock coat. Bankers and shipping magnates, ranch owners and wealthy farmers and merchants stood shoulder to shoulder with the gold and silver barons, and the barbarians were forced to conform to standards that—although shocking elsewhere— were considered genteel in San Francisco.

Culture came to the city overnight. Tom McGuire built his Opera House, and imitators erected gaudier theaters. Joe Lawrence, a writer, editor, and former newspaperman who was, simultaneously, an idealist and a cynic, began to publish one of the most exciting literary journals ever to see the light of print in the United States, the *Golden Era*. Optimists saw cautious reason to hope that San Francisco might be coming of age.

The Civil War proved that, if nothing else, the city was learning to use reason rather than the revolver. There had been many Southerners who had joined the race to the gold and silver fields, so the Confederacy smuggled vast quantities of arms into San Francisco, and there seemed good reason to believe there were enough Southern sympathizers in the area to lead a successful revolt. But the recipients of these gifts left their rifles at home, and carried their new pistols and revolvers only for personal protection. San Francisco, like the rest of California, remained staunchly loyal to the Union.

The city's principal link with the portions of the United

States east of the Rocky Mountains was the Pony Express, which had been inaugurated on an experimental basis in 1860 and had immediately proved successful as a relatively rapid communications link. The telegraph, which followed soon afterward, was—when it operated without interruptions caused by breakdowns in the wilderness of the Rockies—equally effective. But mail and telegrams could do little to ease the basic isolation of San Francisco. That development would not come until the first transcontinental railway was completed near the end of the decade.

In the meantime, a great city that was bursting with wealth, bubbling with energy, and searching avidly for new interests, anxiously awaited the arrival of the most widely discussed actress of the era.

Adah and San Francisco fell in love at first sight. She was enough of a real poet to weep at the beauty of the Golden Gate. But she dried her eyes and repaired the damage to her make-up in time to sweep ashore from the *Palace Queen* in a hat, gown, gloves, shoes, and tasseled parasol of matching pink. With her usual flair for the dramatic, the dress hugged her celebrated figure and was sufficiently low-cut to promise that tickets purchased for a performance of *Mazeppa* would be well worth the price.

San Franciscans were accustomed to seeing fancy ladies in such attire, and the more fastidious immediately jumped to the conclusion that La Menken rightly belonged in the waterfront Red Eye Saloon. The sniffing, head-high-in-the-air minority soon changed its tune, however.

McGuire gave a reception for the visiting celebrity, turning his Opera House into a huge restaurant and bar for invited guests. Even the most conservative of the new gentry were curious, and Adah—who ate heartily but drank neither hard spirits nor champagne—charmed everyone. Her manners were perfect, her speech elegant and, in a gesture that won all local hearts, she could talk of nothing except the wonders of lovely, lusty San Francisco.

The city immediately returned the compliment, and *Mazeppa* was sold out for its entire run before the play opened. McGuire immediately exercised his option and extended the engagement a month.

Adah and her entourage, which included her virtually forgotten husband, were ensconced in a house rented by McGuire and approved by Murdoch. It overlooked the ocean, and Adah was so entranced by the view that she was inspired to write some of her most sentimental poetry while Minnie and two locally hired servants unpacked her belongings. She made herself completely at home in the city, and San Francisco responded with gusto. Crowds gathered to cheer her wherever she went, and on her third afternoon in the bracing climate a group of young gallants insisted on hitching themselves to her carriage. They dragged the coach around the town, showing her the sights, while hundreds of others followed on foot.

Murdoch tried in vain to protect her privacy when, attired in man's clothes—a shocking innovation—she tried out the horse that had been selected for her. A throng estimated at more than two thousand watched her put the mare through her paces. The original name of the horse has not survived for the edification of posterity, but when Adah renamed her Beauty Belle, several saloons, a gambling house, and at least one hotel immediately called themselves Beauty Belle, too.

Newell, the forgotten man, paid a visit to the *Golden Era* office. There, instead of being greeted as a colleague, he suffered the humiliation of being treated as a nonentity who had the good fortune to be Adah Isaacs Menken's husband. Lawrence wrote a flowery invitation, requesting the honor of Adah's presence in his editorial sanctum at her pleasure and convenience, and the members of the staff added their signatures, as did several contributors. Among the latter was a twenty-four-year-old author and part-time editor, whose stories appeared frequently in both the *Golden Era* and a rival magazine, *The Californian*. His name was Francis Brett Harte, and his friends regarded him as a pleasing young man of mediocre talent. Another was Charles Farrar Browne, a humorist who had first gained recognition five years earlier when he had written a series of articles for the Cleveland *Plain Dealer* under the name of Artemus Ward.

Newell handed the invitation to Adah, who was surrounded by admirers in the living room of the rented house. The names scribbled at the bottom of the page meant no more to her than to any other reasonably literate American of the moment, for neither Bret Harte nor Artemus Ward had yet acquired any real measure of fame. But the lure of the literati proved as irresistible to her as the proverbial clang of a firebell to a horse trained to pull a hook-and-ladder wagon. Off she dashed to be with people whom she regarded as her own kind, leaving the disgruntled Newell to entertain her guests.

" 'How do you do? I'm Adah Menken,' the Goddess said as she paused in the entrance to our ink-stained office," the enthralled Lawrence wrote in the *Golden Era,* describing the visit. "At least a dozen of us were sitting around the room. We leaped to our feet, but none had the grace to reply to this vision of rare beauty in white."

Harte, who always liked older women, succumbed wholly to Adah instantly, as did Charles Warren Stoddard, an even younger and more impressionable author, who later became Mark Twain's secretary. "She was pretty enough," Artemus Ward subsequently wrote, "but it wasn't until she started to talk that I paid much attention to her. A talking woman is no rarity, but this one made sense!"

Still another member of the group was Cincinnatus

Hiner of Indiana, a brilliant twenty-two-year-old lawyer who had enjoyed fair luck in the Nevada mines and was now supporting himself as a journalist and poet. He contributed to the *Golden Era* under the name of Joaquin Miller, and eventually adopted the name legally. He was rather scornful of his companions' reaction to Adah, but soon he, too, became one of her ardent admirers. Even more than the others he learned to appreciate her poetry, and gave her some of his efforts to edit.

These authors were united by their youth, their zest for living, and, above all, their love for the Far West. Harte's stories of the frontier were to make him famous, and Ward first attracted national attention by his accounts of his travels in California, Oregon, and Nevada. Stoddard was a California booster who would have gladdened the heart of any West Coast chamber of commerce a century later; when Miller died, in 1913, his ashes were, at his request, scattered over the wilds of the Sierra Nevadas. Mark Twain, the Connecticut Yankee, captured for all time the lively, humorous spirit epitomized by these young men, all of whom he came to know during his own sojourn in San Francisco during the 1860's. Their wit stemmed from a sense of wry exaggeration, and Adah, who told tall tales about herself with a straight face, was a kindred soul.

The authors of the *Golden Era* adopted her at once, and when they discovered that Newell was Orpheus C. Kerr, they had the grace to extend him their apologies. He, too, became an intimate of their circle during his brief stay in California, but as his relations with Adah were so severely strained, they rarely visited the magazine's office at the same time. Newell, in fact, found the burden so intolerable that he left for the East after a stay of only six weeks.

A gentleman to the end, in September, 1863, he allowed

Adah to divorce him, although rumors had it that he had ample grounds and could have named one or two mining tycoons as co-respondents on grounds of adultery. Oddly, he became Adah's friend after she won her uncontested California divorce. They met on several occasions in New York, to which he returned occasionally from the Virginia front, where he served the *Mercury* as a war correspondent. Later Adah wrote to him frequently from England and the Continent, but neither regretted their separation.

"If Adah hadn't been so famous and so wrapped up in her career," Ed James wrote to Newell a year after her death, "she probably would have loved you. I know you were the only one of her husbands she admired. Of course it is a waste of ink and paper to write about 'if,' because you and she wouldn't have met had she not been an actress."

Men slipped out of Adah's life without ceremony, and Newell was no exception. If she missed him, she neither said so nor confided any such thoughts to her *Diary*. She was far too busy in San Francisco to pine for another lost love, another broken marriage.

An intriguing mystery of her visit to California centers on the question of whether she became acquainted with Mark Twain. She later spoke of him and of his work in familiar terms to friends in England and France, but that didn't necessarily mean anything. By the time she reached Europe she had become such an accomplished liar that it was no longer possible for her to distinguish truth from fiction. No account of any meeting is mentioned in the published correspondence of Samuel Clemens or in any of his works written under the Mark Twain pseudonym.

Yet it seems likely that their paths crossed, for Mark Twain became the most prominent member of the *Golden Era* group, and Adah was not one to neglect any literary lion. To the members of the Golden Era coterie, she became "the goddess" (the epithet was probably coined by Stoddard). She became many things to these earnest authors, mother and confidante, colleague and friend and adviser. One thing she emphatically was not: the mistress of any.

From this time forward, with two notable exceptions, all of her relations with members of the writing profession were strictly platonic. Perhaps the failure of her marriage to Newell convinced her that there was nothing to be gained by becoming intimate with a man who wielded a pen as a means of earning his living. Or it may be that, as the sex act was not significant to her, she felt it would be demeaning to go to bed with someone who regarded her as an equal in his profession.

Whatever her reasons, literary friendships and sexual relationships were separate and distinct from the time of her San Francisco sojourn. A great deal is known about the former during her West Coast stay, virtually nothing about the latter. There can be little doubt that she took lovers, whom she entertained in the rented house, but she maintained a discreet silence regarding their identity, and the young men at the Golden Era played guessing games in vain. Adah knew it was wise to keep silent on the subject, something she had learned in Havana.

In San Francisco she formed the pattern she would follow for the rest of her life. She slept until noon, ate a hearty and leisurely breakfast, and then communed with her Muse for an hour or two. She spent the latter part of each afternoon with authors, sometimes meeting with them in what might be described as a very informal version of the salons that had been fashionable a century earlier. Before going to the theater she ate a light meal, either alone or with one or two companions. Then the lady of letters became the theatrical celebrity who made audiences cheer and, on occasion, actually caused riots.

After the performance, depending on her mood, Adah either went off with writer friends for the sort of evening she had known in New York, or, if some gentleman of wealth, standing, and personality appealed to her, she allowed him to buy her a hearty dinner before inviting him back to her house for a cozy hour or two.

Her *Diary* is filled with comments to the effect that she did not accept gifts from men who became her lovers. In her own thinking, at least, she was not acting as a prostitute now, but was preserving at least a semiamateur standing.

Why did she slip back into promiscuity after spending a number of years with one husband at a time or, at the worst, one lover at a time? She herself gives no reason, and it can only be assumed that the final separation from Newell convinced her that she was not made for conventional, matrimonial relations with any man.

She accepted gifts from San Francisco tycoons, to be sure, among them a gold and ruby ring from someone she calls "E." Much to his disappointment, she refused to have an affair with him. Had he been aware of her upside-down standards, he could have seduced her had he given her no gift.

In any event, virtually all of her companions in San Francisco were men. The ladies of the city were not fooled by her diction or manners, and she was invited to few of their homes. She appears to have been groping in a vain attempt to fill the vacuum made by the termination of her marriage, and a letter to Ed James, dated September 24, 1863, indicates her bewilderment:

"If you have a sister, never permit her to marry a 'gentleman.' I am in tears. I have not been in bed all night, and my new gown of Imported French Silk (the green one that I promised to give your niece when I come home) has a rip in it that can't be mended.

"All the sports like me. That's a consolation. Last week I gave a complimentary benefit to St. Francis Hook and Ladder Co. They presented me with a beautiful fire belt and serenaded me with the finest band in the State and finished up with 'Three Cheers for Adah.' I was so choked up that I couldn't thank them as I wanted to.

"I am writing again, which is my only salvation. Joe Lawrence is publishing one of my poems next month. I'm not satisfied with it, but he won't let me make any more changes in it. He says I'll ruin it if I keep altering words and commas, but I am still the perfection-seeker who has never known true happiness and who will, I fear, never know it.

"I miss all of you. There is no zest in the air here, and I think of the falling leaves at home. I'd like San Francisco better if the women didn't throw their ugly noses so high in the air when they pass me on the streets. But I don't care. There is a crowd of sports outside my house to cheer me every day when I go to my errands, so I can't ask for more than that."

The letter was signed "Infelix."

The signature is as significant as the body of the letter. Adah liked to think of herself as unfortunate, as one oppressed by the Fates, even when collecting the highest salary known in the theater. She had become the toast of a continent, but was beginning to learn that success and money could not buy the serenity of mind and spirit that she wanted—or thought she wanted. Most of the poems she wrote in the years that followed were laments bemoaning her sad state.

According to accounts written by the *Golden Era* authors, however, she lived in a gay social and intellectual whirl that gave her little time for tears and less for reflection. She was in constant demand, and quarrels broke out among Harte, Miller, and Ward, each of whom accused the others of trying to monopolize her. Adah solved the problem in a manner that might have pleased a Solomon, but left the authors thoroughly dissatisfied. She refused to see any one of them alone.

There may have been more to her decree than the young men realized. The break with Newell having convinced her that love and literature were not compatible, Adah may have been avoiding possible romantic complications by seeking safety in numbers.

Through these artists who were dedicated to the West, its rough ways of life and its awe-inspiring scenery, Adah gained a new understanding of her native land. She had always been something of a chameleon: in New Orleans she had been a Southern lady, in Havana a Latin trollop, in Cincinnati a domesticity-loving housewife, in New York a brittle and polished celebrity. Now—and for the rest of her life—she would always be an American who bore the stamp of the Far West.

Perhaps the freedom of Western customs impressed her. Certainly she appreciated the bluntness, quick humor, and absence of sham. In any case, for whatever her reasons, she was a symbol of the mountains and prairies when she lived in London and Paris. Even in Vienna she was accepted as the Romantic American. Interestingly, she became a prototype, naïve and shrewd, worldly and innocent, brash and sensitive. Countless Americans who followed her to England and the Continent in the next century fitted the same image.

Part of her appeal, her charm, was that she seemed to be so many different things to so many different men, if not all things to all men. Artemus Ward, hearty and straightforward, exchanged wry jokes with her. Joe Lawrence listened more than he talked when he and Adah discussed

literary trends. Charles Dickens, she told him, had brought
the age of make-believe to an end in prose writing; hence-
forth the emphasis would be on realism and explorations,
in depth, of character. Lawrence, accepting these sound
views as valid, dutifully published them under his own
signature in the *Golden Era*, taking care to credit their
source.

Bret Harte, more than any other man in Adah's life,
was conscious of the ever-present prostitute in her nature.
"B.H.," she writes in her *Diary*, "had the gall to tell me
last night that I'd feel at home in one of the bawdy houses
we passed while driving to supper. When I protested, he
challenged me to deny that I could earn a tidy living in
that profession if deprived of work as an actress. I did
deny, of course, but was none too convincing. I wonder
why it is that young men see things so much more clearly
than their elders? E. treats me like royalty, but B.H. slaps
me across the backside if I don't laugh loudly enough at
his jokes."

The intense Charles Warren Stoddard, who was passing through a moody stage, expressed his opinion of
Adah in a poem that Lawrence obligingly published in
the *Golden Era:*

> Wild was her look, wild was her air,
> Back from her shoulders streamed her hair,
> Her looks that wont her brow to shade,
> Started erectly from her head.
> Her figure seems to rise more high.
> From her pale lips a frantic cry
> Rang sharply through the moon's pale light,
> And life to her was sudden night.

His clumsy verse won no prizes, but he was sensitive
enough to see the shadow of gloom that hovered over

Adah, ready to envelop her whenever there was a pause in her frantic social life.

The sojourn in San Francisco also marked something unusual in Adah's experience, a friendship with another woman. Ina Coolbrith, a young actress who specialized in the classics and was herself something of a poet, came to the city with a company of actors for an engagement of repertory, principally Shakespeare. The ladies of San Francisco took her up, no doubt as a way of showing their opposition to Adah.

But Ina found their supper parties dull, their conversation boring and their moral standards confining. She soon drifted into the *Golden Era* set, and the young authors welcomed a fresh, lovely blonde. The stage was set for a battle royal between two proud actresses and their followers.

But those who expected fireworks made the common error of underestimating Adah. She was incapable of tolerating competition, it was true, but she had climbed so high that she would not demean herself by admitting that such competition even existed. Therefore she solved the problem by taking the flattered Ina under her wing and acting as the younger woman's sponsor.

She praised Ina's verse, and publicly urged Joe Lawrence to print some of the feeble efforts. Lawrence winced, but a command from the Goddess was law, so an Ina Coolbrith limerick appeared on the back page of a *Golden Era* issue. Ina became her mentor's frequent dinner companion, and although actually prettier, was relegated to the background and became little more than a handmaiden. Adah, dressed to kill in the flashiest, most seductive clothes of her age, her manner self-assured and bold, commanded the center of the stage.

Ina, who eventually married a San Franciscan, lived happily ever after. Adah went on to greater and still greater glories. The most dramatically sensational incident in her dramatically crowded life took place soon after the conclusion of her San Francisco engagement.

In December, 1863, the run of *Mazeppa* ended, and Adah was ready to return to New York. Murdoch had gone home soon after the play had opened, leaving the company manager, Thomas C. Browne, in charge of operations. McGuire approached Browne with an offer of a return engagement the following spring, but Adah felt she could not afford to accept. She would have nothing to do for several months; she had been spending her money freely and needed work.

So, in spite of her reluctance to leave the most convivial city and friends she had ever known, she insisted that the entire company of actors go to New York together. Joe Lawrence told her that December was not the best month for the crossing of the Sierra Nevadas and the Rockies, but the prospect of adventure hardened Adah's resolve.

Several stagecoaches were hired, and the troupe departed at dawn one morning in December, following an all-night farewell party given by the staff and contributors of the *Golden Era*. Adah wept, the authors wept, and a hired band played dirges. Everyone had a wonderful time, and the Goddess waved a damp handkerchief as her admirers called to her from the street in front of the magazine's office.

Then, according to James, she turned to her maid. "Minnie," she said, taking a horse pistol from a large carpetbag, "I have a gift for you. Mr. Harte says the Indians of the mountains are the most vicious creatures on earth. Use this if they try to make a slave of you. I have another for myself." She reached into the bag again and produced another pistol.

Minnie recoiled in horror and refused to touch the lethal weapon until reassured.

"Don't worry," Adah said blithely. "It isn't loaded."

The journey from San Francisco to New York resulted in some of the most fanciful tales Adah ever spun. The stories enthralled Europe, and thousands who knew literally nothing about the United States formed opinions of the country based on Adah's imaginative fancies.

The most famous of these fairy tales first appeared in *Bell's Life,* an English sports publication whose editors had fond memories of John C. Heenan. Respectable London newspapers like the *Morning Post* and the *Daily Telegraph* reprinted the story, and it was copied in France and a number of the German states. It was treated with solemnity everywhere, and only *Punch* lampooned it.

Somewhere on the trail—the precise spot unspecified—the stagecoaches were halted by a fierce band of Indian warriors. A bloody battle took place, the coachmen and armed guards were killed, and Adah was taken prisoner. Helpless in the hands of her captors, she was carried to an Indian town deep in the wilderness, the exact location again unspecified.

There the Indians feasted, celebrating their victory for three days and nights while their prisoner remained under heavy guard. At the climax of these barbarian festivities she was led before the whole tribe, and saw that a stake had been erected in the center of a compound. Piles of kindling and brush were heaped nearby, and she realized instantly that the savages intended to burn her alive as a sacrifice to their gods.

On all sides she saw the evil, glittering eyes of primitive men and women who would cheer as they watched her suffering in death agonies. But the intrepid Adah felt no fear, for she had not been idle during her captivity. She had learned from her guards—conversing with them in an unspecified tongue—that the tribe was a nation of snake worshipers. The snake—any snake, apparently—was sacred.

Therefore, before she could be tied to the stake, she began to dance, wriggling sinuously like a snake. The burly warriors on either side released her and watched in open-mouthed admiration. A murmur ran through the crowd, then the entire tribe became quiet. Adah used her arms, her legs, her body as she twisted and writhed. According to *Bell's Life,* several Paris newspapers and one or two in the German states, she was completely naked. The *Daily Telegraph* and *Morning Post,* with due regard for Victorian sensitivities, made no mention of her attire, or lack of it.

The braves, who would have celebrated her death by pounding on rawhide drums, began to beat a rhythm, scarcely aware of what they were doing. Adah danced more rapidly, and the tempo of the drums increased. The throbbing sound filled the air and became still faster, wilder. Adah was in continuous motion now, twisting and wriggling in an imitation of a snake so perfect that even the most ignorant savage recognized the portrait she was painting with her body and limbs.

Glazed expressions came into the eyes of the audience. One by one the drummers fell under Adah's spell, too, and stopped pounding on their crude instruments. Time had lost its meaning, so she had no idea how long she worked in this, the greatest and most important theatrical performance of her life. But at last she knew it was safe to halt. The whole audience sat cross-legged on the ground, transfixed and motionless.

Her dancing had hypnotized the entire tribe.

The rest was easy. She took a strong horse and, being an accomplished rider, escaped before the warriors came out of their trance. Presumably she took time to snatch some clothing before galloping off toward civilization.

One of the leading impresarios of Paris, an Alsatian named Beck, was so impressed by this nonsense that he offered Adah any salary she wanted for a two-week engagement featuring her Indian snake dance. She refused, telling him that her relief was so great when she found herself alive that she vowed never to dance again.

The snake story, and others like it, were for the future, however. The fantastic events that actually took place at Virginia City, Nevada, were more than enough for the present. It may be that, after her experience there, she thought anything possible. It would be hard to blame her.

Virginia City, located high in the Sierra Nevadas, not far from Lake Tahoe and the California border, was a boom town. Silver was king, and Adah Isaacs Menken became queen.

She and her supporting players arrived in Virginia City late one afternoon after spending an uncomfortable day in the mountains. It was Browne's intention to remain overnight, resting the horses as long as necessary and then resuming the journey east on what was known as the Kit Carson Trail.

The miners of Virginia City had other plans. Hungry for culture of the variety that Adah dispensed, a delegation came to her as she and Browne were eating dinner in a saloon opposite the dingy hotel in which the company was staying. The men wanted to see a performance of *Mazeppa,* and were willing to pay a large sum of hard cash for the privilege. So far, the delegates said, a sum of five thousand dollars had been collected or pledged. The total might run considerably higher.

Adah and Browne almost fell over each other in their eagerness to accept. Then they settled down to haggle with each other, finally agreeing that Adah would take twenty-five hundred dollars, the rest of the receipts going to the other actors and Browne, with Murdoch receiving his usual percentage.

The next morning Browne inspected possible sites, and

found so many problems that he reluctantly advised Adah to abandon the idea. But the gleam of pure silver was in her eyes, and she went out on her own tour of the town and vicinity, riding a borrowed horse and accompanied by an enthusiastic escort of several hundred miners.

She was willing to admit that there were complications. For one thing, there was no theater in Virginia City, but even if there had been one, it would have been far too small to accommodate the thousands of miners and prospectors clamoring for admission. The officials of several prosperous mining companies offered suggestions and help, and at last she found a spot that seemed ideal.

On the northeast side of the town was a natural amphitheater located at the base of a rugged hill. Adah proposed that a wooden platform be built there, with a shack at either side to conceal the actors when they were not on stage. The audience would sit or stand on the ground. And at the climax of the play she would be carried through the audience and up the side of the hill.

Browne, who was responsible for Adah's safety, was afraid she might be hurt when a strange horse tore up the rocky slope. He protested vigorously but in vain. Adah had made up her mind, and the rest of the company was anxious to earn a quick profit, too.

Scores of brawny volunteers built a platform-stage, the two shacks rose in a matter of hours, and a third was constructed for Adah's private use. The considerate miners built it with a large window facing the audience, but someone, foiling the architect's intention, put in curtains that concealed its occupant from view. Everything was ready for the outdoor performance in one of America's first theaters-in-the-round.

Nights in the Sierra Nevadas are rarely balmy, and in winter are frigid. The actors shivered in their thin costumes, exhaling clouds of frosty vapor every time they spoke their lines. Presumably they consoled themselves with the thought that they would soon be able to afford expensive new overcoats. The audience was indifferent to niceties, and paid scant attention to anyone except Adah. She was cheered loudly at every appearance, and each of her exits was accompanied by thunderstorms of applause.

At last came the climactic moment, with Adah lashed to the back of a mare belonging to the wife of Henry Godfrey, partner-manager of one of the established mining companies. Adah rode back and forth through the huge throng several times to make sure that the thousands who were watching caught at least a glimpse of her. Then she disappeared up the hill, where three men waited to catch the mare.

A few minutes later Adah appeared on the platform stage for her curtain calls, and there was bedlam, the most extraordinary scene ever to take place in the history of the American theater. Someone threw a chunk of silver onto the stage, narrowly missing the star. Others delightedly followed the gift-giver's example, and a shower of precious metal crashed onto the roughhewn planks. Adah, for the moment solely concerned with the prevention of mayhem, retreated to the rear of the stage.

A one-time Detroit bricklayer named Murphy, who failed in his efforts to locate his own silver lode but did sufficiently well with a pack of playing cards to be known to his intimates as Lucky, came to the rescue of a lady in distress. Shoving through the front ranks, he leaped onto the stage and made a short, pungent speech. According to some of the subsequent accounts, he delivered a polished, polysyllabic address, which is doubtful.

Ed James, who presumably learned of the incident from Adah, has Murphy say, "You damned sons of beggars! Would you kill the poor little thing? Bring your silver to her in your own two hands!"

The relieved Adah rewarded him with a kiss, which

Lucky Murphy did not tire of describing to Nevada mine-field visitors for the next twenty years. A line quickly formed, and men came onto the stage one by one to make their offerings to the Goddess. Each was given a warm embrace, and others in the audience were so stirred that they raced off to their lodging houses, shacks, and tents, where mattresses were upended, treasures were dug up from secret hiding places, and the pile of silver on the stage rose higher. Adah's kisses became correspondingly warmer, and the audience howled gleefully when one sheepish miner handed her a heavy ingot.

She received several ingots before the bizarre ceremony ended. The excitement was so intense that no one kept count of the exact number. Then an honor guard of volunteers, armed with loaded rifles and muskets, carried the treasure back to the hotel for her.

The night's activities merely marked the beginning of Virginia City's love affair with La Menken. Browne had intended to resume the journey east on the morning following the performance, but the troupe's departure was delayed by developments beyond the control of mere mortals.

For the next forty-eight hours Adah was inundated with silver. Men brought her ingots, chunks, and even bags of silver dust. Others handed her stock certificates in a score of companies; it was not the fault of the donors that too many men were working the area and that, consequently, most of these companies failed.

Silver had just been discovered in a hitherto unexplored area a few miles northwest of the town. The prospectors scouring the district named it the Menken, by acclamation; the Menken, as it was known thereafter, became famous when several rich veins were discovered. A group of hard-bitten adventurers from Cleveland changed the name of their organization to the Menken

Shaft and Tunnel Company, and gave Adah one hundred shares of their stock. Each had a face value of five dollars at the time. When she died, the executor of her estate, Ed James, collected fifty dollars per share.

Exaggerated stories of the silver shower followed Adah for the rest of her days. "It is not true," she told the New York *Mercury* in an exclusive interview, "that my dear friends in Nevada gave me gifts worth one million dollars. Would that I were worth even a small fraction of that sum."

Newell estimates that she received one hundred and fifty thousand dollars in silver. James, who was in a better position to know the facts, places the total at one hundred thousand. Whatever the precise figure, Adah received more for a single performance than any actress in the history of the theater, and no one has yet topped her record.

The nest egg provided her with neither security nor peace of mind. Scorning material wealth with the high-handed disdain of a silver miner, she squandered the fortune. Each of the *Mazeppa* actors received a watch fashioned of silver and bearing Adah's signature in a thin vein of gold. Browne, who was engaged to be married, was dazed by a gift of a plot of land in Yonkers, where Adah urged him to buy a house. Friends in New York and San Francisco received handsome presents, and Adah celebrated her return to New York by going on her most intensive clothes-buying spree. She also hired three additional servants, bought a new carriage, and, because her house reminded her of Newell, refurnished it from cellar to attic.

In brief, the fortune flowed through her fingers like quicksilver.

The rest of her journey was uneventful and anticlimactic. Denver, a smaller San Francisco, gave her a roaring welcome, and the Rocky Mountain *News* urged her, in a strongly worded editorial, to perform in *Mazeppa* for the culture-starved citizens of the Colorado metropolis. But she was tired after a rough ride across the mountains and the excitement of her experience in Virginia City.

She refused, and Denver turned its back on her. "Miss Adah Menken thinks we are not good enough for her," the Rocky Mountain *News* said, bristling. "Judging from press reactions elsewhere, we aren't missing much."

The usual crowd was gathered outside Adah's hotel when she emerged after a night's sleep and hearty breakfast. She paused for the usual smile and wave before stepping into her coach, but recoiled when men hissed, shook their fists at her, and cursed. Browne urged her to retreat into the lobby.

"I will not," James quotes her as saying. "Denver may lack refinement, but American men will not assault a defenseless woman."

She was right, up to a point. No attempt was made to lynch her, but her carriage was pelted with rotten eggs and stones. Browne wanted to appeal to the state militia for protection, but Adah wisely preferred to ignore the incident, and encountered no further difficulty.

She had learned a lesson, however, and in Kansas City promised to return for a run in *Mazeppa*. She made the same vow to St. Louis, but kept her word to neither. It was not easy to secure train accommodations in wartime, so she was forced to spend a few days in St. Louis, doing nothing but contemplate the Mississippi River. It reminded her of her childhood in New Orleans, she said, and became so melancholy that she retired to her hotel suite and refused to see anyone.

When Browne secured space on a train, her mood improved, and the Girl of the Golden West returned in triumph to New York.

CHAPTER XI

THE BELLS OF WESTMINSTER

O lonely watchers for the Light! how long must I grope
with my dead eyes in the sand?

Only the red fire of Genius, that narrows up life's chances
to the black path that crawls on to the dizzy clouds.

The wailing music that spreads its pinions to the tremble
of the wind, has crumbled off to silence.

From the steep ideal the quivering soul falls in its lonely
sorrow like an unmated star from the blue heights of
Heaven into the dark sea.

O Genius! is this thy promise?

O bards! Is this all?

—"Miserimus"

FLUSHED with success and silver, Adah expected New
York to give her a heroine's welcome. Instead she discovered, as had some before and many after her, that Manhattan was indifferent to what happened in the provinces
beyond the Hudson. San Francisco was far away, the
Golden Era authors meant nothing to the literati of the
East, and, of course, *Mazeppa* was no novelty to New York.

Adah was annoyed, and became even more irritated
when reports of her reception in Virginia City, which
appeared in several New York newspapers, touched off
the only flurry of excitement. She received a number of

marriage proposals from strangers, salesmen appeared at her house hoping to come away with some of her easily won silver, and a horde of nodding acquaintances descended on her when she dined at Pfaff's and other restaurants.

She retired behind the closed doors of her house and saw only a few close friends. Solitude and inactivity invariably made her spells of depression more severe, and her spirits were not lifted when she received the divorce decree granted by a San Francisco court. Alderman Joe Brice, attorney for the *Clipper,* was called in as a legal consultant by the worried and faithful Ed James.

It was the counselor's opinion that the divorce was not valid as Adah had not been present in the courtroom at the time the decision had been rendered. In view of her spectacularly bigamous past, he urged her to be on the safe side, recommending that she file again in New York. Adah agreed, but took no action for several months.

Bored, with only her new wardrobe to offer her consolation of sorts, Adah was at loose ends. She spent hours writing sad verses, but still they occupied only a small part of her time. She had enough money to coast indefinitely, provided she was reasonably frugal, but the cost of living was the least of her concerns. She had no lover and was interested in no one man. Her friends had their own lives to lead, their own families to occupy their time and attention.

She announced that she intended to search for a new theatrical vehicle, but the New York theater owners were not overjoyed. *Mazeppa's* success would not be easy to repeat, particularly when the talents of the star were limited.

At this critical moment, Murdoch received a letter from E. T. Smith, owner of Astley's Theater in London and one of England's most successful showmen. Would Miss Menken consider coming to London with her own company for an engagement of unlimited duration? The most he could offer, Smith said apologetically, was a salary of one hundred pounds a week, approximately five hundred dollars.

Adah accepted instantly. Murdoch had not yet worked out his own terms with Smith, but Adah could not be bothered with such picayune details. If he did not accept at once, she told him, she would write to Smith herself. Murdoch worked out a compromise with her, giving her his word that he would negotiate successfully with the owner of Astley's. In the meantime, knowing that Adah was impatient, he began to hire a supporting cast and arranged for the company to play a break-in engagement in Baltimore.

Strangely, the hiring of the actors proved to be a major problem. Many of the veterans who had seen long service in *Mazeppa* had taken roles in other plays and were not available. Some, who were currently unemployed, were deemed unsuitable. Murdoch insisted on hiring only actors whose diction would be comprehensible to the English. He himself would receive a royalty, but no guarantee, and he would earn money only if the play enjoyed a long and prosperous run.

Adah insisted on being present when actors were interviewed; she also demanded the right to hear them audition and pass judgment on them. The patient Murdoch rebelled, and the ensuing argument, which took place in his office, sent the members of his staff hurrying into the streets. Adah broke a plaster bust of Shakespeare, a goblet that Edwin Booth had used in *King Lear,* and a number of other unspecified objects.

When the smoke cleared away, Murdoch emerged the victor. Adah was forced to accept his decree that he alone would sit in judgment on the supporting cast. Thereafter relations between director and star were strained and formal.

In March, 1864, the newly assembled *Mazeppa* company entrained to war-weary Baltimore. The principal topic of conversation was the promotion of General Ulysses S. Grant to the over-all command of the Union Army on March 10, news which created a great stir elsewhere. Baltimore, still a border city with divided loyalties, saw no reason to assume that Grant would do better than his predecessors. Confederate commander Robert E. Lee had proved himself a genius, and although lack of men, munitions, and equipment had made it impossible for him to launch a major campaign on enemy soil after his defeat at Gettysburg, Baltimoreans assumed that he would be able to continue fighting a brilliant defensive war for years, perhaps for a decade or two.

Heartily sick of the conflict, with many families on both sides grieving over sons killed or wounded, the people of Baltimore wanted to be left alone. They were in no mood for theatergoing, and Adah's brand of entertainment did not appeal to them. The curious and the thrill seekers, who had already seen her in *Mazeppa,* now preferred to save their money.

The people stayed away. Even opening night the receipts were disappointing, and thereafter dwindled to almost nothing. On the fourth night, there were no more than fifty people in the audience. Adah, hurt in pride as well as pocketbook, felt grossly insulted. A more sensible woman would have made an attempt to understand the situation. A realist would have taken the view that the success or failure of the Baltimore run meant nothing. The actors were learning to work together prior to crossing the Atlantic, and the indifference of Baltimore to the star and the play could have been dismissed with a shrug.

But Adah brooded, and had few distractions. Most of

the city's literati were now in uniform, the few wealthy gentlemen who sent their names backstage were elderly shopworn playboys whose company she found distasteful. She decided that something had to be done to perk up public interest and, consulting no one, she did it.

At noon on March 18 she went to a restaurant owned by a man named Singer and questioned the proprietor at length about a mysterious stranger who was supposed to meet her there. As the stranger was the product of her imagination, Singer was blank. Adah returned at six o'clock in the evening, and giving a better performance than was her custom onstage, she became quite agitated when informed that no one had inquired for her.

"She didn't say the man was a Confederate spy," Singer told the authorities the following day. "But she hinted. I felt certain that's what she meant."

Adah paid her third visit to the restaurant after that evening's dismal performance of *Mazeppa*, and appeared agitated when told that no one had been seeking her. In Singer's words, "She was worried."

Her manner conspiratorial—and probably melodramatic—Adah offered the restaurant owner one hundred dollars in cash to say nothing about the matter. She idled away an hour by eating a large steak, frequently glancing in the direction of the entrance. She did not leave until Singer was ready to lock up for the night, and she emphasized that she would return the following day.

The seeds were now planted, and she hoped the box office would come alive when the newspapers screamed that she was believed to be a Confederate espionage agent. She had been the victim of circumstance, compounded by her own cupidity, in her previous brush with the Union Army at Baltimore, and this time she wanted to cash in.

The first act played perfectly. Adah appeared at Singer's restaurant for a late breakfast at noon the next day, and was taken into custody by a squad of Union soldiers. They escorted her to Army headquarters, where she was informed that Brigadier General Alexander Fish, Provost General for Maryland, would question her. She cooled her high heels while Singer was interrogated, and had every reason to believe that her publicity scheme would succeed. General Fish, a distant relative of the distinguished former Governor Hamilton Fish of New York who was destined to become Secretary of State under Grant, was an exceptionally intelligent man adept at reading human character. He was also overworked and short-tempered.

Adah lost control of the interview at the outset. Her coyness did not appeal to the general, her mock air of bewilderment irritated him and he soon became convinced that she had manufactured an incident out of whole cloth in order to increase her notoriety. It was within his power to dismiss her and forget the charade. But he was annoyed because an actress had dared to ruffle the already turbulent waters of national security, so he surprised her by writing a brief report of the affair and sending her on to Washington under armed guard.

War Department staff officers who were working seven days and nights a week, who subsisted on hastily snatched meals and always needed sleep, were impervious to the beauty of the celebrated actress from New Orleans. Adah was shunted from office to office, questioned briefly by several harassed officers in turn, and, finally, put on a New York train. She protested that she was expected in Baltimore for the remainder of *Mazeppa's* run there.

The unsympathetic War Department informed her that her return to Baltimore was not in the national interest.

Given no choice, she went to New York. Perhaps the most maddening aspect of the pathetic little comedy was that not one word appeared in the newspapers. And Mur-

doch added gross insult to injury by paying the actors
their week's wages out of Adah's salary.

Adah never forgot the incident. Eventually she told a
story that warped the truth beyond recognition. By the
time Alexandre Dumas entered her life in Paris, she was
saying she had been unjustly arrested and thrown into a
dungeon. There, due to crowded conditions and the inevitable confusion caused by a war, she went hungry, had
no blankets, and suffered from the bitter cold. Fortunately,
General Grant himself learned of her plight, ordered her
released, and had a private visit with her at his headquarters. In the interview he apologized on behalf of the
Army, congratulated her for her patriotism, and expressed
the hope that he might, someday, watch her perform in a
play.

Dumas, the master storyteller whose unlimited imagination had earned him several fortunes, accepted the tale
without question. Adah took care not to tell the story in
England, however, as the sympathies of many upper-class
Britons lay with the Confederacy. It is unlikely that Ulysses S. Grant ever heard of Adah Isaacs Menken. And the
possibility that she might have seen him while being
questioned at the War Department is remote. The man
who had just been made President Lincoln's field commander had more important matters on his mind than the
pretended espionage of a publicity-seeking stage star.

There were few farewells as Adah prepared for her
voyage to England in late March, 1864. Most of her friends
had said good-by to her when she had gone off to San
Francisco, and her present home stay was so brief that she
did not resume her earlier regular routines. She wrote to
Whitman, who was in Washington, offering him the use
of her house whenever he came to New York. Hannah
James took a set of house keys, promised to keep an eye
on the place, and arranged to have her own servants dust

and clean it from time to time. Joe Brice told his client he had begun the divorce action against Newell in New York, and he felt certain that, by the time Adah returned, she would be able to go into court at her convenience. In the meantime, he warned her, she was not to marry anyone else, and he stressed the probable invalidity of her California decree.

Murdoch was not on speaking terms with Adah, so he sent her a letter informing her that he would follow her to England in May with the rest of the company. Her reason for leaving earlier was to find a suitable horse in England and break in the animal prior to the start of rehearsals. Negotiations with Smith had been completed, and *Mazeppa* was scheduled to open at Astley's Theater in late June.

Adah sailed for Plymouth on April 3, 1864, with Minnie, high hopes, and twenty-eight pieces of luggage. Still scattering her Virginia City silver, she traveled in style, enjoying the luxury of a suite. Her need for companionship was so great, however, that she spent little time in her own cabins, and instead became friendly with the other passengers, who treated her with the gratifying awe that was the due of one of the most celebrated, notorious women on the face of the earth.

London was bigger and noisier than New York, but Adah felt certain she would conquer it. "I believe," she wrote to Ed James from shipboard, "that *Mazeppa* will repeat its New York success. Why shouldn't it? Men are the same everywhere." She was in a position to know.

Arriving in London, she took a handsome suite of rooms at the plush Westminster Palace Hotel and sent a note to Smith, informing him of her arrival. The next morning he came to call on her, arriving at the hotel while she was still asleep. An hour later she appeared from her bedroom, wearing one of her feather-trimmed negligees and too much make-up. The gaudy American actress and the stiff, humorless British impresario took an instant dislike to each other, and the better part of a year was to pass before steady ticket sales melted their mutual antagonism.

E. T. Smith was a short, pudgy man with side-whiskers, an ultraconservative taste in clothes and a lofty manner calculated to offset the unfortunate fact that he earned his living in show business. Actors made him uncomfortable, dramatists were odd creatures best kept at arm's length, and staff employees were beneath notice. Edward Burne-Jones, the distinguished painter who was prominent in the set that eventually adopted Adah, summed up the producer in a letter to Rossetti, his good friend: "What a pity that Smith is in the theater, for he would be its most severe critic were he engaged in the pursuit for which Nature intended him, that of an embalmer."

Adah and her new employer found it difficult to observe the amenities as they drank coffee together at their initial meeting. Smith could not conceal his disapproval of the flashy American's careless habit of allowing her negligee to fall away from her legs, which she enjoyed exhibiting. Adah, sensitive to every nuance of like or dislike in others, bristled, and exposed still more of her famous body. Then came the blow.

Smith deeply regretted any inconvenience he might be causing Miss Menken, but the opening of *Mazeppa* had to be postponed. The lovely, talented, and intelligent Laura Seymour was doing unexpectedly good business as Lady Macbeth at Astley's Theater Royal in Westminster Road, and her run had been extended for an indefinite period. Miss Menken and *Mazeppa* would have to wait.

The furious Adah made a scene, but Smith had come prepared for a tantrum. His contract with Murdoch, which he produced from his pocket, gave him the exclusive right to determine when *Mazeppa* would open; the only condition he was obliged to observe required him to present the play prior to the end of the year 1864.

Adah sent a blistering letter to Murdoch, but in vain. The director could do nothing, and Adah's peace of mind was in no way improved when the director postponed the sailing of the rest of the company from New York. For a time Adah seriously considered returning to the United States, but finally realized she might be causing herself great inconvenience, as there was no way of determining how soon she would have to turn around and sail back to England.

So she settled down to a bleak existence at the luxurious Westminster Palace. She knew no one in England and, aside from the cold-blooded Smith, had met no one. Her one task was to find a suitable horse, and she spent her days at livery stables, examining mares and testing them.

It was impossible for someone with her restless disposition to remain quiet for any prolonged period. The great Charles Dickens, whose work she admired beyond that of any other living man, was a natural target, and she sent him a letter of self-introduction.

The master novelist, living a smug, snug, and complicated existence at his country retreat, Gad's Hill Place, Higham-by-Rochester, Kent, did not reply. So many unknowns wrote to him that he did not bother to answer fan mail.

Adah tried again, sending him copies of some of her poems and expressing the humble hope that he would condescend to act as her literary adviser.

The poems intrigued Dickens, who made inquiries and discovered that Adah was a celebrity in her own right. Curiosity moved him, and he sent her a short note, offering to meet her for lunch in the restaurant at Cataldi's Hotel on Dover Street whenever he could fit such a visit into his busy schedule.

Adah was elated, but the immediate problem of how to fill her time remained unsolved. She finally decided to investigate her opposition, and assiduously attended performances of every play currently appearing in London. The acting, she wrote Walt Whitman, was remarkably good and far superior to that found in the American theater, but the contemporary plays were dreadful. At last she got around to seeing Laura Seymour in *Macbeth,* and was impressed by the imaginative power of the English actress.

Smith was present at Astley's that night, and Adah overcame the shyness that she usually managed to conceal from others. She asked him to take her backstage to meet the woman whose success was spoiling her own debut. Miss Seymour was the mistress of Charles Reade, one of the most prolific and successful of English dramatists and social novelists, and he happened to be present when Adah was presented.

It would have been too much to expect that two strong-willed women who craved admiration would take to each other. Adah and Laura began spitting, hissing, and arching their feline backs at first sight. But Reade, a crusader for women's rights, was struck by Adah's intellect—and her familiarity with his work. She spoke warmly and at length about his still-popular novel, *The Cloister and the Hearth,* a study of Erasmus' father, which had been published three years earlier. And she demonstrated that she was no intellectual sycophant by intelligently criticizing his most recent novel, *Hard Cash,* a bitter treatise on the barbaric conditions prevailing in English insane asylums.

Reade was charmed, and invited Adah home for supper. Laura, who kept house for him, had to accept the situation with as much grace as she could muster. Adah, who had known nothing about the private lives of her host and hostess, instantly understood the situation and reacted accordingly. She directed most of her conversation to Laura, and made it clear that she had no intention of becoming a man-stealer.

She emphasized that resolve in a thank-you note she sent by messenger the following day. "I entertain the highest respect for you, dear Miss Seymour," she wrote, "as a woman and as an actress. I hope I comported myself with sufficient dignity to warrant another visit to your lovely home."

There was nothing subtle in the declaration, as the house was Reade's, not Laura's. By emphasizing that it was Laura's home, Adah made it clear that she would not trespass. Laura did not accept the statement at face value, as Adah's allure was too intense and too obvious for any woman who did not know her well to trust her. But after a delay of two weeks, another invitation was extended, and again Adah's behavior was impeccable.

Laura then decided she had nothing to fear, and Adah became a frequent visitor at the Reade-Seymour dwelling. The ice was broken, and she had plunged into the waters of the literary world she loved. Laura also wrote poetry, so the two women had a bond in common. Both were alert and aggressive, and shared a contempt for the morals and manners of the Victorian age. Laura, living openly with her lover in defiance of convention, was not one to point a finger at Adah. They became good friends, and Adah steeped herself in Reade's work, which Laura encouraged her to discuss with him.

A two-line note from Charles Dickens caused Adah to spend the better part of a day going through her wardrobe. She should have spent a much longer period at the task, for she appeared at Cataldi's wearing a gown of pink silk that Virginia City, Nevada, would have loved. The habitués of Cataldi's raised their eyebrows when they saw a plunging neckline that belonged in the hellion days of the previous century.

Dickens was mortified, and the lunch was an unqualified failure. Adah's blatant charms and eagerness to expose them numbed him, and although he was usually a fluent, easy conversationalist, he addressed her in monosyllables. She says in her *Diary,* "C.D. stares at his plate. Not once did he look me in the face. For all that, he is brilliant."

The novelist scurried back to Kent, and not until autumn did Adah learn from Reade that she had made an unfavorable impression. Thereafter she went to great pains to correct it, and showed such tenacious patience that eventually she won Dickens' friendship. However, he never again made the mistake of dining with her in a public place, and their relationship was chiefly confined to a running correspondence on the subject of her poetry.

Adah's respect for Dickens was so great that she meekly accepted criticism from him. "Even your best poems lack discipline," he wrote her in November, 1865, "and I feel that when you achieve a sense of discipline, it is accidental."

Adah broke off friendships with people who dared to say a fraction as much, but to Dickens she wrote humbly: "You are right. I am impatient, and do not revise my poems as I should. I hope that I can correct my faults and merit your approval."

He encouraged her, but did not praise her. Adah appears to have been afraid of him, and submitted everything she wrote in her last years to this stern literary father. Others—among them Whitman, Swinburne, and Rossetti—were better qualified than a master of prose fiction to judge her poetry, but she wanted no help from any of them. George Sand suggested that Adah was so uncertain of her work that she was afraid she might borrow the style of another poet. The charge was never admitted, but the simple fact of the matter is that Dickens was the only person to whom she turned for assistance and the only one whose criticism she tolerated.

She acknowledged her debt to him, and paid him the highest compliment in her power by dedicating her one published book of poems, *Infelicia,* to him.

The most popular stage star in the London of 1864 was Charles Albert Fechter, the matinee idol of his day. Born in London of French parents, he had scored an enormous initial success in Berlin and had gone on to become the highest-priced and most temperamental actor in Paris. Now, although in his forties, he was still playing romantic, swashbuckling roles with great gusto, and London was wild about him.

It was inevitable that he and Adah should meet, and their paths crossed at the Reade-Seymour house. Fechter, blithely ignoring the fact that he was married to Eléonore Rabut, a French actress who had given up her career for him, announced that he was in love with Adah. The patient Eléonore, accustomed to his peregrinations after seventeen years of marriage, braced herself for a new humiliation.

But she misjudged Adah, who made it a cardinal principle never to become involved in an affair with a married man. "Sir," she told Fechter in the hearing of a dozen Reade-Seymour guests, "you are too handsome for your own good or the peace of my own sex. If you were single, I would tell you that I love you, too, and we would walk together into the moonlight of Laura's garden. But you are not free, sir. Go, sit beside your wife and hold her hand."

The startled Fechter obeyed, "as if in a trance," the amused Laura Seymour wrote to her sister.

Eléonore Fechter was grateful to her unexpected benefactress, and Adah discovered she had made a friend of another woman. Fechter, having been chastised, had learned a lesson, and did not try again. In time he was to become Adah's business associate and the stage director of her plays on the Continent.

Despite her blazing wrath, the postponement of *Mazeppa* paid dividends from the outset. The first of these came when she moved from the Westminster Palace to Cataldi's, a small hotel patronized by authors and actors. The Fechters had a small suite there, and Eléonore convinced Adah that she would spend far less if she took a suite there, too.

Everyone at Cataldi's knew everyone else, and the restaurant was crowded with dramatists, novelists, essayists, and poets. It was there that Adah first met Rossetti, with whom she formed a platonic bond almost at once.

"You remind me of my sisters," he told her diplomatically, but was guilty of gross distortion. Other than that the Rossetti girls were females, they did not resemble Adah in any way.

Adah later claimed that she met Swinburne during this same period when she was idling away the days, waiting for *Macbeth* to conclude its run at Astley's, but her memory was imperfect. That meeting did not take place until *Mazeppa* had opened.

Late in August, after several months of free-spending inactivity, Adah finally became busy. Murdoch arrived in London with the other members of the cast, and the play went into rehearsal. *Macbeth* had closed at last, but Smith was in no hurry to present *Mazeppa*. After so many delays, he preferred to wait until the muggy heat, which kept theatergoers away, became transformed into the cooler mists of autumn.

The opening was scheduled for October 3, and Adah went to work in earnest, spending the better part of each day and evening at the theater and working out with a horse she named Black Star. Her new friends were curi-

ous and told her they hoped she would succeed, but
Eléonore Fechter confided in her that virtually every au-
thor and actor in England believed *Mazeppa* would fail.
It was too sensational, Eléonore said, for British tastes.

Bell's Life printed a small article saying that intense interest had been aroused, but the other newspapers were
prepared to pay little attention to the event. Adah, working grimly and losing weight, invited some of her new
friends to a dress rehearsal. They attended, and went
away gasping. Rumors began to fly, the newspapers decided they couldn't stand aside after all, and Smith took
advantage of their awakening curiosity by running larger-
than-usual advertisements.

Then the *Daily News* helped the sale of tickets by publishing an attack on Adah, *Mazeppa,* and the exposure of
a seminude female body to the gaze of an audience. Adah,
with a fine sense of timing and publicity, wrote a re-
joinder, which the *Daily News* felt obliged to print:

"In your Leader of last Tuesday on the Moral of American Art," she wrote, "you associate my name with what an
American Journal terms 'The Naked Drama' and express
the hope that Mr. E. T. Smith will not degrade Astley's by
an exhibit of indecency. As I am about to appear at that
establishment, such an observation is calculated to do me
serious injury, and I am sure you will allow me a few
words of explanation, as you confess you know nothing of
the actress or her piece. To begin with, the play is *Mazeppa,* and I impersonate the hero; but my costume, or
rather want of costume, as might be inferred, is not in the
least indelicate and in no way more open to invidious
comment than the dress worn by Cerito Rosati, or even
the grotesque garbs employed by ladies of the London
stage.

"I have long been a student of sculpture and my attitudes selected from the works of Canova present a classi-

cality which has been invariably recognized by the foremost of American critics.

"I may add that my performance of *Mazeppa* had a most prosperous career in America, and as is usual in such cases, my success created a host of imitators. Some of these ladies, I hear, have adopted a style of drapery inconsistent with delicacy and good taste.

"*Mazeppa*, like any other specialty, is easily vulgarized. Let *La Sylphide* be scantily dressed, or ungracefully acted, by an indifferent artist, and what will be more offensive?

"The critics found no fault with Mrs. Charles Kean's embodiment of Don, and the young ladies who exhibit their well-formed limbs in the Haymarket or the Strand pantomimes (notably in such parts as Cupid or Ixion) are not accused of indelicacy.

"Do me the favor, as a stranger, to suspend your opinion of my representation, and after you witness it, I am quite willing to abide your criticism."

Adah's appeal to the British sense of fair play was a canny gesture, and the editors stilled their pens. But nothing could silence the loud whispers of those who foretold that the most scandalous performance in history would soon unfold. All seats for the first four weeks of *Mazeppa's* run were sold prior to the opening, and *Punch* solemnly declared, "Mr. E. T. Smith is said to have smiled."

On the night of October 3, 1864, Adah Isaacs Menken repeated her New York triumph. The *Daily Telegraph* said that she took twenty-two curtain calls, the *Morning Post* counted twenty-three, and *Bell's,* not bothering with mere numbers, summed up the audience reaction by observing, "The most popular of America's actresses has conquered us."

The reviewers did not share the enthusiasm of the first-night audience. The *Times,* which had been expected to thunder in righteous wrath, confined itself to the prim an-

nouncement that Miss Adah Menken was playing in
Mazeppa at Astley's. The *Daily News* slyly remarked that
no member of Queen Victoria's court had been seen in the
audience, adding, "Small wonder, for Miss Menken leaves
little to modesty or the imagination."

"There is no excuse for nudity on our stage," the *Telegraph* declared. But the reviewer was a gentleman, for he
continued, "If nudity there must be, Adah Menken de-
serves the many plaudits she has received."

"One is not bored," said the *Morning Post*. "One is too
startled by the immodesty of the leading lady to feel the
weight of an oppressive, old-fashioned play."

The country's leading professional critic, Mark Lemon,
made his views known in *Punch*. First reminding his
readers that an actress named Cartlich had played in the
creaking *Mazeppa* in 1831, he turned to rhyme:

> Here's half the town,—if bills be true,
> To Astley's nightly thronging,
> To see The Menken throw aside
> All to her sex belonging.
> Stripping off woman's modesty,
> With woman's outward trappings,
> A bare-backed jade on a bare-backed steed,
> In Cartlich's old strapping.

Belted earls, members of the House of Commons, and
blue-blooded Guards officers lined up at the stage door to
pay their respects to a lovely and daring young woman.
Murdoch, income assured for months to come, quietly
left the theater without saying good-by to Adah. He sailed
for New York a few days later, their feud unhealed, and
their paths did not cross again.

Word of the success of the play spread quickly, and a
long line formed at the box office on the day following the

opening. Everyone who was anyone wanted to see *Mazeppa*, and seats became almost impossible to obtain. Smith was besieged with requests, and had so little privacy that he worked at home rather than submit to a crossfire at his office.

Crowds formed outside Cataldi's to catch a glimpse of the American actress who, it was said, appeared on stage completely nude. Adah waved graciously whenever she climbed in and out of carriages, and was shocked when three women attacked her one afternoon, ripping her cloak, tearing her hat from her head, and screaming, "You harlot!"

Smith requested constabulary protection for her, but the police refused to give it, thinking he was merely seeking publicity for his star. Various gentlemen gallantly leaped into the breach, and Adah was provided with male escorts whenever she left her hotel. The assault was not repeated, which led various cynics to side with the police, but nothing was ever proved.

Adah was launched on a dizzy whirl that made her New York reception mild by comparison. "She has told me herself," Laura Seymour wrote to her sister, "that she can accept no more supper or luncheon engagements for the next month." The man-about-town who wanted to maintain his reputation as a gay blade was obliged to appear in public with Adah on his arm—or retire.

Charles Dickens cast aside his reserve and, descending from Olympus, tried to obtain tickets for *Mazeppa*. He failed, but Adah, learning of his plight from Reade and Laura, immediately obtained the royal box for him. He courageously paid her a backstage visit after the performance to thank her, but kept his critical opinion to himself. "C.D. was embarrassed by *Mazeppa*," Adah tells her *Diary*. "I believe he is uncomfortable when dealing with women other than those he creates in his novels."

Among the many who saw the play was a homely young man with red hair who looked as though he had outgrown his clothes. Algernon Charles Swinburne, son of an admiral and the titled daughter of an earl, had heard of Adah from his good friend and mentor, Rossetti. Just recently returned from a walking tour through France and Italy, he had not met Adah, but heard her mentioned so frequently at the Rossetti home in Cheyne Walk that he decided to investigate this exciting phenomenon for himself.

Painfully—almost pathologically—shy, yet at the same time inclined to boisterous turns of enthusiasm, Swinburne was one of the most complicated geniuses of his century. A homosexual and an alcoholic, he failed for many years to recognize his disturbances, much less come to terms with them. He enjoyed periods of great elation, living wildly, then plunged into such deep moods of depression that his family and friends feared that his health, at best never robust, would give way completely.

Late in 1864 and early in 1865, when he was infatuated with Adah, was a time when he was producing some of his finest work. He wrote the brilliant lyrical tragedy, *Atalanta in Calydon,* was blocking out *Chastelard,* and in his spare time working on the magnificent *Poems and Ballads.* His energy was inexhaustible, and he often spent as long as eighteen or twenty hours at a stretch sitting at the desk in his Dorset Street lodgings. For the moment he felt strong enough to conquer the world.

Swinburne saw three performances of *Mazeppa* and, his head whirling in a cloud-strewn fantasy, imagined himself in love with Adah. Rossetti, in whom he confided some of his feelings, offered to arrange a meeting; Swinburne recoiled, preferring his dreams to the reality.

But Rossetti refused to accept the refusal, and told Adah about her new admirer. She was unfamiliar with Swinburne's work, so Rossetti lent her a copy of *Rosamond,* a play in blank verse that Swinburne had written in 1860, while at Oxford. She was flattered that someone so talented should be interested in her, but Rossetti hastened to put her straight.

Swinburne, he said, was too shy to love a woman except in his daydreams.

Adah was amused, replying that no man on earth was that shy.

The result of the discussion was a ten-guinea wager. Adah volunteered to go to Swinburne's lodgings, unannounced, and felt certain he would overcome his diffidence sufficiently to make love to her. Rossetti accepted the wager—with misgivings.

Canceling another engagement, Adah had herself driven to Swinburne's house one night after her performance. The poet himself came to the door in response to her knock, and was so stunned that Adah thought he would faint. She asked if she might come in, and he nodded, speechless.

What had started as a joke in dubious taste became something else. Adah felt deep sympathy for the awkward, inarticulate young man and, using all her experience and cunning, worked hard to put him at his ease. Discussing the occasion many years later with his friend, Theodore Watts-Dunton, Swinburne said, "We sat in the kitchen for hours, drinking ale and spearing cheese."

Naturally they discussed poetry. Swinburne, who loved an audience, recited some of his work. Adah, realizing she was in the presence of a great talent, in her turn became shy, and Swinburne had difficulty persuading her to recite some of her own poems. Finally he succeeded, and was astonished to discover that the goddess was literate. His cup of joy overflowed.

Adah needed courage to tell him of the wager with Rossetti, but could not bear to fool him. Swinburne, whose sense of humor was juvenile, whooped with delight, and when she revealed that Rossetti would appear in mid-morning, insisted that she must remain as his guest, using his bedroom while he slept on a divan in the little drawing room.

They didn't retire until dawn, however, for both became engrossed in their discussion. Each was delighted to find that the other was a rebel who scorned convention, middle-class attitudes, and the judgment of a scandal-mongering society. They were kindred spirits, and were completely relaxed and at home with each other by the time they went off to separate rooms.

Rossetti, appearing at Dorset Street in the late morning, was solemnly greeted by Adah and Swinburne, attired in dressing gowns. Swinburne watched gleefully as the ten guineas were paid over to Adah.

That evening the gangling young poet saw *Mazeppa* again, this time as the guest of the star. He soon started showing up every night, and when Adah canceled other engagements in order to dine with him after her performance, people began to talk. A few words even crept into the columns of the caustic London *Review:* "The Menken looks like Lady Godiva in a shift. Of course, respectable people go to see the spectacle, and not her figure. One can only speculate on the motives of a poet."

It was inevitable that the affair that had been a fancy should become a fact. Literary and intellectual circles found the combination incredible but entertaining. It was easy to understand what the inexperienced Swinburne saw in the glamorous Adah, but no one could understand why she was attracted to him.

She kept a discreet silence and confided in no one except Ed James in New York, to whom she wrote, "You've heard stories of a new romance, I imagine, but don't be worried, and tell Joe Brice I don't intend to do anything foolish.

"I am not in love. He is a dear, unpredictable boy who has much to learn, and I enjoy being his teacher. He behaves like a spoiled child, but I forgive him because his poems soar to Heaven like angels. His lyrics will live for centuries after we have turned to dust."

Her interest seems to have been twofold. Like so many women of great experience, she enjoyed tutoring a shy novice. And his poetry, expressing so much that she had tried without success to say, enthralled her. For a short time the ill-matched couple enjoyed a honeymoon.

Excerpts from the poem Swinburne wrote for Adah, *"Laus Veneris"* ("The Praise of Venus") best express his feelings during this idyllic period:

Asleep or waking is it? for her neck,
Kissed over close, wears yet a purple speck
   Wherein the pained blood falters and goes out;
Soft, and stung softly—fairer for a fleck.

. . .

Lo, this is she that was the world's delight;
The old grey years were parcels of her might;
   The strewings of the ways wherein she trod
Were the twain seasons of the day and night.

. . .

Behold, my Venus, my Soul's body, lies
With my love laid upon her garment-wise,
   Feeling my love in all her limbs and hair
And shed between her eyelids through her eyes.

. . .

Love is not glad nor sorry, as I deem;
Labouring he dreams, and labours in the dream,
   Till when the spool is finished, lo I see
His web, reeled off, curls and goes out like steam.

Night falls like fire; the heavy lights run low,
And as they drop, my blood and body so

Shake as the flame shakes, full of days and hours
That sleep not neither weep as they go.

. . .

Ah love, there is no better life than this;
To have known love, how bitter a thing it is,
    And afterward be cast out of God's sight;
Yea, these that know not, shall they have such bliss.

High up in barren heaven before his face
As we twain in the heavy-hearted place,
    Remembering love and all the dead delight,
And all that time was sweet with for a space?

For till the thunder in the trumpet be,
Soul may divide from body, but not we
    One from another; I hold thee with my hand,
I let mine eyes have all their will of thee,

I seal myself upon thee with my might,
Abiding alway out of all men's sight
    Until God loosen over sea and land
The thunder of the trumpets of the night.

"S. read me a poem written for me," Adah tells her
Diary in February, 1865. "He says it is not yet finished,
but I don't see how he can improve on it. He will find
some way, of course, for he won't rest until a line is perfect. I can't help wishing he pursued other things with the
same intensity."

It appears that she was beginning to tire of him as a
lover. She also found it inconvenient to have her name
linked exclusively with his. Other men no longer sought
her company, and she found the antics of the immature
Swinburne wearing. She had become a member of the
inner circle of literati that met daily at the Sabloniere
Hotel in Leicester Square, and was intensely interested in
the discussions of the Pre-Raphaelites who were seeking a

return to classical purity in their work. But Swinburne made it difficult for her to concentrate.

When she listened to another man, he jealously interrupted. When she asked questions, he invariably answered, regardless of whether he really knew the answers to her queries. And when she tried to express her own views, he cut in to correct her.

The refusal of his family to recognize her existence further increased tensions. Lady Jane Swinburne, the poet's mother, made a number of brief trips to London to visit her son, but refused to meet his spectacular mistress. Admiral Charles Swinburne sent his son a firm letter, urging him to terminate the liaison, and the young man carelessly left the communication on a table, where Adah saw it. She was hurt, or professed to be hurt, and they quarreled.

Late in the winter of 1865 his behavior became erratic and unpredictable. He failed to appear at Astley's after a performance to escort Adah to supper, and she was stranded. She considered it absurd that someone in such great demand should be forced to eat alone, and upbraided Swinburne for his negligence.

He sulked, drank too much, and began to stay away for three or four evenings at a time. Adah, never one to tolerate indifference from any man, began making other engagements. Swinburne reacted with jealous violence, and not only fought with her privately, but staged a scene in the presence of Rossetti, Burne-Jones, and others at the Sabloniere round table.

"I shall not be surprised," Laura Seymour wrote her sister, "when Adah Menken gives up her Swinburne. She respects his talents as a writer, and so has tolerated his vile tempers with better grace than I could show. She is a woman and he a boy. She needs a man, and I am surprised they have spent this long a time in each other's company.

She begins to avoid him, so the end will not be long in coming."

There was a task Adah wanted to complete, however, before she said farewell to Swinburne. She had been working on a poem to him, a reply to *"Laus Veneris,"* and late in the spring of 1865 it was ready. She called it "Dreams of Beauty" and, perhaps because it was influenced by him, it was one of her better works. It began:

> Visions of Beauty, of Light, and of Love,
>   Born in the soul of a Dream,
> Lost, like the phantom-bird under the dove,
>   When she flies over a stream—
>
> Come ye, through portals where angel wings droop,
>   Moved by the heaven of sleep?
> Or are ye mockeries, crazing a soul,
>   Doomed with its waking to weep?
>
> I could believe ye were shadows of earth,
>   Echoes of hopes that are vain,
> But for the music ye bring to my heart,
>   Waking its sunshine again.

She confided to Eléonore Fechter that she hoped *"Laus Veneris"* and "Dreams of Beauty" would be published jointly in one volume. Certainly she was too intelligent to imagine that she was in Swinburne's class as a poet, but she pictured the little book as a permanent memorial to a grand passion. The fact that he had bored her as a lover, even though stimulating her intellectually, was beside the point. Adah always thought in self-dramatizing terms.

Others knew of the scheme before Swinburne learned of it. Reade advised against it, and the diplomatic Rossetti expressed careful, hedging doubts. But Adah, dreaming of seeing herself immortalized in print, refused to listen. She wrote a total of thirteen verses, the first of six cantos that she planned.

Then she showed her efforts to Swinburne. He could have let her down gently, but the demands of his own ego forced him to condemn her work in scathing, mocking terms. Adah, who found it hard to accept criticism, could not tolerate ridicule. She lost her own explosive temper, smashed furniture in his Dorset Street lodgings, and terrified him by cursing fluently in French and Spanish as well as English.

Then she stormed out, and the affair was ended.

"Laus Veneris" first saw the light of print when privately published in January, 1866. Adah did no more work on "Dreams of Beauty," and what had been intended as the first canto appeared as a complete poem in her posthumously published *Infelicia.*

One of her most famous, vicious, and crude remarks was widely repeated soon after the relationship with Swinburne was terminated. "He doesn't know and won't learn," she said, "that there's more to love-making than biting."

CHAPTER XII

MARRIAGE À LA MODE

In the Beginning, God, the great Schoolmaster, wrote upon the white leaves of our souls the text of life, in His own autograph.

Upon all souls it has been written alike.

We set forth with the broad, fair characters penned in smoothness and beauty, and promise to bear them back so, to the Master, who will indorse them with eternal life.

But, alas! How few of us can return with these copybooks unstained and unblotted?

—"The Autograph on the Soul"

THE ENORMOUSLY successful London run of *Mazeppa* finally concluded in midsummer of 1865. E. T. Smith, who had never made such a huge profit from any one play, wanted Adah to appear again at Astley's in the autumn. She was agreeable, provided he found another vehicle for her. She had grown heartily sick of *Mazeppa,* even though it had brought her wealth and international fame. The producer, now her good friend, promised to begin a search for a new play at once, and Adah packed her many trunks for a quick trip to New York.

Joe Brice had been urging her to return so she could complete her divorce action against Newell, and she agreed. She had no other reason to go home, but there was nothing to keep her in England, either. A large crowd of

English friends saw her off, and she landed in New York on August 24, 1865. Two days later she went into court and was granted her freedom from Newell.

Times were changing rapidly, Adah had been absent from the United States for a year and she found her native land strangely alien. President Lincoln had been assassinated, the Civil War was over, and the controversial Tennesseean, Andrew Johnson, was now in the White House. A spirit of vengeance against the conquered Confederacy enveloped the land, and the arts were not flourishing. Mark Twain's *The Celebrated Jumping Frog of Calaveras County* and James Russell Lowell's "Ode Recited at the Harvard Commemoration" were, perhaps, the only literary works of merit published during the year. The theater was relying on plays of light-weight stature, and Adah could have done *Mazeppa* again, had she been in the mood.

Most of her friends had scattered, many were growing older and grayer, and a younger group of hopefuls now sat at the table in the far corner at Pfaff's. Ed and Hannah James were faithful, but other friends were occupied with their own problems. The United States and Adah, the international star, had drifted apart.

She spent only a few weeks at her Seventh Avenue house, and a letter from Smith telling her he had found the right play sent her hurrying back to her suite at Cataldi's in London. She was greeted so enthusiastically by a crowd of authors, actors, and gallants that she observes somewhat plaintively in her *Diary*, "I seem to have more friends here than in New York."

Her life's pattern was set: she made new friends quickly, but the old fell away rapidly, too. She neither demanded nor gave long-term loyalty. Undoubtedly her self-absorption was one reason for the constant turnover, and probably her hedonism was another. Adah lived for the pleasures of the moment, and there were few who could maintain her pace.

Work was her most immediate concern, and she was delighted when she read the play Smith had selected for her, *Child of the Sun,* by John Brougham. Smith had chosen it for blatantly obvious reasons. The leading role was that of a pagan girl in the tropics, a part that would give Adah the opportunity and excuse to wear a variety of scanty costumes. She liked the play because the star's role was long, arduous, and melodramatic. She would be required to spend the better part of her evening on-stage, and would play opposite three different leading men.

She plunged into rehearsal with enthusiasm, unable or unwilling to see that *Child of the Sun* was a weak, artificial drama. Only an actress of great sensitivity and talent could have sustained it, and Adah was lacking in both qualities.

Friends brought down the house when the play opened on October 9, 1865, and Adah took repeated curtain calls. She was the guest of honor at a supper party given by Smith that night and, as the champagne flowed, the happy crowd predicted a long and joyous run. The newspaper critics deemed otherwise. *"Child of the Sun,"* said the *Daily Telegraph,* "is as puerile as its title."

"Foolish," echoed the *Morning Post.* "Boring," declared the *Daily News.* "A mistake," said *Bell's,* summing up the reactions.

Adah's personal reviews were a trifle better, but comments on her performance were sparse. Instead, the critics concentrated their attention on her body, and agreed that she had lost none of her curves since they had seen her the preceding year. It was galling that she wasn't taken seriously, and she was humiliated when the *Morning Post* asked, "Why doesn't she play in *Mazeppa* again?"

Smith thought the suggestion eminently sensible. Adah

had enough of a following to give *Child of the Sun* a four-week run, but business subsequently dropped off so sharply that the engagement was terminated on four days' notice to the actors.

Adah, who had been spending money freely in her usual openhanded manner, became panicky. She had anticipated a long engagement, and had made commitments accordingly. Rooms at Cataldi's were scarce, and she had taken a lease on her suite until March 31, 1866, at fifty pounds a week. Minnie had to be supported, and so did the other two servants who were now permanent members of her ménage. She had sent for a number of expensive new gowns from Paris, and had ordered a small coach which she intended to use for daily drives.

Under the circumstances, Smith found it easy to persuade her to play *Mazeppa* again. A local supporting cast was recruited, and Adah broadened her own accent to mesh with that of the English actors. Day and night rehearsals were scheduled, and the opening was set for November 20. An unexpected hitch developed when the horse Adah had used the previous year proved to be unavailable, but she recklessly agreed to use another.

The runway that Smith had stored in the cellar was hauled out, dusted off and joined together. Adah began practicing with her new horse, and the animal, unaccustomed to the frenzy of theatrical life, reacted violently. Adah claimed she could tame the mare, but the horse bolted one afternoon, and raced up and down the runway while Adah was lashed to her back. Trainers and stagehands were unable to intervene, but Adah freed herself, climbed onto the animal's back and calmed her.

Everyone in the theater applauded, and the frightened Smith promised to get another mount at once. Adah, quietly feeding sugar to the mare, said she was satisfied there would be no more difficulty. She was right; there-

after the mare behaved beautifully, and *Mazeppa* opened
on schedule.

The box office came to life immediately. Thousands who
had not seen Adah carried through the audience in her
pink tights bought tickets, as well as other thousands
anxious to repeat their previous experience. "The Menken
shines once more in her firmament," said Mark Lemon in
Punch, "and all's right with the world."

London may have been happy, but Adah was not. She
needed a challenge in order to maintain her interest in
life. She had been playing in *Mazeppa* for so long that the
part, the play, and her very existence bored her. Although
she still enjoyed the company of such friends as Reade,
Laura, and Rossetti, she needed something more to spark
her. She patched up her feud with Swinburne, but did not
resume her affair with him. They spoke civilly when they
met at the Sabloniere, but Adah was deaf to hints that he
might like to reestablish a closer relationship.

It was during this period that she began to think seriously of publishing a book of poems. Reade and Laura encouraged her, as did the Fechters, and the diplomatic
Rossetti could see nothing wrong with the idea. Adah con-
templated making a weekend trip to Kent to discuss the
project with Dickens, and wrote him a note, suggesting
that she come to see him.

He preferred to keep his reputation intact. "Dear Adah
Menken," he wrote to her, "I regret that my schedule
won't permit a visit at present. But I hope you'll allow me
to assist you in every way."

Adah took him at his word, and sent him sheafs of her
poems with the request that he select those he deemed
most suitable for inclusion in a book. The winnowing
process would take the better part of two years, and
Dickens proved to be a faithful correspondent. Like so

many other members of his profession, he was interested in her as an artist rather than as a woman.

Lovers visited the suite at Cataldi's several nights each week, and what shreds of reputation had clung to Adah were now blown away by the strong breeze of fresh gossip. Her *Diary* indicates virtually nothing on the subject of these brief liaisons, and it must be assumed that Adah did not consider them important. She had time on her hands, men wanted to take her to bed, and she saw no good reason to refuse them. She hated being alone, and if she got nothing else out of the affairs, she could console herself with the thought that she wasn't lonely.

An unverified and unverifiable story made the rounds of London to the effect that a gentleman-in-waiting at the royal court inadvertently mentioned Adah's name in the presence of Queen Victoria. Her Majesty supposedly sniffed, glowered, and said icily, "We have not heard of such a person."

The high society doors that had been opened to Adah were now slammed in her face. The ladies who had been willing to condone a single affair, that with Swinburne, could not tolerate the company of a woman who took many lovers. Once again Adah found herself in the familiar position of living outside the invisible pale. She pretended not to mind, but her depression deepened, and in the winter of 1865–66 she wrote some of her gloomiest poetry.

A letter sent to an unidentified intimate from Cataldi's in January, 1866, sums up her mood:

"Today, Roberto, I should like to see you if you are good-tempered, and think you could be bored with me and my ghosts. They will be harmless to you, these ghosts of mine; they are sad, soft-footed things that wear my brain, and live on my heart—that is, the fragment I have left to be called *heart.*

"Apropos of that I hear you are married—I am glad of

that; I believe all good men should be married. Yet I don't believe in women being married. Somehow they all sink into nonentities after this epoch in their existences. That is the fault of female education. They are taught from their cradles to look upon marriage as the one event of their lives. That accomplished, nothing remains.

"Byron might have been right after all: 'Man's love is of man's life a thing apart; 'tis woman's whole existence.' If this is true we do not wonder to find so many stupid wives —they are simply doing the 'whole existence' sort of thing. Good women are rarely clever, and clever women are rarely good. Now I am digressing into mere twaddle from what I started to say to you.

"Come when you can get time, and tell me of our friends, the gentle souls of air; mine fly from me only, to fill my being with the painful remembrance of their lost love for me—*even me!* once the blest and chosen. Now a royal tigress waits, in her lonely jungle, the coming of the king of forests. Brown gaiters not excluded." She closed it: "Yours, through all stages of local degradation, Infelix Menken."

The pall lifted in early March when Adah received a letter from R. R. Kupfer of Vienna, inviting her to appear there the following month in a German-language version of *Mazeppa* at the world-famous Theater an den Wien. Here was a challenge worthy of her steel and, as business had started to fall off, Smith agreed to release her at the end of March.

Adah had never spoken German extensively, and Fechter hastily translated her part for her, then coached her in it. She canceled all social engagements and threw herself into the task with such furious energy that Fechter, a man abundantly supplied with reserves of vitality, soon was exhausted.

An April 1, Adah invaded the Continent of Europe for

the first time, accompanied by an entourage consisting of Minnie, an English butler and housemaid, one black mare, two poodles, and thirty-eight pieces of luggage. She tarried in Paris only long enough to change trains, and went on to Vienna in the brightest mood she had enjoyed in years.

The capital of the Austro-Hungarian Empire was unlike any other city on earth. Peasants might be oppressed, national minorities might be silenced, and anti-Semitism might be rife, but nothing was allowed to disturb the serene façade that Emperor Franz Josef demanded. The beautiful blue Danube flowed sluggishly past the metropolis, its waters a muddy gray-brown. Johann Strauss the Younger was the Waltz King, and the family orchestra, which he had inherited from his father and in turn had handed to his brothers, Eduard and Josef, joyously played his new compositions, which the citizens hummed, whistled, and sang. The Burg-Theater and the magnificent new Opera House were crowded nightly, bands played in the Prater and families sat at benches beneath the trees, eating sausages, drinking beer, and exchanging the basic staple of Viennese society—gossip.

On the surface, Vienna was a frivolous city, and her cozy culture was as *gemütlich* as her many composers, authors, actors, and singers claimed. Beneath the façade, however, was a corset of steel. Franz Josef, who had ascended the throne as a result of the Revolution of 1848, had a long memory and did not intend to permit liberals and radicals to draw a deep breath. Count Moritz Esterhazy, Count Richard Belcredi, and other conservative members of the old aristocracy held the reins of power tightly in their manicured, gloved hands.

A wit who observed that the Empire was a submerged iceberg and that Vienna was an ornately shaped mound of *schlag* (whipped cream that floated on coffee) was sent to prison for his audacity. Certainly the stranger saw only the gay frivolity and, after gazing in awe at the many palaces inhabited by archdukes, dukes, princes, and counts, might have concluded that the royal court was a maraschino cherry sitting at the apex of the *schlag*. Dragoon and Hussar officers in high boots kissed the hands of magnificently gowned ladies, and the Emperor benignly allowed the nobles to dance their sedate waltzes and mazurkas.

The royal emphasis on propriety was discreet but ever-present. England's Victoria was gaining the reputation as the guardian of middle-class virtues, but Franz Josef privately deplored English moral standards. The behavior at his court was impeccable, and if couples sometimes sneaked off to a country castle for an extra-marital liaison, they took great pains to conceal the truth from His Majesty.

The decorous but fun-loving Vienna fell in love with Adah, and her *Diary* contains the completely false notation, "A European San Francisco!" She would soon learn better.

Kupfer, who met her train, had engaged a suite of rooms for her at the old, splendid Three Hussars Hotel, and presented her with an armload of roses. There were more roses waiting for her in her rooms. Adah was enchanted, and when she went for a stroll in the Prater, a crowd formed and followed her. She accepted the tribute to her fame, not realizing that the Viennese were unaware of her identity and that her low-necked, tight-fitting lavender gown with matching accessories was causing the furor.

The disciplined actors at the Theater an den Wien were respectful, polite, and so talented that, even at the first rehearsal of *Mazeppa*, they made Adah look like a rank amateur. Kupfer pondered, rubbing his bald head, and quietly postponed the opening until mid-May. A few days later he concluded that Adah was incapable of rising to Viennese theatrical standards on her own, and sent a plea to Fechter for help. In the meantime, of course, he said nothing to disconcert the star, knowing she would become angry if he criticized her performance in a play that she had, for all practical purposes, made her own.

The extra time gave Adah more leisure, and she plunged into a round of social life. Poets, dramatists, and novelists flourished in the city, and although their names were strange and their work unfamiliar to the woman from New Orleans, their obvious admiration warmed her. She felt completely at ease with them, and happily allowed a platoon to escort her to dinner every evening. As always when dealing with writers, she was in her element.

One night she was presented to Johann Strauss, and took pains to charm Frau Strauss, a former singer. The move paid dividends, and she was invited to their home, where she listened raptly to dozens of Strauss compositions played on the piano. One of Adah's great talents was her ability to draw shy creative artists out of their shells, and Strauss responded to her like all the rest. She was flattered, but not surprised, when he promised to dedicate a new waltz to her.

Then, suddenly, Adah's past caught up with her. She returned to her hotel suite after rehearsal early one evening in mid-April to find Baron Friedrich von Eberstadt waiting for her.

She greeted him civilly, but her *Diary* contains the icy declaration, "I could have carved out his heart."

The Baron was older, grayer, and heavier, but was still the lighthearted playboy who had not hesitated to seduce a teen-aged girl, take her to Havana, and abandon her. He asked Adah to dine with him, and was refused. Making it plain that he was still enormously attracted to her and that he wanted to resume their relationship after all these years, he begged her to reconsider. Adah asked him to return the following day for her answer.

Throughout all of her stormy life Adah had frequently

lost her temper, but had never treated anyone with calculated, vicious anger. Von Eberstadt, however, held a
place in her "esteem" and "affections" that was unique,
and she had spent many years thirsting for revenge. He
was handing her the chance on a baronial platter, and she
concocted a scheme as diabolical as it was clever.

Adah made it her habit in social relations with men to
remain silent and let the male animal talk. Therefore,
even though she had been in Vienna only a short time,
she had already learned that the Emperor's court was
prim, formal, and stuffy. According to Ed James, who later
gleaned at least a portion of the story—without ever learning why she hated the Baron—that was all she needed to
know.

Von Eberstadt arrived punctually, confident of Adah's
decision. She informed him she would be willing to live
with him again, discreetly, provided that he took her to
the royal court and presented her to the Emperor. The
Baron was shocked, and with good cause, as Franz Josef
was not in the habit of receiving foreign actresses of
dubious reputation. But Adah insisted, waving aside the
financial offers that meant nothing to her.

At last the Baron capitulated, and although he could
promise no miracle, said he would do what he could. For
the next six days Adah heard nothing. She rehearsed, went
sightseeing, and dined with her new friends; she behaved
as though all was normal. Only her *Diary* reveals her
tension.

Von Eberstadt returned to inform her that he had accomplished the impossible through the help of a royal
chamberlain who was indebted to him. The Emperor's
next "informal" reception was scheduled to be held at the
Hofburg on the afternoon of May 8, and an invitation
would be sent to the American actress. The Baron made
it clear that he intended to confine himself to a brief re-

mark or two when he presented her to His Majesty, who
would not appreciate details about the nature of the entertainment offered in *Mazeppa*. Luckily the court was in-
bred, interested only in its own doings, and as the play
had not yet opened, it was unlikely that the gentlemen
who combed undesirables from the list of guests would
know either *Mazeppa* or its star.

Considering his mission completed, the Baron wanted
his reward, but Adah firmly held him off. In the light of
past experience, she told him, the bargain would not be
concluded until she had curtsied before Franz Josef. Von
Eberstadt grumbled, complaining that she was causing
him all sorts of difficulty, including the need to send his
wife off to their country estate. Adah remained unimpressed.

The following morning a dressmaker was summoned,
and Adah went into a secret session with the woman. Rehearsals were postponed while she examined materials and
stood for fittings. Kupfer was sympathetically understanding; after all, a woman didn't receive an invitation to the
court of Franz Josef every day in the year. That afternoon
Charles and Eléonore Fechter arrived, and Eléonore later
supplied some of the details that Adah failed to pass along
to Ed James.

Fechter took charge of rehearsals, Adah's performance
improved, and the atmosphere at the Theater an den
Wien became brighter. Adah worked hard and, always
professional in her attitude, made no complaints. Visits
from the dressmaker were her only distraction, and she
became so nervous as May 8 approached that the Fechters
wondered if she might be working too hard.

No rehearsals were held on the great day. The Baron
arrived at Adah's hotel in his court uniform, complete
with decorations and a plumed helmet. She greeted him in

a floor-length cloak of embroidered, beaded silk and, following the custom of the Austrian court, wore a small veil.

Imperial troops stood at attention in the Hofburg courtyard, and household guards taken from a score of prominent regiments lined the corridors. Thousands of candles burned in magnificent crystal chandeliers, and Adah, making her way slowly toward the throne room with Von Eberstadt, caught glimpses of rooms with damask-lined walls. The sumptuous elegance of the ancient palace of the Holy Roman Emperors was breathtaking.

Forty or fifty guests waiting to be presented to Franz Josef were milling in anterooms, and Adah's name was checked off several lists. The Baron was nervous, but she maintained a deceptive calm, which vanished when they were admitted to the throne room. Still more troops were in place, swords drawn, and the guests were herded together behind velvet ropes at one side of the chamber. Dukes and archdukes entered and moved to the positions near the throne to which royal protocol assigned them.

Then the swords were raised in salute, and Franz Josef, imperturbable in side-whiskers and a white uniform, came into the hall. Men bowed low, ladies curtsied and he took his throne. The velvet ropes were removed, and the presentations began. Members of the nobility came first, so Adah's wait was long. With nothing better to occupy her, she watched the Emperor, and saw that sometimes he nodded, and only occasionally did he deign to speak. The routine of the "informal" reception was dreary, and time dragged.

At last it was Adah's turn. Von Eberstadt led her forward, bowed, and spoke her name. She sank to the floor in a graceful curtsy, throwing aside her cloak. There was a moment of stunned, disbelieving silence, and no one moved. Adah Isaacs Menken, The Naked Lady, was wearing a snug-fitting gown of flesh-colored jersey, remarkably similar to the *Mazeppa* costume she had made famous. From a distance of ten feet she looked nude.

A woman in the throng giggled hysterically, and several men coughed. Then Franz Josef stood, his face wooden, and, looking neither to the right nor the left, stalked from the chamber. The reception had come to an abrupt end.

Adah quietly gathered her cloak around her and walked to the courtyard, where carriages were waiting for the guests. The apoplectic Baron had stomped off, so the next scene of the drama was decidedly anticlimactic. One of the officers was forced to obtain a public carriage to take Adah back to her hotel.

She was pleased with herself, and had good cause to believe she had evened the score. Friedrich von Eberstadt was a ruined man. Not until much later did she learn how thorough was his disgrace. He was banned from the imperial court, and retired to his country estate. Then he hoped to escape to a foreign refuge until the incident could be forgotten, but the autocratic Franz Josef issued an order prohibiting him from leaving the country. He spent his last years at his estate, bitter, lonely, and shunned by everyone who knew him.

Adah celebrated the occasion at a gay dinner with the Fechters, who were astonished and horrified by what she had done; no woman could treat one of the mightiest monarchs on earth so cavalierly. But Adah didn't care, and actually drank several glasses of champagne. "Few women," Eléonore wrote to Burne-Jones in London, "have hated as she hates. I would love to learn how the poor man incurred her ill will."

That evening Adah paid the inevitable penalty for her vulgar jest. A civilian official from the Ministry of the Interior and three uniformed officers were waiting at her hotel, and she was informed that she had been banished from the empire. If she failed to leave Vienna within forty-eight hours and if she dared to pause anywhere within the imperial borders she would be placed under arrest. The American legation, she was told, had been informed of the ruling.

Kupfer made frantic efforts to have the order rescinded, but his cause was hopeless. Franz Josef had been made to suffer a personal affront, and the offender could not and would not be allowed to remain. The Theater an den Wien would have to change its bill. Kupfer filed a lawsuit against Adah, and although a Viennese court eventually awarded him damages, he was unable to collect, as she never returned to Austrian soil.

The incident created a sensation, although the newspapers, which were subject to censorship, printed nothing about the scandal. The novelists, dramatists, and poets who had been Adah's companions made themselves conspicuous by their absence. And Johann Strauss protested vehemently to friends that it had never been his intention to dedicate a waltz to Adah. Only the Fechters, who carried French passports, dared to be seen with her. They saw her off when she departed, but no one else appeared at the railroad station. She had obtained her revenge, but her pocketbook had suffered.

Nevertheless there was a bright spot on the horizon. Adah had been discussing a new project with Fechter, who knew how intensely she hated *Mazeppa* and, being an actor himself, sympathized with her. He believed that a seldom-played comedy, *Les Pirates de la Savane,* by Anicet Bourgeois and Ferdinand Dugue, might be an excellent vehicle for her. He promised to obtain a copy of the script and felt certain that, if she liked it, he could arrange a Paris production.

Adah's hopes were high as she set out for Paris, but she had no intention of remaining in France through the rest of the spring and summer. There was no reason for her

to visit London again, so she decided to return to the
United States, and sailed from Le Havre after spending
a week getting acquainted with Paris. The voyage marked
another major turning point in her life.

A fellow passenger was "Captain" James Barkley, a
suave, extraordinarily handsome man in his forties with
courtly manners and the massive build of a John C. Heenan. Adah met him in the main saloon, where he was playing cards, and they were attracted to each other at once.
By the end of the voyage they were inseparable companions, and their romance flourished after they reached New
York.

"I thought I was dead," Adah says in her *Diary*, "but
J.B. awakens my soul."

Ed and Hannah James did not approve of the "Captain," who said he had been a cavalry officer in Grant's
Western Corps during the war. But Adah refused to hear
a word against him, so they kept quiet, aware of her fierce
loyalties to a new love.

A thrice-married woman who had also entertained
countless lovers would have been foolish to erect a barrier
of false modesty, but Adah went overboard. Much to the
distress of the Jameses and of Joe Brice, Barkley moved
into her house. Public opinion, as usual, meant nothing
to her.

Barkley, who dressed in expensive clothes but had no
visible means of support, tried to take over the complete
management of Adah's life, but she refused to let him
interfere with her career. She was offered a return engagement at the Broadway Theater in *Mazeppa*, but she
refused. Barkley disagreed with her decision, and they
quarreled. Thereafter their relations were stormy, although they continued to live together.

Fechter kept his word and sent Adah a copy of *Pirates de
la Savane*. She loved the play, which would not tax her

talents and would give her innumerable opportunities to wear abbreviated costumes as the prisoner of a pirate crew. She also found a spot in the last act which, with rewriting, would give her the chance to ride a horse, and she wrote to Fechter, telling him enthusiastically that she would be delighted to do the play provided the change was made. It had been understood from the outset that he would be her director.

Fechter wrote again, saying that he had obtained the Théâtre de la Gaité for the engagement, and that all Paris was awaiting the actress who had set the court of Franz Josef on its ear. Adah booked passage for herself and her entourage on August 19, and it was tacitly understood that Barkley would accompany her. He had intimated to her that he had retired from business and was living on his investments, which made it possible for him to live and travel where he pleased.

The question of marriage had arisen, and Barkley was anxious to make Adah his wife, but she sidestepped. Three husbands had been three too many, and she saw no reason to marry again. Then, late in July, she discovered that what she had suspected for some weeks was true—she was pregnant. Two physicians confirmed the diagnosis, and it seemed likely that the baby had been conceived on board ship in May.

New plans had to be made at once. Adah wrote to Fechter, telling him the opening of *Pirates* would have to be postponed until late February or early March. She planned, however, to sail as scheduled, and would have the baby in Paris. Suddenly concerned about her reputation—or what might be left of it—she believed there would be less talk in France, where she was not yet well known. Also, under the circumstances, it now became mandatory for her to marry Barkley. It was arranged that the weary alderman, Joe Brice, would marry the couple at Adah's home on August 19, a few hours before they sailed.

A week before the wedding, Ed James went privately to Adah with shocking news. As editor of the *Clipper* he knew everyone in sporting circles and, having distrusted Barkley from the start, had made an intensive private investigation. In his own words, taken from his biography, "Barkley's claim that he had served as an officer in the Union Army during the recent hostilities was without foundation. He was neither an officer nor a private on either side during that conflict.

"For many years he had been a professional gambler, earning his living at cards on Mississippi River boats. After the end of the war he transferred his activities to steamships crossing the Atlantic, and had sailed many times between New York and the ports of England and France. He was a penniless scoundrel and a despicable rogue."

Adah, with unerring instinct, had made another bad choice. But her pregnancy made it necessary for her to go through with the wedding.

She confronted Barkley with what James had told her, and the scene that followed might have been taken from a second-rate contemporary drama. Unfortunately, it was all too real. Adah had assumed that Barkley was what he had represented himself to be, a wealthy, retired businessman. He, on the other hand, had falsely concluded that she was rich. According to James, he was highly indignant when he discovered she was almost out of funds, and accused her of deceiving him. He was enough of a gentleman, however, to make an honest woman of her.

The last days before the wedding were hectic. Minnie and the English servants busily packed Adah's luggage. The bride-to-be hastily had some maternity clothes made. In her spare time she visited Joe Brice at his office, and instructed him to draw up a new will for her. She directed that 80 percent of her estate be given to her child and 10 percent to Ed and Hannah James. The remaining 10 percent was to be spent on "the publication of new editions of my book, *Infelicia,* which is nearing completion." Barkley was specifically excluded from sharing in the estate, "for reasons best known to myself, which I deem sufficient to give me valid cause for such exclusion."

On August 17, Adah indulged in a quixotic, almost inexplicable gesture, and had lunch with Newell. He was now a man of great prominence in the newspaper world, having become a principal editor and writer at the *Herald.* She sent a note to his office, asking him to meet her at Pfaff's, and he agreed.

"I did not know then and I do not now know the purpose of that meeting," Newell declares in his biography. "I can but assume that Miss Menken felt lonely, and hoped to obtain solace from one who had been close to her."

She mentions the meeting briefly in her *Diary:* "Saw N. He is much the same as ever, a bit thinner, and wears stronger eyeglasses. He needs a wife. Hope he finds one."

Newell is far more complimentary. "On this, the last occasion I was to see Miss Menken, she was far lovelier than I had remembered her. She glowed with a youthful radiance that made all who set eyes on her stare in wonder."

If she told him she was going to have a baby, he was tactful enough to remain silent on the matter in his biography. Presumably she did reveal that she intended to marry again, and he probably wished her good luck, knowing she needed it.

On August 18, Adah made another bow to the past, writing a last letter to Isaac Menken's parents in Cincinnati. "I am ashamed to confess to you that I rarely attend Services at Synagogue," she told them. "But in my own way I still feel close to God, and know He is close to me."

She concluded the letter with a quotation from her poem, "Hear, O Israel!" Knowing nothing of her predicament, they could not have understood why she should say:

> Courage, Courage!
> The Lord of Hosts is in the field,
> The God of Jacob is our shield.

Turning from her unhappy past to her clouded present and unsettled future, Adah was married to James Barkley on the morning of August 19, 1866, at her home, 458 Seventh Avenue. Joe Brice, who was becoming expert at this sort of thing, having married Adah to Heenan, performed the ceremony in his capacity as an alderman. Ed and Hannah James were the only witnesses.

Barkley immediately departed, walking permanently out of Adah's life. They neither met nor, according to James, communicated with each other again, and apparently Barkley knew nothing and cared less about the subsequent birth of his child. There is no record of his activities thereafter until, early in 1869, he was killed in Denver after a drunken argument with another gambler.

Adah, who had planned her wedding day with great care, now signed her new will, with Brice, Ed, and Hannah as witnesses. Then she sat down with her friends to a quiet lunch, after which they accompanied her to the ship that would take the groomless, pregnant bride to France. Few experiences in Adah's life were as grotesque as that voyage.

She left her native land for the last time, keeping her regrets to herself. After dinner, on the first night out of New York, she settled down in her cabin to study her role in *Pirates*. Unbowed and indefatigable, she looked—as always—toward the future, hoping it would be bright.

CHAPTER XIII

LA VIE PARISIENNE

Angels, is this my reward?
Is this the crown ye promised to set down on the foreheads
of the loving—the suffering—the deserted?
Where are the sheaves I toiled for?
Where the golden grain ye promised?
These are but withered leaves.
Oh, is this all?

—"Drifts That Bar My Door"

NEVER in the history of Europe had there been a gayer, more brilliant city than the Paris of Napoleon III in the years preceding the Franco-Prussian War of 1870–71. The City of Light was dazzling, generating and reflecting her own glory, and neither she nor Western civilization was ever the same again.

Baron Georges Haussmann, acting under an imperial mandate, was energetically carving grand boulevards and beautiful parks out of tortured alleyways that had endured for more than one thousand years. France was prosperous, and Napoleon, who loved money, good food, and fine drink, set the moral tone for his people by keeping a young English lady as his mistress, a liaison he foolishly believed to be a state secret.

The Spanish-born Empress Eugenie consoled herself by setting the fashion styles for the women of the world. Sleek and chic, she had a flair for clothes, if not for the management of a wayward spouse, and her feathered hats, décolletage, and high-heeled slippers were copied everywhere. Jewelers and perfume makers competed bitterly for her patronage, and dressmaking became a major Parisian industry.

Jacques Offenbach, who made light opera synonymous with his own name, composed scores with blinding speed, sometimes writing tunes on a small spinet installed in his carriage as he dashed from one theater to another, sometimes rehearsing as many as four light operas at a single time. Hector Berlioz had set the standards for more serious music, and Georges Bizet, still in his twenties, was just emerging as a new giant.

There were probably more gifted artists working with brushes and easels than at any time since the Renaissance. Paris was crowded with such brilliant painters as Monet and Renoir and Sisley, Manet and Cezanne, Daumier and Degas. There was a surfeit of genius, and men of lesser talent were ignored.

The titans of the literary world inspired awe, and their monumental quarrels shook the foundations of the magnificent new buildings rising on the boulevards. Victor Hugo was king, but members of the new generation declared their loyalty to the careful Alexandre Dumas the Younger, who carved his words with loving care. Flaubert created gems on paper, and the young Emile Zola was beginning a brilliant career as a reformer. George Sand, known to her family as Amandine Lucie Aurore Dupin Dudevant, was now an elderly woman, several times a grandmother, her scandalous affairs with Musset and Chopin far behind her. But she was still the grand old lady of French letters, and she sat enveloped in clouds of blue cigar smoke, issuing verdicts and judgments on everyone and everything.

Jules Verne daydreamed and spun fantasies of a type that a later generation would call science fiction. People smiled indulgently as they read his stories, and neither he nor anyone else realized that he possessed amazing prophetic gifts. The learned Theophile Gautier no longer wrote the poems that had brought him fame, but devoted his whole time to criticism of all the arts. His scathing wit was universally feared, and only a few members of the older generation remembered when this middle-aged man had been a wild young rebel who had worn crimson waistcoats and absurdly long hair.

Still present on the scene was the most popular author in French history, Alexandre Dumas the Elder. Now in his mid-sixties, his great days were behind him, and he no longer turned out his richly romantic novels, his countless essays on every conceivable subject, his travel books on countries he had not actually bothered to visit. Younger men smirked when they heard stories of his many mistresses, his incredible extravagances, and his unquenchable zest for life. But he still carried himself with the dignity of one who had carved a niche for himself that was unique in the annals of letters. And he could still thunder like a wounded bull when he wrote replies to the mocking jibes of striplings.

Into the maelstrom that was Paris came the pregnant Adah Isaacs Menken, seeking balm for her wounded pride, gold for her flat purse, and pleasure for her deflated ego. Thanks to her, Parisian women now smoked cigarettes in public and cut their hair short. Thanks to her, too, seminudity had become respectable on the Paris stage. The city was in her debt.

Charles and Eléonore Fechter had engaged a suite for Adah at the fashionable Hotel Suez, a literary and theatri-

cal gathering place. The news that she was expecting a
child had not surprised the Fechters. Anyone who knew
her was bound to expect the totally unpredictable. But
various arrangements had to be made, and chief among
them was the postponement of the *Pirates*. The owners
of the Théâtre de la Gaité had suggested that, rather than
risk the opening of an untried play, Adah should do a
French version of *Mazeppa* as soon as she could appear
on a stage.

She groaned, but Fechter pointed out that the idea was
sensible. The other members of the cast could be rehearsed, and she could use her time of enforced idleness
to learn her role in French. Fechter promised to direct
her privately, and predicted that she would need no more
than a day or two of co-ordination with the other actors
to be ready for the opening. This Gallic logic was unassail-
able, and Adah reluctantly agreed.

The frugal Eléonore, who had spent many years curbing
the extravagances of a husband unaware of the value of
money, took charge of Adah's personal life. The two English servants, who were unnecessary luxuries, were dismissed and sent back to London. Only the faithful Minnie
remained. A smaller suite was rented, and an inexpensive
stable was found for the mare Adah had taken from England to Vienna, then to the United States and now to
Paris.

Fechter gave his star a copy of the French version of the
hated *Mazeppa*, and Adah went to work. But the number
of hours she was willing to spend studying her part was
limited. She decided to become better acquainted with
the city, and ignored the advice of a cautious physician
who warned her that physical exercise would be harmful.
She explored Paris on foot, a delightful pastime, since
followed by thousands of her fellow Americans, and she
fell madly in love with the city.

"I'm reminded of all that is good in New Orleans, New York and London," she wrote to Ed James. "At last I have found my real home, and I pray I will be a success here."

The Café Suez was located on the ground floor of the hotel, and Adah soon adopted the local custom of sitting at a small sidewalk table and watching the world go past. A spare erect man in his fifties, who often sat nearby, thought the mother-to-be was an exceptionally handsome woman. He made inquiries, learned her identity, and presented himself.

Theophile Gautier always did things the hard way. He could have said a word to the Fechters, who were in and out of the hotel constantly, and thus saved himself the bother of an awkward introduction. Apparently it did not occur to him that, as he was virtually unknown in the United States and at best a minor figure in England, Adah might not have heard of him.

Luckily, she had become an avid reader of the mass-circulation newspapers of Paris, the *Siècle*, the *Presse*, the *Patrie*, and the *Constitutionnel*, among others. She was also acquainted with the stately *Moniteur*, for which Gautier frequently wrote, and the newest of the papers, the sharp-edged *Figaro*, to which he also contributed. Thus she was able to recognize him, and a literary friendship in Adah's familiar pattern was formed.

She was even more fortunate than she knew, for Gautier not only reviewed novels, philosophical treatises, poetry, and art, but was Paris' foremost drama critic. He was considered incorruptible, particularly by both the friends and enemies of Napoleon III's regime, which included virtually everyone in France. Even his close friends failed to realize that he had no interest in politics, and therefore refrained from either lauding or attacking the government, so they praised his high-minded abstention.

His reputation was based on his scalding sarcasm, and

he himself probably would have been startled had anyone pointed out to him that he treated his intimates with rare and gentle kindness. He had carried on a long feud with Victor Hugo, who had been living on the Isle of Jersey in exile for fifteen years after an unsuccessful foray into the political arena, but Hugo quarreled with everyone. Gautier had fought with the late Honoré de Balzac, who had indiscreetly crossed pens with him, and he had delighted in stinging Sainte-Beuve, the busybody of the era.

But he wrote elevated critiques of the novels of George Sand, whom he considered extraordinarily gifted. And he refused to join the pack baying at the heels of old Alexandre Dumas. "His work," he said quietly in the *Moniteur,* "will long outlive the thrusts of his detractors." But Gautier could be vicious when he chose. "All that distinguishes one Offenbach opera from another," he wrote in the *Figaro,* "is the title someone thrusts into his too busy little hand. How monotonous it must be to live with a single, simple tune running constantly through one's mind."

Adah's intellect fascinated Gautier, as did her easy command of the French language. She defied the cliché conventions of the Frenchman: English actresses were stupid, at best, and Americans were savage barbarians. Adah, of course, was the first American he had ever met. She knew more than he had dreamed possible about French literature, and was thoroughly familiar with the work of his own god, Voltaire. But there were gaps in her education, and he hastened to fill them, bringing her many volumes of prose and poetry from his own library.

Then he made the error of trying to arouse the interest of his friends in his protégée. Dumas, who considered pregnancy a state more to be feared than death, recoiled and fled. "The actress who is expecting a child," he wrote to Gautier, pretending to scold him, "is a woman who contradicts her own reason for being and therefore commits a crime against Nature."

Young Emile Zola, whose first novel, *Contes à Ninon*, had created a sensation, and who was finishing work on his second, *Thérèse Raquin*, thought Adah brash. Earnest, hard-working, and burning with a great zeal to reform society, Zola saw in Adah a representative of all that he considered degrading in the world. Within a matter of weeks, however, he changed his mind after discovering that she had struck a defensive pose at their first meeting. Thereafter he became her good friend, but there does not seem to be any basis for the speculative guess made by some of his contemporaries that he had borrowed details from Adah's background for his most sensational work, *Nana*, the story of a prostitute, which was published in 1880. Adah had told no one about her career in Havana, and there is no reason to assume that she confided in Zola.

George Sand received the American actress with gracious curiosity that quickly turned to hostility. Herself extraordinarily forceful, the colorful old novelist could not tolerate aggressive instincts in other women, particularly those who did not agree with her views. Their quarrel was caused by Adah's unswerving loyalty to her friends. George Sand, hearing that her guest knew Dickens, launched into a scathing attack on him, declaring that he represented the very middle-class hypocrisy he attacked. Adah leaped to his defense, hot words were exchanged over teacups, and Gautier led his angry protégé away.

"You are a fool," George Sand told him in a note. "The most that can be said for you is that, under the circumstances, you cannot play the role of seducer."

Adah's baby was born prematurely on January 1, 1867. In the morning she complained of indigestion, but insisted she would be better within a short time. Her pains grew more intense, however, and eventually the alarmed

Minnie summoned a physician. The doctor, eating his New Year's Day dinner of roast goose, tarried at his table, and arrived at the Hotel Suez just in time to take charge of the delivery.

The child was a boy, small but in perfect health. No verification can be found for the remark allegedly made by Adah when she first looked at the infant, "I had no idea the wages of sin could be so lively."

The efficient Eléonore Fechter engaged a wet-nurse and a governess, and Adah, who was anxious to resume a more active life, ignored her doctor's advice and stayed in bed for only a few days. As it was customary then for ladies to rest for three or four weeks after giving birth to a child, it was subsequently said that Adah ruined her health by her eagerness to appear on the stage. Later medical theories dispute that claim.

Impulsive, as she was in all things, Adah decided to name her son Louis, after the father of Napoleon III, Louis Bonaparte. Enemies of the regime promptly declared that she was displaying partisanship in French politics, but she paid no attention to the charge. She was too busy rehearsing *Mazeppa*.

The opening at the Théâtre de la Gaité was scheduled for January 21, and a barrage of articles in the widely read popular newspapers alerted Paris to the fact that the city would soon be treated to the spectacle of the age. The Emperor decided to attend the opening, as did the King of Greece and the Duke of Edinburgh, who were visitors in the metropolis. The demand for tickets soared, and Alexandre Dumas, who displayed a child's enthusiasm for circuses, found it difficult to obtain a seat. Finally he appealed to Fechter, who secured two for him, and he invited his intellectual son to accompany him. The offer was refused, much to the subsequent regret of Dumas the

Younger. "Had I gone with my father," he said, "I could have prevented him from making a fool of himself."

The curious and contemptuous George Sand agreed to go with old Dumas, and it was she who recorded the dramatic events that took place in Adah's dressing room after the performance. Gautier attended the play in his professional capacity as critic for the *Moniteur,* the most influential newspaper in France. Zola was there, too, as the personal guest of the star.

The sophisticates went wild. Adah's ride through the auditorium was greeted with such a storm of applause that she broke precedent and made a second tour of the runway. Napoleon III led the cheers, standing in his box, shouting and clapping his hands. Staid gentlemen jumped onto their chairs, and Adah was pelted with flowers when she appeared to take her curtain calls.

She made a deep curtsy before the Emperor, who responded by throwing her a bouquet of roses. Others followed his example, and soon the floor of the stage was covered with petals. Cynics wondered how it happened that so many men had come to the opening prepared to throw flowers at the actress, and speculated in print whether the blossoms had been supplied by a thoughtful management. Adah paid no attention to these small mosquito bites, for she had repeated her New York and London triumphs.

Napoleon III paid her the honor of going to her dressing room after the performance, and congratulated her at length, calling her a "great artist." She replied "modestly," according to George Sand, who stood outside in the corridor with Dumas. The approval of the Emperor guaranteed the success of *Mazeppa,* and it no longer mattered what the critics might say. Adah's solvency was guaranteed for months to come.

At last the burly old Dumas shouldered his way into the

crowded dressing room, with George Sand at his heels.
The next morning she gave the Younger Dumas a written eyewitness account of what was seen by a score of
well-wishers. "I was numbed," she said, "when he fell to
one knee and declared in a loud voice, 'Fairest of the fair,
delight of delights, wonder of wonders, I have lost my
heart to you.'"

The streak of ham in Adah was not as broad as that
which made the author a natural actor, but she responded
with gusto, "Sir, you take my breath away. I do not de-
serve such praise from the greatest of living novelists."

Years had passed since anyone had called Dumas great,
and he seized her hand, kissing it fervently.

Had Adah been capable of blushing, color would have
risen to her face. She did the next best thing; she pretended to be overcome by confusion.

The disgusted George Sand left the dressing room and
went back out into the corridor, so there is no authentic
account of what happened next. Within a few weeks, of
course, dozens of Parisians claimed to have been present
in the room that, at best, could hold fifteen or twenty
persons. Some said that Dumas embraced Adah and that
they kissed. Others declared that the couple arranged to
meet privately at Dumas' house on the Boulevard Malesherbes, where—according to legend—dozens of innocent
maidens, experienced matrons, and wise prostitutes had
been seduced.

Such stories were premature and exaggerated. Dumas
saw an opportunity to move back into the limelight, and
seized it. Adah, also publicity-conscious, unhesitatingly
fell in with him. Dumas meant no more to her than had
Edwin Booth at the time of her pretended elopement
with the great American actor. Several weeks were to pass
before her relationship with Dumas became complicated
and embarrassing.

The Paris newspapers treated Adah and *Mazeppa* with far greater kindness than had the New York and London press. Gautier set the tone in the *Moniteur:* "She is a beautiful and elegant woman, svelte and admirably proportioned, who mimes with rare intelligence. *Mazeppa* is a fragile drama, but so great is her skill that the audience loses sight of its faults."

The *Siècle* threw caution to the winds, declaring, "Paris must rejoice! Long have we waited for the incomparable Menken! We have not waited in vain! She is superb!"

The *Constitutionnel* scarcely bothered to mention the play as it went overboard in a hymn of unrestrained praise: "No woman since the Greek goddesses of antiquity possessed such perfection of body. The world is in the debt of La Menken, who shuns false modesty and permits us to feast on the glories of her undraped body."

The *Presse* and the *Patrie* were equally enthusiastic, and *Le Petit Journal,* the youngest, most brash and frankly sensational of the popular newspapers, printed a drawing of an almost-nude woman beneath the caption, "La Menken is gorgeous!"

The respected critic, Hippolyte de Villemessagent, waited a week before reporting to the readers of *Figaro,* and he concentrated solely on Adah, too, blithely ignoring her vehicle. "Her astonishing beauty and charm," he said, "have turned all masculine heads, and her throng of admirers, among whom can be counted the most illustrious Bohemians of Paris, excite the jealousy and envy of her own sex. Out of the barbaric jungle of North America has been plucked a flower of rare beauty and grace."

Even Adah was surprised by the excitement she had created. "I can do no wrong here," she wrote to Ed James. "Fechter tells me that Paris is very loyal to its theatrical players, and I can stay here forever, playing in as many parts as I can find. It is nice to know I am so welcome."

She was not prepared for the ferocity of her admirers' pursuit. English blue bloods had been gentlemen, and wealthy Americans had demonstrated some measure of restraint. The French did not bother with nuances, and Adah was under a state of siege, whether at her hotel, at the theater or dining in public. Men camped on her doorstep, bombarded her with flowers, jewels, and clothing; they bribed stage-door attendants to let them pass, they wrote her impassioned notes which waiters delivered, and they promised her everything from a fortune in cash to a chateau in tne country.

Adah, still recovering from her experience with Barkley, plunged into a new round of social life more frantic than any she had ever enjoyed. Parisians were realistic, and therefore did not expect actresses to behave like middle-class housewives. Adah would have been considered odd had she not taken lovers. She found it surprisingly easy to do what was expected of her.

Her first act was to take a larger suite at the Suez so she could entertain guests without being embarrassed by the wails of her infant son. "Louis is a dear baby," she tells her *Diary*, "but he has not yet learned there are times when silence is preferable to noise."

When she moved into the new suite, gentlemen who stayed for breakfast were not embarrassed by the shrill howls of a newborn infant. Adah refused to permit her son to cramp the style to which she had been so long accustomed.

Whether she relaxed her post-Havana rule and accepted money from men is not clear. A Parisian gallant who spent a night with an actress expected to pay for the privilege, and certainly Adah received many direct, straightforward offers. Her *Diary* is silent on the subject, so the matter is open to conjecture. "Her escorts," said *Le Petit Journal* with typical candor, "include many of the wealthiest men in our city, and she is also seen with prominent residents of Brussels and other foreign places."

She continued to devote her afternoons to her literary friends, and Alexandre Dumas now joined Gautier every afternoon on the pilgrimage to the Hotel Suez for tea and conversation. The old man, like a firehorse seeing flames, was not content to be just a friend, however, and began to write Adah little love notes. She refused to believe he could be serious, so he stepped up the pace of his assault. Matters would come to a climax in the spring.

In the meantime, Adah reveled in fame. The Restaurant Printemps, a favorite of the Empress Eugénie and a much frequented haunt of authors, visiting royalty, and artists willing and able to pay its outrageous prices, placed several dishes "à la Menken" on its menu. One was a crayfish bisque to which wine was added, another was a succulent beef and oyster concoction marinated in a secretly blended sauce, and a third was a compote of fresh, pitted cherries soaked in Armagnac. Only two dishes had been named in honor of the Empress herself, so—according to the standards of the boulevardiers—no one could have scaled a higher peak than Adah.

There were problems, of course, and chief among them was a statuesque brunette singer, Hortense Schneider, the reigning queen of light opera, who had been the primary target of every gallant in Paris. The buxom Hortense still had her admirers, to be sure, but overnight lost her throne. The dashing man-about-town who wanted to create an impression now walked into a restaurant with the divine Adah rather than the sublime Hortense on his arm. The sublime Hortense, who had inherited a Gallic temperament from her mother and a stubborn Germanic streak from her Alsatian father, was not one to sit back meekly and suffer in silence.

"The Menken woman," she announced to a group of

some thirty or forty intimate friends helping her celebrate the opening of a new Offenbach light opera, "is a fraud."

Le Petit Journal, its life blood dependent on such fare, gleefully reprinted the comment, then sent a representative to learn the American's reaction.

Adah, who had attended a rough, tough school of guerrilla warfare, struck for the jugular vein. "Who," she inquired blandly, "is Hortense Schneider?"

Paris girded itself for the coming battle. Wagers were placed on the two contestants, and the managements of their respective theaters fanned the glowing embers. All seats for both ladies' performances were sold out many weeks in advance. Gautier, as a friend of Adah's who had long praised the singing voice of her enemy, tried to act as a mediator, with results that could have been predicted. La Schneider cursed him and La Menken laughed at him. Baffled by the illogical females, he retired to his library.

It was inevitable that the paths of Adah and Hortense should cross, and they finally met one night at the Restaurant Imperial, one of Paris' most elegant eating and drinking places. Both were wearing feather capes and, as the *Constitutionnel* reported to its faithful readers, everyone present expected the air to resemble that of a barnyard at feeding time. All conversation ceased, waiters halted, and customers sitting at tables in the far corners stood to obtain a better view.

A nervous Comte de Prenne made the necessary introductions, then ducked for cover. There was a brief, tense pause, and everyone in the Imperial held his breath. Then Adah smiled, and at the same instant Hortense smiled. They glided into each other's arms and embraced warmly, like two childhood friends who had not met for many years.

The customers were disappointed, the waiters became surly, and *Le Petit Journal* hinted to its loyal followers that the two actresses had conspired together, in some way, to cheat the public.

The peace was illusory. Two women who were rivals in a popularity contest could not become real friends. Soon each was being quoted again, to the detriment of the other, and the sniping tactics continued until Adah's death. On the other hand, the enmity may not have been genuine. Each had all the lovers and would-be lovers she could handle, and there was nothing to gain by blasting one's competition. Like actors and actresses of a later era, Adah and Hortense may have discovered that a mock feud paid heavy publicity dividends.

Le Siècle reported, late in the spring, that the ladies met amicably on a number of occasions at the house of Alexandre Dumas, who was promptly dubbed "the peacemaker." A veteran whose hide had been made callous by the slings and arrows of outrageously brash newsmongers, he wisely held his own fire and pretended to be unaware of the commotion.

Neither tact nor nobility of purpose was responsible for Dumas' silence. By the time he persuaded the warring ladies to meet in his bric-a-brac cluttered living room over a soothing samovar, he himself had become involved with Adah in one of the most highly publicized romances of the age. His pretended fancy had given way to real interest, sparks of opposition were created by his son and fanned by George Sand, and all Paris watched, holding its breath, as an old man made a fool of himself over a young woman.

CHAPTER XIV

THE FINAL FLING

O love! I waited—I waited years and years ago.
Once the blaze of a far-off edge of living Love crept up my
horizon and promised a new moon of Poesy.
A soul's full life!
A soul's full love!
And promised that my voice should ring trancing shivers of
rapt melody down the grooves of this dumb earth.
And promised that echoes should vibrate along the purple
spheres of unfathomable seas, to the soundless folds of the clouds.

—"Resurgam"

THE AFFAIR of Adah Isaacs Menken and Alexandre Dumas opened on a comic note in her dressing room immediately after the initial performance of *Mazeppa* at the Théâtre de la Gaité. It soon became half-serious, then degenerated into wild farce. Dumas, hurt because it was commonly believed, by editors and publishers as well as by the reading public, that he had passed his peak and was now in a severe literary decline, was making frantic efforts to focus attention on himself once more.

Adah, the most discussed person in Paris, gave him the opportunity to use her as a steppingstone, and he was too shrewd not to grasp his chance. She, on the other hand, was flattered by his interest in her, regardless of whether it was genuine. He was by far the most renowned of living French authors, and certainly his reputation in the United States, where her opinions had been formed, far outweighed that of any other French writer.

It must be understood that, by no stretch of the imagination, did Adah fall in love with the old man. She liked him, she enjoyed his company, and she used him, as he used her. They were two expert fencers in the fine art of love who crossed foils, then decided to raise their swords in unison against common foes. The man who had invented D'Artagnan was a superb duelist, and the Queen of the Plaza needed instruction from no one.

The affair would have gone smoothly if Dumas had not made the almost fatal error of breaking the ground rules. He fell in love with Adah, which spoiled everything.

He first appears in Adah's *Diary* on April 5, 1867, under the brief notation, "A.D. spent the night. He boasts a great deal, but is fascinating. Would he were twenty-five years younger and I not so jaded. He would have made a wonderful husband. I know I could have tamed him."

The old lion was tame enough now, after a lifetime of self-indulgence, but he could still roar like the king of beasts. At first friends refused to believe that Adah had become his mistress, as they could imagine no reason why she would choose him when there were so many others who wanted her. The scoffers failed to take Dumas' experienced charm into consideration, and were unaware of the magnetic attraction members of the literary fraternity had for Adah.

The couple went away for short weekends after Adah's Saturday night performance at the theater, usually traveling to the much-utilized Dumas estate at Bougival. They were following an accepted tradition, and had they curbed their excessively high spirits, Paris might have smiled sardonically, shrugged cynically, and let them go their way in sin-laden peace. But neither the hero nor the heroine wanted to hide from an adoring public.

Adah was able to spin tall tales with the dexterity of the master himself. Dumas was part Negro, of course, so she dreamed up a new genealogy for his sake, making herself part colored. Whether he believed her is open to question, but he admired her extravagantly. One day in early May, 1867, he wrote her a letter in which he declared, "If it be true that I have talent, how much truer it is that I have love—and both are for you."

Proud of the neat turn of phrase, he made a copy of the letter before sending it to her, and then read the glowing words to friends in cafés. They listened politely, and waited until he departed before bursting into loud laughter. Inevitably, the sentence found its way into print in *Le Petit Journal.*

Dumas' distinguished son, who was recognized as the most successful of the serious dramatists in France, was horrified. He had tried in vain over a period of many years to persuade his father to behave with dignity, and even though he realized that the old man never listened to him, he made another attempt. Paying an early morning visit to the house on the Boulevard Malesherbes, he was fortunate enough to find his father in bed alone.

A one-sided stormy scene followed. "I tried," the younger man—then in his mid-forties—wrote to George Sand, "to pound a few grains of sense into his head. I tried to make him see that the American cares nothing for him, and I begged him not to play the role of a clown at his age.

"He listened to me, which was so unusual that I felt encouraged, and dwelt at some length on the need for one in his position to set an example. Not once did he interrupt any dissertation, but when I was finished, he cocked his head and said what I have heard so many hundreds of times, 'Alexandre, you missed your calling. You should have taken Holy Orders.'

"He no longer disgraces me, but himself only. So monumental is his vanity that he will not see he is a jester with whom the American woman toys. I am disgusted, and will not visit him again."

The angry son returned to his father's house again and again, of course. His own reputation demanded that he do something, for he was considered a moral and ethical purist, and it would have been unthinkable for him to refrain from trying to reform the person nearest and dearest to him.

Perhaps his meddling, which always infuriated the elder Dumas, was in part responsible for an act in such bad taste that even the most Bohemian of Adah's friends on both sides of the Atlantic were startled, shocked, and dismayed.

The hero—or perhaps the villain—of the incident was a professional photographer named Liebert who was one of Alexandre Dumas' many cronies. Photography was a new, developing art, and Liebert was engaged in a long, hard struggle for success that evaded him. Badly in debt, with creditors hounding him, he needed to make a sensational photograph in order to bail himself out.

He discussed the problem at length one night with Dumas and Adah in the untidy living room of the house on the Boulevard Malesherbes. They sympathized deeply, knowing from their own experience how difficult it was to live without funds. Then Liebert, in his desperation, had an inspiration that, he declared, could make him solvent.

At least, according to what Adah later wrote apologetically to Ed James, the idea was Liebert's. The photographer, trying to take shelter when winds of hurricane velocity buffeted him, insisted that Dumas and Adah were responsible and that he, a mere nobody, had been a pawn in the hands of the wealthy and famous. Dumas, in his majesty, refused to discuss the matter with anyone.

No matter who sparked the venture, nothing could have been done without the willing co-operation of the two principals. In brief, they agreed to pose for a photograph. Adah rummaged through her wardrobe and found the very low-necked, very tight-fitting gown of flesh-colored jersey that had been made according to her specifications when she had wanted to rock the Imperial Austrian court. It was so revealing that, she felt certain, Liebert could sell many copies of a photograph that showed her off to her best advantage in it.

Dumas appeared at her suite in his newest frock coat and high, stovepipe hat. Liebert arrived with his camera, and Adah served her guests champagne. Soon everyone was in the jolliest of friendly moods, one thing led to another and it was agreed that the photograph would be an even better seller if Adah posed sitting on Dumas' lap.

She perched on his knee, he steadied her with one hand and clutched his hat with the other. Liebert fussed with the lights and fiddled with the camera. By the time he was ready, Adah's sultry expression had become glazed and Dumas' smile had become a fatuous smirk. The camera clicked, and Liebert raced off to his studio to develop the precious negative. It turned out better than any picture he had yet made.

A few days later, the newspapers heard through the mysterious but ever-present grapevine that such a photograph was in existence. They began to bid for it, and Dumas told Liebert to demand at least double the highest offer. The *Presse* was the winner, and its readers were treated to a rare spectacle. All Paris gagged, blinked, and looked again.

Liebert was just beginning to cash in. Anticipating a demand for prints, he had been working day and night in his darkroom, and now the world beat a path to his door for a livelier mousetrap. So many people wanted prints that he was forced to hire an assistant who acted as his salesman while he returned to his darkroom. Soon nobody who was Anybody could hold up his head unless he could boast that he owned a private, personal copy of the photograph.

Never before had renowned people advertised a sinful relationship with the casual blatancy that Adah and Dumas displayed. The London *Daily News* paid handsomely for the English reprint rights, and in New York the *Mercury* successfully outbid its competitors. In an age when husbands and wives bold enough to venture together before the all-seeing lens of a camera took pains not to touch each other, people could scarcely believe what they saw. Not only were Adah and Dumas unrelated, but she was actually sitting on his lap. What was more, she was wearing a gown that caused good women to sniff and, as soon as they stomped out of the room, prompted their husbands to examine the photograph more closely under a magnifying glass.

The last shreds of Adah's reputation were destroyed. For all practical purposes she now wore a huge, scarlet "A" on her generous bosom. Even Paris, too stunned to laugh, could only gape.

Queen Victoria told members of her court that Dumas' smile made her ill. Obviously she had seen the photograph. For days no one spoke of anything else in the great cities of the Western world. Liebert became wealthy almost overnight, and there was a new flurry of interest in *Mazeppa,* which delighted the owners of the Théâtre de la Gaité But no one else rejoiced.

Theophile Gautier paid a call on Adah, and came away from the interview in a confused state. "She doesn't understand," he wrote to George Sand, who demonstrated an exceptionally active interest in the matter, "that she has done anything wrong. I was unable to make her understand that the world must condemn such vulgarity."

Emile Zola sympathized with Adah, but he was a young man striving for his place in the sun and prudently stopped calling at the Hotel Suez for a time. And the gallants who sought Adah's company made it plain that, although they were still anxious to spend an hour or a night with her, they didn't want to appear in a public place with her.

The younger Dumas was so crushed that he stopped speaking to his father again. The old man cheerfully accepted the blow and made no change in his way of living.

On May 30, George Sand finally took pen in hand and wrote a brief note of condolence to the prodigal's son. "How this business of the photograph must have annoyed you!" she said. "The consequences of a Bohemian life make a sad spectacle in old age. What a pity it all is." Having conveniently forgotten the wild oats she herself had sown, she could sit back comfortably and shake her head.

Dumas the Younger held off as long as he could, but his conscience nagged at him, and finally, early in June, he stormed into his father's house at an hour when he knew Adah would not be there. He delivered a long, sonorous lecture. He quoted at length from his father's works, usually an effective technique, in order to make his point. He talked himself hoarse.

Then Dumas the Elder smiled the beatific smile of a man in love, and said, "My dear Alexandre, in spite of the burden of my years, I have at last found the Marguerite with whom to play the role of your Armand Duval."

The son wrote a dutiful report to George Sand, who took it upon herself to chastise the elderly knight errant. She was one of the few persons on earth for whom he entertained any real respect, and he went home from the interview in a depressed mood.

Adah tried to ignore the hubbub, but it was difficult when the normally ebullient Dumas suffered guilt, gazed listlessly into space, and told her he thought they would be wise to dine in private so they wouldn't call undue attention to themselves. She could tolerate abuse but not obscurity, and her unhappiness increased.

She reached the breaking point when a jingle written by Paul Verlaine, a young Montparnasse poet who was gaining considerable renown, became the refrain of Paris. He had written:

> L'Oncle Tom avec Miss Ada,
> C'est un spectacle dont on rêve.
> Quel photograph fou soude,
> L'Oncle Tom avec Miss Ada?
> Ada peut rester à dada,
> Mais Tom chevancher—t'il sans trêve?
> L'Oncle Tom avec Miss Ada,
> C'est un spectacle dont on rêve.

Ladies repeated the rhyme in their drawing rooms, gentlemen recited it at café tables, and little children chanted it in the streets. No one knew or cared that Verlaine himself was a wild Bohemian and agnostic who delighted in ridiculing every institution that other men held dear. Dumas refused to leave his house, and when Adah first stepped onto the stage of the Théâtre de la Gaité every evening, she could hear titters in the audience. Her blood, never cool, began to boil.

"I spent yesterday (Sunday) with poor A.D.," she wrote to Eléonore Fechter, now in London, "and my heart and I ached for him. He is a gentle, sweet old man who has wished harm to no one. If his enemies do not stop persecuting him, I shall become his champion. Then, dear friend, what a battle will be fought!"

Eléonore and Fechter replied in a joint letter, urging her to do nothing rash. Dumas, they reminded her, was an ink-stained veteran of countless campaigns, and could take care of himself. He, the author of so many successful works that no one had ever been able to count his entire literary output, needed no assistance from anyone.

Adah was too upset to listen. She conceived the idea that Verlaine was a protégé of George Sand's, and it didn't matter that the concept was completely false. The elderly one-time rebel who had become the most respectable woman in Paris had no connection with the amoralists of Montparnasse, and it is doubtful that she had ever read any of Verlaine's odd, experimental works. But such details were irrelevant, and the American tigress decided to launch a direct attack.

Adah dressed in her frilliest outfit, an act of defiant disrespect to the cigar-smoking George Sand, and summoned her carriage. Gautier, to whom she confided her intent, shuddered and begged her to reconsider. No sane person locked horns with the formidable George Sand, whose tongue was as sharp as her razor-edged quill pen. But Adah felt she had nothing to lose.

"A virago stormed into my drawing room," George Sand wrote Dumas the Younger, "demanding justice and, I believe, my head on a platter. I fully expected her to decapitate me and dance through the streets with her trophy in the manner of Salome celebrating the beheading of John the Baptist."

Adah was so furiously angry that, for the first time in many years, George Sand could not break into the monologue, much less dominate the conversation. "If she is a harlot," the letter to Dumas the Younger continued, "she is a learned one. Her command of French adjectives is impressive, and she delivers insults in the grand manner."

The communication ended with the astonishing declaration, "I enjoy her company."

The stormy meeting was the beginning of a remarkably close relationship. George Sand respected intellect, particularly when it was displayed by members of her own sex, and really cared nothing about the moral standards of others. Adah, in turn, discovered that the old woman was witty, compassionate, and wise. How much time they spent with each other, straightening out their differences, is unknown. But a scant two days after Adah paid her initial, vengeance-seeking call, the two women dined together in public, George Sand immersed in a cloud of cigar smoke, Adah puffing on cigarettes.

Now Paris had a new sensation to discuss, and people shook their heads in astonishment. "She is intelligent," George Sand allegedly told an inquirer, "and her poetry is no worse than most of the verse being published these days."

The most immediate, tangible result of the new friendship was a diminution of the campaign of ridicule directed against Dumas. Perhaps the sensation caused by the appearance of the photograph would have died out in any event, as stale gossip becomes stifling. But George Sand made certain that people would stop talking by sending Dumas off to his country place at Bougival. Adah, who was growing weary of his purple rhetoric, urged him to go, too. He finally agreed, saying he intended to write the play of plays for her, a drama that would live for all time as an enduring monument to his love for her.

She breathed more easily after he was gone, and settled down to enjoy her newest literary friendship. George Sand was surprised by the purity of Adah's taste, and Adah discovered she had a great deal still to learn about the written word. Virtually all of her teachers had been men, but now she had an instructress who thoroughly understood the subjective feminine approach to writing. Adah brought a stack of her poems to her new friend, and they went over them together, line by painful line. "In my ignorance," Adah wrote to Ed James, "I believed I could write poetry, but the most sensitive of all authors has taught me that I am still a babe."

During the summer of 1867, with George Sand's encouragement, help, and practical advice, Adah finally made up her mind to publish a book of her poems. The project, as first conceived, was enormously ambitious. The book would be published simultaneously in London and New York, and a French edition would appear at the same time in Paris. There would be five thousand copies printed in each edition, and all copies would be autographed by the author.

George Sand considered the plan economically foolhardy, and told her protégé some of the facts about book publishing. Total printings of fifteen thousand copies would bankrupt even a wealthy author, and unsold copies would rot in warehouses, whose proprietors would charge a stiff fee for storage. It would be far wiser, she explained, to limit each edition to one thousand copies, then print new editions if sales warranted such a move.

Adah reluctantly agreed, and began the arduous task of translating many of her poems into French. She had ample time for the purpose now, as the run of *Mazeppa* finally came to an end in early July, 1867. George Sand helped in the task of selecting the poems that would appear in the volume, and Adah was tortured by the limitations of the printers, who wrote to her from London that the cost would be prohibitive if the book exceeded one hundred and forty-two pages. How could she compress the work of a lifetime into that space? It was impossible, obviously. How, then, to select representative samples that would blend into a balanced whole? There was a great deal of work still to do.

Adah also conceived a grandiose scheme typical of her approach to people. She wanted to dedicate the French edition to George Sand, the English to Charles Dickens, and the American to Walt Whitman. George Sand said she was flattered, but thought it more appropriate to offer the dedication to someone she had known longer. A letter went off to Whitman in Washington, where he was still earning his living as a clerk in the employ of the United States Government. His reply was warm and delicate. He treasured their friendship, he declared, but felt himself unworthy. Also, he told Adah, such a dedication would not help the sales of her book. Not too many people were familiar with his own work, and most of his readers considered him controversial. She would do far better to dedicate her book to a popular, universally recognized author of stature.

Charles Dickens accepted unequivocally, with great pleasure. Eventually, when *Infelicia* was published in the United States, England, and France, all three editions were dedicated to him.

A great deal more than poetry occupied Adah during the summer of 1867. George Sand had launched a vigorous campaign to give the younger woman a patina of respectability, and Adah, obeying her injunctions, dismissed the gallants whose one desire was to share her bed with her. Then Liebert was summoned, and made several new photographs of Adah. All were conventional portraits, and in each she was modestly, fully clothed in demure dresses that buttoned securely at the throat. These portraits became Adah's "official" photographs, and in the next twelve months, the final year of her life, she used no others.

Dumas, tiring of his rustic exile, returned to Paris, and George Sand immediately collared him for a long talk.

Neither of these two exceptionally verbose people wrote one word about their meeting, but George Sand's will prevailed, as it always did when she was dealing with men. Dumas was permitted to see Adah occasionally, but was not allowed to escort her anywhere in public, and was instructed not to discuss her with his many cronies. Alexandre Dumas in his prime would have scoffed at prohibitions of any sort, but an elderly man, still groping for the true love he had never found in countless affairs, meekly and pathetically accepted the conditions.

His son was grateful. Sometime during the summer George Sand had succeeded in bringing Adah and Dumas the Younger together. The brilliant moralist and the trollop who understood authors managed to achieve a rapport that became stronger when the dramatist learned that Adah had no real interest in his semisenile father. The new arrangement was particularly pleasing to the playwright, who reasoned that if the old man maintained just enough of a spark to chase discreetly after Adah, he would neither find the time nor feel the inclination to get into trouble elsewhere.

The campaign to give Adah respectability was gaining momentum, but the largest task was still ahead. George Sand, as a mother and grandmother, was disturbed by Adah's casual relationship with her child, who was supervised day and night by a governess. The baby's mother, she decreed, should be seen taking him for a daily stroll. Adah obediently pushed a carriage down the broad boulevards. Their photograph should be taken, with the loving mother holding her son in her arms. Liebert was summoned again.

Then, said George Sand, he should be baptized. That demand presented problems, for there was no baptismal ceremony in Judaism. But George Sand was not a woman who allowed obstacles to stand in the way of what

she believed right. Adah had been a Catholic prior to her
conversion to Judaism, she declared, so it would be only
right for her child to be baptized a Catholic. The question
was simplified by Adah's complete blank regarding what
faith, if any, Barkley held. She readily agreed, and George
Sand took charge of the arrangements.

Dumas the Younger agreed to become the baby's god-
father. George Sand insisted that she herself be the god-
mother. The Sacrament was administered on August 9,
1867, at Notre Dame, with a few friends, Gautier among
them, in attendance. The baby was christened Louis
Dudevant Victor Emanuel Barkley. "Dudevant," of course,
was a curtsy to George Sand. "Victor Emanuel" reflected
Adah's awareness of her friends' political enthusiasms.
King Victor Emmanuel II of Italy, a bluff, simple, and
hearty constitutional monarch who, with his brilliant
prime minister, Cavour, was uniting his country, was very
popular in France and was a particular favorite in Parisian literary circles. Whether Adah knew much about him
is questionable, for none of her correspondence shows
much interest in politics and she managed to omit one
"m" in naming her son after the monarch. Apparently
it was enough for her that George Sand and Dumas the
Younger admired the Italian King.

Thanks to George Sand's efforts, Adah was no longer
the talk of the boulevardiers. It was impossible to white-
wash someone who had been wallowing in mud for years,
of course, but she was now considered no worse that Hortense Schneider and a dozen other ladies of the theater
whose beauty was indisputable, whose talents filled the
houses, and whose elastic morals were their own business.
"I love this town!" Adah wrote to Ed James. "Even
duchesses invite me to their homes for dinner, and treat
me as an equal."

It was true that, after a lifelong struggle, she had become

socially accepted. Blue-blooded hostesses and the wives
of newly rich financiers included her on their guest lists,
and Adah returned the compliment by rejecting the advances of the ladies' husbands. For two or three months
she enjoyed the social whirl, accepting every invitation
sent to her. And on one occasion she met the Emperor
and Empress, who stopped spitting at each other long
enough to appear together at a supper party given by
P.-J. Robert, a cannon manufacturer who was acquiring
a fortune as a result of the growing tension between France
and Prussia.

"I spent a quarter of an hour chatting with the Empress
Eugenie last night," Adah wrote to Ed James. "I was in
awe of her until I was seated near her in the drawing room
while we waited for the men to drink their after-dinner
brandy. Then I saw that she wore a great deal of rouge
and blackened her lashes, just like an actress.

"She talks like an actress, too, and I suspect that em-
presses are mortal, just as we are. My French accent is
better than hers. She asked me who had made my gown, and
I told her. Then, to be polite, I asked her the same question, and everyone was shocked. I hadn't known it was
poor manners to ask such questions of royalty. But she
was kind, and after the men had joined us, took me aside
and told me in confidence the name of her dressmaker.

"I wanted to laugh, for everyone here knows that every
stitch she wears is made for her by Worth-Dobergh. But
I thanked her solemnly, as though she had told me a great
secret. She is lively and, I fear, a trifle stupid. All the
same I feel sorry for her because her husband appears to
hate her. She is very delicate and sweet, while he is a
gross man who eats and drinks too much, becomes boisterous and is quite careless in his language. The good ladies
of New York would swear he is no gentleman, and they

would be right. He is a Bonaparte, which counts for much more in this country than being a gentleman.

"It would have been easy for me to take the Emperor aside for a private talk, I don't mind telling you. Every time I changed my position in my chair I found him staring at me, and his expression reminded me of the soldiers who were always waiting for me outside the Broadway Theater.

"I've had my share of troubles in the world, and don't want a king asking me to join him for a secret weekend in the country. Nothing Napoleon does is really secret. His wife would find out what had happened, and would have me expelled from the country. That would be too bad, as I like it here and am now in rehearsals for the *Pirates*.

"Besides, I like the Empress Eugenie, even if she is lightheaded."

The Queen of the Plaza, who had walked the streets of Havana offering herself to strange men, had come a long way.

She discovered, however, that high society life did not appeal to her. A stiff, polite façade made it impossible for anyone to behave naturally or spontaneously. Conversation was confined to noncontroversial subjects, with the result that the aristocratic guests at a party devoted most of their talk to gossip about the affairs of friends who did not happen to be present.

Adah's curiosity was satisfied, and she returned to the literary and theatrical people with whom she had more in common. In any event, she had to curtail her party-going, for she faced a new and exacting challenge. Fechter had returned to Paris from London, and was directing rehearsals of the *Pirates*. The play was scheduled to open at the Théâtre de la Gaité in late September, and Adah was justifiably nervous. So far her career had consisted of a success of triumphs in *Mazeppa,* and she had failed to score even a moderate success in any other play. Sensitive to the jibes of fellow actors who said she was incapable of acting in anything except *Mazeppa,* she was determined to prove them wrong.

She attacked her role in the *Pirates* with such concentrated fury that she upset the members of her supporting cast, who were reluctant to indulge in such heavy-handed histrionics. Fechter kept her after rehearsal for private tutoring, and her performance improved somewhat, but still failed to satisfy him. "Charles is afraid," Eléonore Fechter wrote to the sympathetic Laura Seymour in London, "that Adah will make herself ridiculous by trying too hard."

The opening was postponed for a week, and the director wisely added a new scene to the last act which copied the climactic moments of *Mazeppa.* The scantily clad heroine, attired in a very short, semitransparent gown of chiffon, was required to make a desperate attempt to escape from the pirates who held her captive. Inasmuch as it was difficult to escape from a ship, the action was transferred to a lonely island on which, providentially, a herd of wild horses was grazing.

The rest was simple. The heroine sneaked away from the brutal pirates who were intent upon violating her, caught a wild horse and rode madly across the island, where a waiting sloop took her to safety. The frugal owners of the Théâtre de la Gaité saw no reason to build a new runway, and used the same one that had seen service in *Mazeppa.*

Adah protested, but in vain. One runway, she was informed, looked exactly like any other runway.

The action perked up, but Adah was not strong enough to carry the play, and the opening was put off for another ten days. This time Fechter added songs and dances, giving some to pirates who, luckily, were endowed with rich baritone voices. Then he made the mistake of injecting several other female captives into the script so that he could utilize a few soprano voices.

His star hit the roof and stayed there. There was only one woman in the cast of an Adah Isaacs Menken play, she said. Fechter, tired after long weeks of hard work, lost his own temper and replied that she was too poor an actress to appear without adequate support. Adah stormed out of the theater, vowing never to return.

She locked the door of her suite, and refused admittance to Fechter. Eléonore made an effort to soothe the injured artistic temperament of the great lady. Adah listened, but insisted that she planned to return to New York by the first available ship. Old Alexandre Dumas bumbled onto the scene, and made matters worse by agreeing wholeheartedly with Adah. He told her she was a great actress and should stick to her guns.

Fechter tore his hair, and hoped the management would not be forced to refund the money pouring steadily into the box office. Eléonore counseled patience, hoping that Adah would grow calmer after a night's sleep. But the next morning Minnie was sent to the nearest steamship office to inquire about reservations.

For the first and only time in her life, Adah was behaving like a stage star, and undoubtedly relished every moment of the commotion she was creating. Whether she really planned to leave the *Pirates* and Paris is open to conjecture. Fechter, however, could not afford to take the risk. At the same time, he had to strengthen the play, no matter how much Adah's pride might be injured.

In his desperation he appealed to George Sand for help. The old lady responded immediately, had herself driven to the Hotel Suez and delivered a blistering speech. "We could hear her voice at the far end of the

corridor," Eléonore—who was obviously eavesdropping—
wrote to Laura.

Adah, like so many before her, could not tolerate the
withering scorn of George Sand and wilted. At least she
went down with her colors still flying, and merely agreed
to discuss the situation with Fechter. At the request of both
combatants, George Sand remained to act as mediator.

The director made it plain that there were places
throughout the play that were flabby, and courteously but
firmly indicated that he thought a group of female singers
would add depth and liveliness to the *Pirates*. Adah adamantly refused to permit other women to take the spotlight
from her. The dilemma seemed insoluble, but George
Sand asked permission to attend a rehearsal, explaining
she believed she knew of a possible way to satisfy everyone.

All three repaired to the theater, and Fechter gave the
grand old lady a copy of the script to study. She read it
carefully, followed every line of the rehearsal, and caused
Adah considerable nervousness by conferring for some
time with the director at the rear of the auditorium. Then
the trio went off to a nearby café, and George Sand revealed her plan. There were scenes, she explained diplomatically, that in her opinion needed strengthening.

This could be accomplished by using a small singing
chorus, as Fechter wanted, but handling the group in a
way that would add to Adah's glory rather than diminish
it. The singers would stand at one side of the stage and
provide the equivalent of background music in a number
of scenes. Neither the tactful author nor the harassed
director said that these were Adah's weakest scenes, which
badly needed bolstering.

Adah could not refuse such a reasonable suggestion, and
agreed to try the plan. The singers appeared that same
evening, and by the following day were working in har-
mony with the rest of the cast. Adah, who was intelligent

enough to be aware of her own limitations, was delighted. She was far more attractive than the singers, and had nothing to fear from them as feminine competition. And, precisely as George Sand had indicated, their singing in the background made her lines sound richer and fuller.

Peace was restored, and Eléonore Fechter presented George Sand with a silver bowl as a token of the director's gratitude.

Les Pirates de la Savane opened on the night of October 16, 1867, before a capacity audience which squeezed into the Théâtre de la Gaité. The excitement of the *Mazeppa* premiere was missing, and people were in a far different mood now. Adah was no longer a novelty, and Paris was prepared to judge her critically.

She was conscious of the hostility, writing later to Ed James, "They kept on their gloves during the first act, and if there was any applause after my first entrance, I didn't hear it."

Adah worked harder in the second act, as did her supporting players, and gradually the audience came alive. Surprising Fechter, Adah revealed hitherto concealed gifts as a comedienne. Soon she mastered her audience, and eventually people were standing and cheering. Long before the play reached its climax Adah had scored a resounding success. Then her familiar ride through the audience, clad in an even flimsier costume than she had worn in *Mazeppa,* brought down the house. Fechter wearied of keeping count of the curtain calls at the end of the play.

No longer was Adah Isaacs Menken a one-play actress. She had scored in a new triumph, and the *Pirates* could support her in style for years, with runs in London and New York following the Paris engagement. The newspaper critics were gentlemen, and refrained from saying that, aside from an unexpected flair for comedy, she had displayed no developing talent. Nor did they stoop to attacks on her play, which was as transparent as her last-act costume.

Gautier treated her with such kindness in the *Moniteur* that the café crowd felt certain he must be her lover—which he was not. "Paris," he wrote, "enjoys a rare privilege. Mlle. Menken gives a performance that is a delight of beauty and grace. Let those who want tragic eloquence go elsewhere and attend the plays of Racine. The young in heart, spirit and mind will find all they seek, and more, at the Théâtre de la Gaité. The new season has truly commenced!"

The popular press was less tactful. "Those who saw La Menken in *Mazeppa*," *Le Petit Journal* declared brashly, "will see even more of her now. It is astonishing that anyone could wear even fewer clothes, but she has done it, and we are glad."

"Her form is exquisite," the *Constitutionnel* declared, then asked rhetorically, "What more can be asked?"

A solid phalanx of gallants besieged Adah in her dressing room after the opening performance, and it was rumored that she received a note from Napoleon III, asking her to meet him for a private rendezvous. She received no such communication, which would have been tantamount to a command, for she went off to the Hotel Suez, where a relieved and beaming Fechter was the host at a supper party for more than a hundred people in a private dining room. Adah sipped champagne, fended off would-be lovers, and in general comported herself with dignity. She was growing accustomed to success and to her status as a glittering international star.

Nothing better illustrates her dignity than her gracious acceptance of compliments from the members of five foreign legations. Her bearing was regal, her smile warm but impersonal as she raised her hand for the diplomats to kiss. She had come a long way from a shanty in Milne-burg, Louisiana.

Although few people realized it at the time, a new era in theatrical history had begun. Adah had broken the ice in *Mazeppa,* and now, in the *Pirates,* had confirmed a trend. Thanks to her daring, nudity had become a respect-able theatrical commodity, and the stages of Europe and North America would never again be the same.

George Sand was better able than most to peer into the future. "Your heroines," she wrote to Dumas the Younger, "will need fewer costumes and better shapes. Audiences who have seen La Menken will demand naked-ness as their right, and authors who fail to give them what they want will play to empty theaters."

CHAPTER XV

THE CURTAIN FALLS; OMNES EXEUNT

O, Death! Death! loose out thy cold, stiff fingers from
my quivering heart!
Let the warm blood rush back to gasp up but one more word!
O, Love! thou art stronger, mightier than all!
O, Death! thou hast but wedded me to Life!
Life is Love, and Love is Eternity

—"Dying"

"SUCCESS, like failure, can be very boring. The only difference between them is that, in the former situation, one
eats regularly and heartily, while in the latter but rarely.
So, when I am asked if I don't grow tired of playing in the
Pirates, I must reply in candor that I do not. The food
in Paris is excellent, and I hope I shall continue to eat it
for many years to come."

The *Presse,* quoting Adah in an interview, did not indicate that she might have smiled while delivering her
weighty opinions. She failed to add that she not only
liked food, but had become accustomed to countless luxuries and extravagances. Her triumph in the *Pirates* sent
her on a new clothes-buying spree, and this time she went

to the Empress Eugenie's dressmaker, Worth, who charged a king's ransom for a single gown. Adah bought twenty.

Having "loaned" her carriage in London to someone whose identity she could not bother to recall, she ordered a new one, custom-made, with a portable vanity table in the interior so she could make up in the evening while driving to the theater. She embarrassed her friends by giving them gifts so expensive that they cringed. Old Dumas received a walking stick with a solid gold handle, a bauble similar to those he bestowed on his intimates. George Sand tried in vain to refuse a gold inkwell, saying she could not use anything so elegant to hold ordinary ink. Zola flatly declared he would not take anything other than books, so he received a tooled leather set of the works of Boileau. Fechter insisted that his business relationship with Adah made it impossible for him to accept anything from her, so she gave Eléonore a bracelet studded with tiny rubies.

Money poured through Adah's hands in a golden stream. Fechter had renegotiated her contract after the triumphal opening of the *Pirates,* and she now received a staggering fifteen hundred dollars a week, the highest salary ever paid to a star in Paris, up to that time. And it seemed likely that money would continue to flow in forever. E. T. Smith wrote urgent letters from London, begging Adah to play in the *Pirates* at Astley's, and she received several communications from the owners of the Sadler's Wells Theater, promising to pay her a larger sum than Smith offered for a London run, no matter what the figure. Ed James wrote from New York, telling her she could name her own price there, but urging her to remain loyal to George Wood and his Broadway Theater.

The theater was not Adah's only source of income in 1867 and 1868. Dazzled by temptations greater than any she had ever before known, she gave in to them. "Baron de F.," she says in one of her few *Diary* entries on the subject, "has offered me as much as I earn in a week if I will spend a night with him. Just one night! How can I refuse?" The question was purely rhetorical.

The wealthiest men in Europe were throwing themselves at her, and their money at her feet. Even if she hadn't been a professional prostitute in her youth, even if she hadn't taken more lovers than she could count, she would have found it difficult to reject the offers. She had long been the leading international sex symbol, and was being subjected to constant pressure. It may even be that she was the first of the modern theatrical stars used as a substitute for Aphrodite by both the press and the public.

She herself probably had no idea how many lovers she entertained, or how much they paid for the privilege. Life was moving at too fast a clip, and she had enough trouble trying to maintain the dignified façade that George Sand had urged her to adopt. The men who remained overnight at the Hotel Suez suite did not leave until noon the following day, when eyebrows would not be lifted if they were seen walking down the stairs. And, no matter how wild or debauched the previous night, Adah always managed to take Louis Dudevant Victor Emanuel Barkley for an airing after her late breakfast.

The surface calm was broken in December. Success always breeds imitation, and a half-dozen generously endowed young ladies were appearing nightly at as many Paris theaters in various states of undress for the edification of predominantly male audiences. So far, Adah alone attracted women into the theater; society, in its mystifying wisdom, had decreed that it was not improper to attend her performance, but other, lesser stars who specialized in nudity were still taboo. One of these actresses, Marie Muller, decided to make herself respectable.

A tall Alsatian blonde, Marie was a handsome girl in

her mid-twenties who had acquired a reputation as a comedienne of some distinction in the plays of Molière before turning to the greener pastures of exhibiting her body. Still a country girl at heart, in spite of her surface polish, Marie associated in the main with other actors, and most of her lovers were members of the expanding merchant class.

Someone—possibly a colleague, possibly a vintner from Cognac, a silk manufacturer from Lyons or a ship owner from Marseilles—urged her to challenge Adah's supremacy. The advice was bad. Marie was appearing at the Théâtre Place Royale in a hastily written, sloppily produced comedy called *Elle,* and the highlight came in the closing moments when, clad in no more than was essential under the law prohibiting complete nudity on a stage, she soared back and forth over the bald heads of her audience on a swing suspended from the high ceiling of the auditorium. *Elle* was doing a fair-enough business, and Marie should have been content. Unfortunately, she took herself seriously, and the knowledge that Adah was accepted by the aristocracy, was close to the giants of the literary world— and attracted admirers who made her own lovers seem like paupers by comparison—stirred the viper of envy in her ample bosom.

Being a direct and literal young woman, Marie believed a challenge was literally a challenge. One day a surprised Adah received a long, badly spelled letter bearing Marie's signature and informing her that she had stolen one of Marie's lovers. "I demand satisfaction for this injury!" the blonde wrote dramatically.

Adah, who may or may not have been aware of the younger woman's existence, paid no attention to the communication.

But Marie was just beginning to work up steam. Several evenings later, when Adah and a group of friends returned to the Hotel Suez for supper after the performance of the *Pirates,* an outraged blonde awaited them at the entrance to the hotel's restaurant. Stunningly clad in a scarlet satin gown and feathered hat, with a coterie of well-wishers to cheer her on, Marie violently denounced her "rival," and slapped Adah's face. Several gentlemen who were members of Adah's party hastily intervened and hustled the bewildered and angry American into the hotel. All were of the opinion that Marie was out of her mind and dismissed the incident.

But Adah's gorge was rising, and her state of mind did not improve when, the following day, she received another letter challenging her to a duel. One of her closest business associates, Louis Hostein, head of the syndicate that owned the Théâtre de la Gaité and the Théâtre du Châtelet, told her to pay no attention to someone who, obviously, was trying to cash in on the greater publicity value of a higher-ranking star.

Marie made it impossible for anyone to forget her. She waited twenty-four hours for a reply, then sent two superbly dressed young men to the Hotel Suez, bearing still another letter issuing a challenge. Reporters for *Le Petit Journal* and *Le Siècle,* the newspaper with the largest circulation in France, just happened to be present.

Adah could have been rid of the nuisance by laughing contemptuously and giving the press a statement ridiculing her would-be opponent. But her patience was exhausted, and she fell into Marie's trap. "Very well," the newspapers reported her as saying. "I do not know the man to whom she refers. I feel certain that no gentleman of my acquaintance would demean himself by associating with someone like this Muller person. But, if she wishes a duel, she shall have one."

The boulevardiers went wild with delight. The prospect of two attractive actresses slashing at each other with swords was almost too good to be true. And everyone joined in the guessing game, speculating on the identity of the lucky man in question.

Adah's friends tried to dissuade her from her folly. "My own duels," old Dumas wrote her, "never brought me anything but grief. Let your sword rest in its sheath."

Fechter, who had returned to London, heard of the incident, and immediately sent Adah a long letter in which he begged her not to make a fool of herself.

None of her French friends would have anything to do with the affair for fear of making themselves appear ludicrous. So Adah appointed two young Englishmen as her seconds. John Thompson, Swinburne's friend and secretary, had come to Paris for the purpose of editing *Infelicia* and putting it in final shape for the printers. The Honorable Henry Hurst-Bowen was spending a year or two in Paris, rounding out his liberal education. Both were young enough to be adventurous, and still close enough to their public school days to enjoy horseplay and travesties.

The pair made an appointment with Marie's representatives, dressed solemnly in top hats and tail coats, and conducted themselves with the mock dignity that the English achieve so well on such occasions. Adah, they informed Marie's representatives, was the challenged party, and therefore had the choice of weapons. She elected to fight with pistols under the "American code," which meant that the principals would fire alternate shots, continuing to fire until one drew blood or it was agreed that honor had been satisfied. Marie's friends had not bargained for such terms, but had to accept them.

It was not easy to settle on a site for the match. There were laws against duels, and it seemed reasonable to presume that the police would not hesitate to crack down on two women who were making the whole system look absurd. A spot too close to the city would not only draw the officials, but would attract a large audience. Marie, of course, wanted as big a crowd in attendance as possible, and was anxious to have the press present, too.

Hurst-Bowen protested, and with true aristocratic British disdain declared that Adah sought neither newspaper representation nor a throng wanting to see a free show. Her one concern, he said loftily, was her honor.

It was finally agreed that the duel would take place on the Sunday before Christmas in some woods outside the town of Versailles. All parties were sworn to secrecy, but the news spread quickly, of course, and all of the newspapers were familiar with the details. Some of Adah's friends actually asked the authorities to intervene, hoping to prevent a farce, but the police refused. They indicated that they didn't believe any real fight would take place, and they washed their hands of the whole affair.

The weather was cold and raw on the appointed day, but a large crowd of well-dressed ladies and gentlemen drove out to Versailles from Paris. There were picnic hampers filled with food and wine in most of the carriages, and people were in a holiday mood. Old Alexandre Dumas drove out with two friends, and walked up and down the clearing in the woods, pounding the frozen ground with the gold-headed cane Adah had given him. Only he sensed that the occasion might not be as amusing as everyone assumed. Only he knew Adah sufficiently well to realize she might be in earnest.

Marie was the first of the principals to arrive. She and her escorts drove up in a carriage, and the crowd cheered. The actress came into the open, and people shouted even more loudly when they saw how attractive she looked in a handsome gown of emerald green velvet and a matching, broad-brimmed hat, heavily feathered in the style made popular by the Empress. Four or five representatives of the press "happened" to be present, and Marie gave them a long statement exuding confidence. They took careful notes.

There was a long wait, and Marie ventured the opinion that her opponent was afraid to meet her. The happy reporters scribbled again. Then another carriage appeared, and people gaped when Adah followed Thompson and Hurst-Bowen into the clearing. The two seconds were dressed in somber black, and neither smiled. Adah, scorning cosmetics of any kind, was bareheaded. She wore a pair of old breeches, boots that she had obviously owned for a long time, and a man's shirt, over which she had thrown a short cloak. She pretended not to hear the applause of the spectators, and failed to acknowledge the presence of Marie.

Reporters hurried to the dazzling American for a statement. She informed them that she had nothing to say, and turned her back to them. The gentlemen of the press were confused, and thought her unco-operative.

Thompson and Hurst-Bowen conferred with Marie's seconds, who carried old, cumbersome pistols which Thompson coldly rejected. Such weapons, he indicated, were incapable of being fired accurately. Hurst-Bowen then produced a pair of fine dueling pistols which he himself owned, and Marie's seconds, not really caring what weapons were used, accepted them.

No one had been appointed as referee, an oversight that was corrected by asking Dumas to officiate. He demurred, but was persuaded to change his mind, and he supervised the loading of both weapons. It was then his duty to reconcile the principals, if possible, and he asked them if they were willing to embrace.

"My honor," Marie trilled, "makes it impossible." She smiled at the crowd.

"No," Adah said bluntly.

According to the account Thompson subsequently wrote

to Swinburne in London, Dumas began to show considerable nervousness. His hands trembled as he gave the principals their weapons. Then it was incumbent on him to help them decide who would fire first, and he suggested that he flip a coin. Adah waived the privilege and gave Marie the right to fire the first shot. A few of the more observing gentlemen in the throng noted that Adah held her pistol confidently, as though she knew something about firearms.

Dumas asked the principals to stand back to back, and to start pacing, taking one step at a time, as he counted to fifteen. Men laughed and ladies giggled as Marie strolled seductively toward the far side of the clearing. Adah's steps were firm, emphatic and businesslike. At the count of fifteen, Dumas paused, then ordered the combatants to turn and fire.

Adah whirled around, and waited calmly.

Marie was still playing to the audience as she turned. It seems reasonable to assume that she had never before held a pistol, and in her ignorance she accidentally discharged the weapon. Luckily the shot plowed into the ground, harming no one, but Marie was so frightened that she screamed.

She would have left the clearing at once, but Dumas called to her, ordering her to wait, and his command was echoed by Thompson and Hurst-Bowen.

Then Adah slowly raised her pistol and peered down the barrel. "At that instant," Thompson wrote to Swinburne, "I realized this was no charade."

She squeezed the trigger, the pistol barked and a puff of smoke rose in the air. The horrified spectators stared at a hole in the brim of Marie's hat, only a fraction of an inch from her temple.

"My aim will improve with my next shot," Adah said, sounding regretful that she had missed.

At last Marie knew that her opponent was not playing a game for publicity purposes, but seriously intended to commit murder. The knowledge overwhelmed her, and she conveniently swooned.

Adah did not budge, and informed her seconds that the next round would be fired when her opponent recovered.

The crowd was stunned and silent now. A number of ladies covered their faces with their hands, but no one left the clearing. Marie's seconds revived her with difficulty, and a long discussion followed, carried on in an undertone that others could not hear.

Hurst-Bowen, pale but composed, asked that the referee load the pistols again.

Marie knew when she was beaten. Looking as though she would faint again, she stood, supported by her escorts, and stammered an apology.

Adah listened in silence, then nodded. "I accept," she said, handing her pistol to Hurst-Bowen. Thompson draped her cloak over her shoulders, she shook hands with Dumas and walked straight to her carriage, followed by her seconds.

The press accounts that appeared in print the following day were brief and cautiously worded. None made fun of the affair or of the principals, and it was clear to anyone reading the stories that Adah had been in earnest. Boulevard humorists promptly declared that any man who crossed her did so at his life's peril.

Marie Muller subsided into obscurity when her run in *Elle* ended a few weeks later. Her method of seeking a more conspicuous place in the sun at the expense of someone more renowned failed miserably because of her inability to understand the temperament of her opponent.

Adah never clarified her reasons for treating the affair seriously. Perhaps she really felt that she had been made to suffer unfairly. On the other hand, knowing herself to be

an expert shot, she may have gambled on her ability to
achieve a near miss and reap a bounteous publicity harvest.
If so, she succeeded brilliantly, but the suspicion remains
that she regarded the entire incident as trivial and beneath notice. No mention of it appears in her *Diary,* nor
did she refer to it in a letter written only a day or two
later to Ed James.

Regardless of how she felt, a legend had been created, of
course. In 1873, shortly after the furor created by the
Franco-Prussian War had subsided, three plays, all presented within the span of a single season, featured duels to
the death between female antagonists. At the time of the
affair itself, Adah may have benefited, for she had become
the talk of the boulevards again. But it was impossible for
the *Pirates* to do better business, as there had been no
empty seats prior to the duel.

For a short time life became somewhat calmer, and
Adah interrupted her normal routines to spend the better
part of her days working with Thompson on *Infelicia.*
She had decided to include a total of thirty poems in the
book, and had translated them herself for inclusion in
the French edition. A sudden decision to print a small
line-drawing illustrating each poem delayed publication
by several months. Adah was inexperienced in art work,
but made up her mind to draw the illustrations herself.
The results were so crude that Thompson protested, and
she agreed to hire a professional artist.

Dumas and George Sand suggested several, but they
were too independent to suit her. She knew precisely what
she wanted, and Thompson promised to find someone in
England who would carry out her wishes. He proved as
good as his word, and an artist named Frederick Becker
submitted several samples, by mail, that delighted Adah.
He was employed as an engineering clerk in the War

Office, and therefore could not make a trip to France to consult with her. So she decided to visit him in London.

There was no sense in making an ordinary trip, Adah concluded. A visit should more than pay for itself, so she notified Smith and the owners of the Sadler's Wells Theater that she might consider doing the *Pirates* in London late in the winter or early in the spring. Smith offered her fifteen hundred dollars a week, which was her salary in Paris. She notified Sadler's Wells accordingly, and the proprietors agreed to pay her the staggering sum of two thousand dollars a week for eight weeks.

She accepted, and notified Fechter, who was in London, to start rehearsing an English company. He went to work immediately, late in February, and had his hands full. First the play had to be translated into English. Then there were actors to hire, costumes to be made, and scenery to build. A contract was sent to Adah, and she agreed to open in London on March 30, arriving two weeks earlier for final rehearsals.

She did not notify Hostein and his partners of her decision until mid-February, and she must have braced herself for their reaction. They were wildly angry, of course, as the play was still selling out at the Théâtre de la Gaité. They would not prevent her from leaving, however, as her contract granted her the right to terminate her engagement on four weeks' notice.

Adah wisely wanted to remain on good terms with the people who had provided her with the highest income she had ever enjoyed, and she saw to it that their parting was amicable. She considered Paris her second home now, and had no reason to want to remain in London beyond the eight weeks of her guaranteed run. So it was agreed that she would take a one-month holiday after she closed in England at the end of May, and would then play the *Pirates* in Paris again, remaining in the part as long as

Hostein wanted. The producers felt they had struck a good bargain, and everyone was satisfied.

The final performance of the *Pirates*, on March 14, was a gala occasion. Adah was inundated with bouquets of flowers from friends, admirers, and the management. Her supporting players gave her a gift of a silver vase, and she presented every member of the company and all of the backstage crew with expensive tokens. Various gallants had requested the pleasure of spending her last night in the city with her, but she had turned them down, and had also refused to let her friends give her a farewell party.

Instead she spent the night with Dumas. "I feel so sorry for A.D.," she tells her *Diary*. "It is sad, but I believe he truly loves me."

The following day, accompanied by her child and servants, she departed for London. Cataldi's was too crowded to accommodate such a large group, so Adah went instead to a private home the Fechters had rented for her in the fashionable Belgravia district, just off Grosvenor Place. The faithful Eléonore attended to the hiring of the additional servants Adah believed she needed, and the star plunged into rehearsals so frantic that she had no opportunity to confer with Becker.

Nor did Fechter allow her time to see friends or go out on the town with the clamoring gentlemen who adored her and were anxious to spend large sums in order to prove it. The requirements of a new cast and a different language occupied all of Adah's waking hours. "I must be growing old," she wrote to Ed James in a hastily scribbled note. "I've never felt so tired. It may be that the dampness of the climate here has seeped into my bones. You'd laugh if you could hear them creaking."

On the night of March 30 a capacity audience watched Adah drag her aching bones onto the stage of the Sadler's Wells Theater. If she felt tired that night, she succeeded in hiding her exhaustion, and was so lively, so spirited that the audience cheered her at every entrance and exit. Her last-act ride around the runway in flimsy chiffon lived up to everyone's expectations, and she had the satisfaction of knowing that she had now become a two-vehicle actress in another country.

The London newspapers were less than lyrical about her performance and damned the play, for its inherent weaknesses were more obvious in English than in French. The *Times,* as usual, confined itself to an austere announcement and did not lower itself to pass critical judgment. The other newspapers agreed that Adah had never been in better form, and *Punch* airily observed, "The most justly renowned shape may be viewed nightly at Sadler's Wells. What more can a man ask? It matters not that The Menken recites her lines prettily. As in times past, one is too busy gazing at her divinity to hear what she may be saying."

A long line formed at the box office, and within ten days of the opening the management announced that all seats had been sold for the rest of the engagement. Efforts were made to persuade Adah to extend her run, but she refused. Fechter's aid was enlisted, and he tried to talk her into remaining in London for an extra four weeks. This would have meant canceling her vacation, and she could not even contemplate the idea, telling Fechter that she badly needed a holiday.

He hated to see weeks being wasted when she could be filling a theater, and accused her of planning to meet some wealthy man in France for a long liaison. Adah indignantly denied the charge, and stopped speaking to her director. Fortunately, Eléonore intervened before the rift became too serious, Fechter apologized satisfactorily, and peace was restored.

Almost immediately after the opening, Adah went to

work on the illustrations for her book. Becker had prepared large numbers of drawings for her inspection, but none met her approval. Her own ideas were simple but dramatic, and she explained them to him carefully.

On the title page of "Dreams of Beauty" she wanted a bird, soaring through the sky, with its shadow reflected on the earth below. "My Heritage" was also to feature a bird, this one sitting on a twisted, dead tree limb with a large, pointed star visible in the sky directly above its uplifted head. "Judith" was to display an angel, a shapely brunette in filmy chiffon, from whose shoulders sprouted large wings. For added effect, the angel was to be drawn with her hands held to her face as she either wept or otherwise grieved.

"Working and Waiting" was to show a woman in a long dress with hair falling forward over her face, who was sitting on a pile of stones that suggested ancient Grecian ruins. "The Release," a serious poem like all the rest, would appear with a plump, realistic frog leaping out of a small, round object that resembled a miniature ship's life preserver.

Warming to her work, Adah waxed even more enthusiastic. The title page of "In Vain" would show the billowing, silken tent of a slain warrior, stretched out on a bier with a pot of incense burning in a Grecian-type container near his head. On the floor, with her head laid on his breast, would be the figure of a grieving woman with long, black hair. All of the women to be depicted in the book would be brunettes, as a matter of fact, and all—with a single exception—would resemble Adah. That one would illustrate a poem called "Adelina Patti," and for its title page Becker drew a reasonably recognizable likeness of the great singer, whom Adah admired.

Raging seas were to be shown realistically. Skulls were to appear frequently, blood would drip from crowns and huge tears would fall from the invisible eye of an unseen female. All women would be dressed in clinging, classical gowns. Becker had his work cut out for him.

He came daily to Adah's house, and together they scanned every illustration. Adah's energy was inexhaustible, her critical taste unappeasable. The artist grew haggard, but she soothed him with praise—and money, promising to double his substantial fee of seven hundred and fifty dollars. She got her money's worth, as she always did, when it occurred to her that it might be nice to print smaller illustrations at the end of each poem. Becker went back to his drawing board, and Adah made the gay rounds of the city after each night's performance.

She found time for her many friends in London, too, seeing a great deal of Reade and Laura, and often appearing at the round table in Cataldi's, where Rossetti and his fellow Pre-Raphaelites gathered. She saw Swinburne on a number of occasions, and their relationship was friendly, with neither showing visible strain. They actually dined together once or twice, but did not resume their affair.

At last, early in May, Becker was finished. Adah went into consultation with the printer, and was disturbed when she discovered there would be a blank page at the end of the book. Rather than leave it blank, she summoned Becker again, and he drew a pen-and-ink sketch of a lovely brunette who wore pearls in her short, black hair and a string of pearls at her throat. It was not coincidence, of course, that Adah wore identical pearls in the climactic scene of the *Pirates*.

Infelicia was now completed, and the printer agreed to send engravings of the drawings to the New York and Paris publishers. Only one detail remained: the cover. Adah decided that dark green, padded linen would be effective. In the upper left-hand corner would be the single word, *Infelicia,* and in the lower right-hand corner would be a simple, "Menken," both written in her own, bold hand, and both to be sure, in gold. Reade laughingly told her she was spending too much money on the volume and could not possibly show a profit, no matter how many copies might be sold.

"I don't care," Adah replied. *"Infelicia* will be my only monument."

Her friends soon had good cause to remember her words.

She played her last London performance on the night of May 30, and was so tired that she didn't want her friends to give her a farewell party. Instead, she said, she would give a party for them when she returned to London the following year. She had no way of knowing that, when she walked to her dressing room after taking her final curtain call, she had appeared before an audience for the last time.

The English servants were dismissed, and Adah, accompanied by her son, her staff, and her horse, went to Dover to catch a steamer for France. The faithful Dumas was waiting for her at Le Havre, and brought her news that, a year or two earlier, would have thrilled her. He was at work on a play for her, and considered it his greatest masterpiece.

It was to be a declaration of his abiding love for her, but he refused to give her any details, preferring that she wait until he completed and polished it. Adah expressed her gratitude, but gently explained that she was committed to the *Pirates,* which Hostein and his partners intended to open at the Théâtre du Châtelet. Dumas accepted her decision with remarkable calm, which was caused by the fact that the play actually existed only in his perennially fertile imagination.

He thought he had impressed her, and was satisfied. Women had become his willing slaves for far less. Adah saw through his ruse, which she described in a brief note to Laura Seymour, but pretended to accept it at face value so he could save his pride. Rarely had she shown such sensitive consideration for another's feelings; but she was not behaving like herself in the late spring and early summer of 1868.

She had made arrangements to spend a few weeks at the little English Channel town, Deauville, which was just beginning to attain popularity as a fashionable summer resort. Sending most of her servants to Paris, she went to the seaside spa, accompanied only by her child, Minnie, and the governess. She had been invited to spend her holiday at the villa recently acquired by Eugene Rouher, the finance minister in the government of Napoleon III, and nothing better indicated her rise in social status than the willingness of Rouher and his family to receive her. The most controversial political figure in France, and possibly the most powerful, Rouher had been known as the "vice-Emperor" and had held a position equivalent to that of premier before his enemies had united against him and forced him to take a somewhat less conspicuous position.

Rouher must have known there would be talk when the gossips of Paris heard that the world's most notorious woman was his house guest, but he was enough of an iconoclast not to care. Visitors to Deauville found Adah spending her days sitting in the shade with the ladies of the Rouher family, and it was said that her evenings were devoted to reading and quiet discussions. Those who jumped to conclusions and assumed that she was Rouher's mistress apparently were mistaken. Her holiday seems to have been completely innocent and uncluttered.

Rehearsals for the new production of the *Pirates* were scheduled to begin on July 1, and an opening date of August 3rd was announced. Most members of the company were veterans who had played in the previous cast, so Hostein took charge of rehearsals rather than send for

Fechter, whose expensive services were not needed. Adah's presence at the early rehearsals was not required, and she paid her first visit to the Théâtre du Châtelet on July 8, having arrived in Paris a day or two earlier.

She remained for a short time, meeting newcomers to the cast and chatting with Hostein before returning to the Hotel Suez to supervise the unpacking of her usual mountain of clothes. Most of her friends were off in the country, the weather was hot and sultry, and Adah seemed to be in unusually low spirits. But when Hostein inquired after her health, she told him she had enjoyed her holiday enormously and had never felt better.

The following day, July 9, she went to the theater in the afternoon, at the producer's request, to rehearse a brief but particularly active second-act scene with several actors who were new to the company. At first she merely walked through her part, but her enthusiasm gradually increased, and finally she was throwing herself into her role with abandon, obviously enjoying her work after having been absent from the stage for nearly six weeks.

Suddenly, as she was standing in the center of the stage, delivering a speech, Adah collapsed.

The startled actors who gathered around her realized that she had lost consciousness, and a physician was summoned. Hostein had revived her by the time the doctor arrived, and she was sitting up, but complained of dizziness and nausea. The physician suggested taking her to a hospital, but Adah indignantly rejected the idea, and insisted on returning to her own suite at the Hotel Suez.

Her legs would not respond to her will, so she was carried to her coach and was put to bed when she arrived at the hotel. The physician made an examination, and although he said he would need a day or two of study to diagnose her ailment, he assured the worried Hostein that her condition was not serious.

The next day Adah felt much worse, and said there were severe shooting pains in her left side. The doctor arrived late in the afternoon and gave her an elixir. She took the medicine, but spent a sleepless night and felt no better the following morning. Minnie was deeply concerned, as was Hostein, and several other physicians were called in, among them the distinguished Claude Hector, who had treated the Empress Eugenie.

Adah was subjected to a long series of tests over a period of several days, and after the physicians finally gathered for a consultation in the living room of her suite, Dr. Hector announced that she was suffering from a bad case of inflammatory rheumatism. By this time she could not move her legs and was unable to leave her bed. The pain in her left side was constant and intense, but she refused the sedatives offered her, preferring to keep a clear head. The doctors informed her that she would recover, but that there was no known cure for her illness, which would have to run its course.

As there seemed to be no choice, Adah became reconciled to pain. But she wanted no one to know she was ill, and begged Hostein to keep the news secret. It was not difficult to conceal the truth, for very few people had known of her return to Paris, and most of her friends were off in the country enjoying vacations. It was easier for her to suffer in silence, alone.

The galley proofs of *Infelicia* arrived, and gave her considerable pleasure, but she needed days to check them thoroughly, as the pain, combined with a fever that sometimes made her delirious, forced her to work very slowly.

She lost weight steadily and became much weaker. After almost one month in bed, Adah began to lose courage, but Dr. Hector still assured her that she would recover and urged her to show patience. She was still seeing no one. Dumas and a few other friends who called were told by

Minnie that Miss Menken had felt the need of a longer rest and had left the city again. The reopening of the *Pirates* had been postponed quietly, and the suspicions of the press had not been aroused.

On August 4, Adah finally broke her silence by writing a letter to Swinburne, to whom she described the symptoms of her ailment in some detail. She was deeply depressed now, and said, "I am lost to art and life. Yet when all is said and done, have I not at my age tasted more of life than most women who live to be a hundred? It is fair, then, that I should go where old people go."

Two days later she started another letter, this one to Ed James, but lapsed into a coma before she could finish it. Early on the morning of August 10 she died without having regained consciousness. Only Minnie was at her bedside, Dr. Hector arriving too late. A post-mortem examination indicated that she had been suffering from an internal abscess that had broken, spreading poison through her system.

Dumas, the only close friend who was in Paris, was notified, and tried to take charge of Adah's chaotic financial affairs. She had paid all of the printers' bills for the publication of her book, and had virtually no money left. After the Hotel Suez bill and servants' wages had been paid, the estate was practically bankrupt.

On August 12 Adah was buried in the Jewish section of Père Lachaise, the "poor man's cemetery." Dumas walked in the tiny procession, followed by Minnie, the governess and two other servants, one of whom led the star's saddled mare. There were no other mourners, rain fell steadily, and the rabbi who performed a brief graveside ceremony did not tarry when he had completed his task.

Adah's unexpected passing was a one-day sensation in the press, and a handful of her friends were shocked, but there were few repercussions and most people forgot her almost overnight. Eléonore Fechter and Laura Seymour made it their business to insure that Adah's son would receive adequate care. They arranged for him to be adopted by an English family of substance, a couple who insisted on changing the child's name and concealing their own identity. Louis Dudevant Victor Emanuel Barkley disappeared from the face of the earth, and a child with a new name took his place.

Infelicia was published on schedule in New York, London, and Paris in October, 1868. But, with Adah dead, it aroused little interest. Few literary critics reviewed it, and only people who had been Adah's close friends bought copies.

The press, however, was moved to comment on her death. "No one cared less for money," the Boston *Courier* said, "and had her income been a thousand dollars a minute, she would have been poor at the end of an hour."

Punch printed a short, pungent verse:

> Ungrateful animals, mankind!
> Walking his rider's hearse behind,
> Mourner-in-chief her horse appears,
> But where are all her Cavaliers?

There were a few who did not forget. Ed and Hannah James sold Adah's Seventh Avenue house and used the money to start a fund for the building of an appropriate memorial. Whitman contributed a small sum, all he could afford. Early in the spring of 1869 James made a trip to England and France, and received contributions from Reade, Rossetti, and Swinburne, among others. Dumas, who was in financial difficulty, nevertheless gave generously, as did George Sand and Zola.

A monument of stone, approximately ten feet high, was erected in Montparnasse, on a site that James purchased,

and permission was obtained from the city fathers of Paris
to move Adah's remains and bury them beneath the monument. The inscription carried her name and the brief line,
"Thou Knowest," from Swinburne's "Ilicet." City grime
ate into the soft stone, and in 1875 the monument was torn
down because it impeded a street-widening project. There
is no record indicating that the coffin of the world's most
glamorous, wicked, and celebrated woman was moved
again.

BIBLIOGRAPHY

Much of the raw material of Queen of the Plaza *comes from a primary source, Adah Isaacs Menken herself. Her* Diary *and the autobiographical prose fragment, which she intended to publish as her* Memoirs, *are in the Adah Isaacs Menken Collection, Harvard University Library, Cambridge, Massachusetts, and I am grateful for the privilege of having been allowed to study them there. I also appreciate the generosity of Henry Ewing Hibbard, New York City, who trusted me sufficiently to let me keep his duplicate copies of these documents in my own care for several months, and who also gave me access to the letters and other papers of Adah Isaacs Menken which he has been collecting so assiduously for more than a half-century.*

I have made use, too, of Adah's one-volume book of poetry, Infelicia, *which was published simultaneously, in 1868, in New York, London, and Paris. I am grateful to Elsa Lichtenstein of Barnes and Noble, Inc., New York City, for finding me a copy.*

I cannot refrain from noting that many of Adah's flights of fancy have taken what appears to be permanent root in the pages of major encyclopedias. One accepts her claim that she was originally Dolores Adios Fuertes, and another states, with equal solemnity, that she began life as Adeline McCord. The facts stated in the Dictionary of American Biography, which refuses to be taken in by myths, are accurate, as always.

Bauer, Henry, *Alexandre Dumas*, L'Echo de Paris, Paris.

Brisson, Pierre, *Les Deux Dumas*, Le Temps, Paris.

Brooks, Noah, "Bret Harte in California," London *Times*, London.

Cincinnati *Israelite*, Vols. 2 and 3.

Clouard, Henri, *Alexandre Dumas*, Albin-Michel, Paris.

Diary of Charles Dickens, William Allingham (ed.), Macmillan, London.

Felton, Cornelius, *Familiar Letters from Europe,* Ticknor & Fields, New York.

Giraudeau, Fernand, *Napoleon III Intime,* Le Temps, Paris.

Golden Era (1863, 1864), Jos. Lawrence (ed.), San Francisco.

Gosse, Edmund, *The Life of Algernon Charles Swinburne,* Macmillan, New York.

Hare, Humphrey, *Swinburne, a Biographical Approach,* Witherly, London.

Hornblow, Arthur, *A History of the Theater in America,* Lippincott, Philadelphia.

Howe, Richard H., "Bygone Celebrities," *Gentleman's Magazine,* New York.

James, Edwin, *The Life and Times of Adah Isaacs Menken,* Burney & Smith, New York.

Johnson, Edgar, *Charles Dickens, His Tragedy and Triumph,* Simon & Schuster, New York.

Lafourcade, George, *La Jeunesse de Swinburne,* Publications of the Faculty of the University of Strasbourg, Paris.

Marks, Edward B., *They All Had Glamour,* Messner, New York.

Maurois, André, *Lelia, the Life of George Sand,* Harper, New York.

—— *The Titans,* Harper, New York.

Newell, Robert Henry, *My Life with Adah Isaacs Menken,* Howell, New York.

Pemberton, T. E., *Life of Bret Harte,* Houghton Mifflin, Boston.

Sand, George, *Diaries* (1867, 1868), Paris.

Scott, Clement, *The Drama of Yesterday and Today,* Macmillan, New York.

Stoddard, Charles Warren, "La Belle Menken," *National Magazine* (1905), New York.

Winwar, Frances, *The Life of the Heart, George Sand and Her Times,* Harper, New York.

INDEX

INDEX